SCIENCE, EVOLUTION, AND RELIGION

A Debate about Atheism and Theism

Michael Peterson

and

Michael Ruse

New York   Oxford
OXFORD UNIVERSITY PRESS

Oxford University Press is a department of the University of Oxford.
It furthers the University's objective of excellence in research,
scholarship, and education by publishing worldwide.

Oxford   New York
Auckland   Cape Town   Dar es Salaam   Hong Kong   Karachi
Kuala Lumpur   Madrid   Melbourne   Mexico City   Nairobi
New Delhi   Shanghai   Taipei   Toronto

With offices in
Argentina   Austria   Brazil   Chile   Czech Republic   France   Greece
Guatemala   Hungary   Italy   Japan   Poland   Portugal   Singapore
South Korea   Switzerland   Thailand   Turkey   Ukraine   Vietnam

For titles covered by Section 112 of the US Higher Education
Opportunity Act, please visit www.oup.com/us/he for the
latest information about pricing and alternate formats.

Published by Oxford University Press
198 Madison Avenue, New York, New York 10016
http://www.oup.com

Library of Congress Cataloging-in-Publication Data

Names: Peterson, Michael L., 1950- author.
Title: Science, evolution, and religion : a debate about atheism and theism /
    by Michael Peterson and Michael Ruse.
Description: New York : Oxford University Press, 2016. | Includes
    bibliographical references and index.
Identifiers: LCCN 2015038356 | ISBN 9780199379378
Subjects: LCSH: Science and religion. | Evolution (Biology)--Religious
    aspects. | Atheism. | Theism.
Classification: LCC BL240.3 .P485 2016 | DDC 215--dc23 LC record available at
http://lccn.loc.gov/2015038356

Printing number: 9 8 7 6 5 4 3 2 1

Printed in the United States of America
on acid-free paper

For our wonderful wives,
Rebecca and Lizzie

TABLE OF CONTENTS

PREFACE

The relation of science and religion continues to be a hot topic in academic circles and general culture—and evolution makes the subject particularly dicey. Does modern science tip the scales toward atheism? Or does religion have the intellectual resources to support its credibility and relevance? And how does evolution influence our consideration of the relation of science and religion? At the most fundamental level, the issues in this area are philosophical and ultimately rooted in worldview commitments. That is why a thorough debate between two professional philosophers who are deeply involved with science, one an atheist and one a theist, is particularly illuminating.

Although we structure the book around the impact of evolution on atheistic and theistic perspectives, we navigate the key topics and interact with the major voices in a way that provides a comprehensive and creative introduction to the larger science–religion discussion. We follow a debate format because it is always engaging and enables the reader to compare and contrast positions. We seek to strike a respectful tone that is inviting to all while rigorously developing our ideas and arguments—a novel ideal in a day when debates are too frequently personal and acrimonious. Since the book originated in a public debate, our exchanges reflect a conversational quality. Because of these features, we dare to hope that both academic and lay readers will find the presentation here to be accessible and helpful at a number of levels.

No project of this sort could be purely a product of our own efforts as writers. We are grateful to have profited from insightful comments from reviewers and colleagues: Mark Balok, Yavapai College; David Blanks, Ohio State University; Craig Boyd, St. Louis University; David Calhoun, Gonzaga University; Philip Clayton, Claremont School of Theology; Chris Doran, Pepperdine University; Darrel Falk, Point Loma Nazarene University; Michael D. Haltenberger, Hunter College; William Hasker, Huntington University; Thomas McKenna, Concord University; Tim O'Connor, Indiana University; Hollis Phelps, Mount Olive College; Kevin Seybold, Grove City College; Michael Slater, Georgetown University; Kirk Wegter-McNelly, Institute for the Bio-Cultural Study of Religion; and David Wilkinson, Durham University.

Other persons were also important to the successful completion of this work. Michael Ruse acknowledges the Stellenbosch Institute for Advanced Study and its director, Hendrik Geyer, where he spent a semester during which he put the final touches on his share of the debate. We both deeply appreciate the guidance and advice of our editor, Robert Miller, and his assistant editor, Alyssa Palazzo. Robert was excited about this project from the beginning, and Alyssa worked diligently on the details of its production.

We recognize with great delight two other important supporters—our wonderful wives, Rebecca and Lizzie—and dedicate this book to them.

Michael L. Peterson
Asbury Theological Seminary

Michael Ruse
Florida State University

August 2015

Introduction

Toward the end of the nineteenth century, some thirty years after Charles Darwin had published his *Origin of Species*, the High-Church Anglican theologian Aubrey Moore wrote,

> Science had pushed the deist's God farther and farther away, and at the moment when it seemed as if He would be thrust out altogether, Darwinism appeared, and, under the guise of a foe, did the work of a friend. It has conferred upon philosophy and religion an inestimable benefit, by showing us that we must choose between two alternatives. Either God is everywhere present in nature, or He is nowhere. He cannot be here, and not there. He cannot delegate his power to demigods called "second causes." In nature everything must be His work or nothing. We must frankly return to the Christian view of direct Divine agency, the immanence of Divine power from end to end, the belief in a God in Whom not only we, but all things have their being, or we must banish him altogether. (Moore 1890, 73–74)

The dichotomy to which Moore draws our attention frames the debate running through this book.

Both authors, Michael Peterson and Michael Ruse, accept that Darwin's theory of evolution through natural selection is the true explanation of organic origins; both accept that the world was changed forever by Darwin; both accept that Darwin's thinking applies to science, to religion, and to the relationship between the two. And both authors accept that Moore is right in this crucial respect: after Darwin, either you are confirmed in your faith, better able to understand the God whom you worship, or you see that faith can never be for you, that the world is empty and without ultimate meaning or purpose. After that, they part company. Michael Peterson is a theist who thinks that the world was created by a good God, that humans have a special place in this creation, and that this God seeks to redeem humankind and indeed the whole universe. Michael Ruse is a nonbeliever, skeptical about most questions but sure that theism is false and that Christianity has no acceptable answers. In this sense, he is an atheist, thinking that religion is false and that its promises are empty. His own version of philosophical naturalism emerges through the debate.

Moore had his reasons for arguing as he did. We live and write more than a hundred years later—years that have seen great advances in science and technology and huge changes in social arrangements, especially in regard to women, people of color, and others against whom traditionally there has been much prejudice, and yet years that have seen horrendous conflicts and mass purges and evils unrivaled in the history of humankind. We live and write also in a time when there are extremists about religion and about science. On the one side, we have those who, in the name of their faith, deny evolution and generally think that religion trumps science. On the other side, we have those, no less shrill, who think that all human ills can be traced back to religious training and prejudice and that nothing will change unless and until science vanquishes religion.

No further justification therefore is needed for taking up Moore's disjunction and seeing how it fares today. Forget the extremes that Darwinian evolution is false or that religion, particularly the Christian religion, is inherently evil. Accept the science; be open to, if not accepting of, the religion. Recognize that people of good will and sound mind can come to the table and work through the issues. Recognize that those with whom you disagree may be mistaken intellectually but that this does not make them idiots or knaves. How do theism and atheism relate to science? What is the most helpful way for a Christian theist today to respond to evolution? What response does the skeptical atheist make to evolution? These are the questions that drive the discussion of this book. There are real issues. There are real disagreements. We shall not evade them.

We interpret our dispute in the broadest sense and cover a wide range of topics, which gives the reader a large sense of the science–religion discussion in both academic circles and general culture. The book is framed by ten topics—and we engage each other on the issues related to those topics. First we shall tell you a little about ourselves, both to give human faces to the discussion and also to orient you toward our different stances. This will help you understand how our philosophical outlooks have shaped our lives and how seriously we take issues related to science, religion, and evolution. We shall next give a brief sketch of our different philosophies and attitudes toward science and its general relationship to religion. With this background, we turn to the science. Strictly speaking, cosmological evolution is not Darwinian evolution, the latter interpreted as being about organisms, but we see the origins of the universe as being part of the greater picture with implications for our thinking about organisms (and indeed about everything). This is justification enough to make the physical world and its beginning the start of our discussion.

We move then to organisms, first the origins of life and then the evolution of plants and animals, meaning here the story as given by Darwin in his *Origin*. Then we consider the impact of Darwinian evolution on the science of biology and on William Paley's widely accepted design argument. Next comes the path to and the arrival of humans. In the *Origin*, Darwin made it clear that our species is part of the story, and some twelve years after this book, in his *Descent of Man*, he dealt directly with *Homo sapiens*. Both for scientists and for religious individuals, humans are conscious intentional beings, and we shall explore this and the related topic of rationality. Continuing, we turn to the ethical aspect of human beings and our beliefs about morality and its foundations. Drawing to the end, we look at matters of vital concern to Christian theists: our propensity to sin, its origins, its implications for our understanding of the deity, and, more generally, its relevance to the problem of evil. Finally, in summing up the discussion, we turn back to the underlying principles guiding our interaction and ask whether the disagreements between our theistic and atheistic positions may share certain concerns and strivings for understanding. Yet we conclude that the different worldviews we develop— theism and naturalism— anchor different orientations toward the question of meaning and purpose in the universe.

Returning to Aubrey Moore, our main focus is on evolution—on Darwinian evolution—and what this means for a traditional theist and also what it means for a traditional atheist. We take pride in our ability to use the word "traditional" because neither of us wants to dodge the real issues by treating, on the one side, an understanding of theism that is nonstandard or of Christian doctrine that most would consider heretical, or by considering, on the other side, a form of nonbelief that most would find insufficiently radical and unable to serve as a significant alternative to theism.

Since this is a comprehensive debate, the book must encompass a large variety of elements. Since the major issues in the science–religion debate make an appearance in our discussion, the book actually becomes an attractive introduction to the field. The reader will come to know the larger lay of the land. As we stake out our positions in relation to each other, we often dialogue with and critique prominent thinkers of all stripes in the science–religion arena. Thus, the reader will be able to participate in the fuller process of critical reasoning about the relevant issues. The book unfolds, then, as a genuine contribution to the science–religion field that not only covers the major topics but also exhibits thoughtful engagement with them. The debate format predictably offers an added level of and interest and energy.

Although we are not intending to present a tome on the history of science or even the philosophy of science, a wealth of fascinating information about the history and philosophy of science will be woven throughout. Major scientists and major scientific theories—as well as significant philosophical issues regarding the nature and scope of science—inevitably play into our exchange and are crucial to how each of us navigates the terrain. Furthermore, although we are not setting out to provide an introduction to the philosophy of religion, a number of important issues in that area will inevitably arise here—such as the coherence of the concept of God, the nature of divine action in the world, and the problem of evil.

The manner in which we approach the debate is important for the reader to grasp. We think of each essay as involving several important ingredients incorporated into our own recipes. Since science and religion is a large and rapidly growing field, each author here must take some time describing certain scientific facts and theories that allow him to make his philosophical point—defining, defending, and differentiating his position. Each of us must situate himself within the general logical space, so to speak, where all the relevant issues reside—the larger intellectual arena. Yet, since this is a debate between two thinkers holding opposing philosophical positions—theism and naturalism—we primarily accent key points of disagreement between us and make our distinctive arguments. However, we do not line up our points in wooden one-by-one fashion; rather, we find our own voices and develop our cases in our own ways. Each essay by each author, then, addresses the broader field of controversy, articulates his own view, and engages the position of his interlocutor.

Each chapter in the book is composed of a pair of essays, with one essay by each of us. We alternate who goes first and second in each pair of essays, although, in a real sense, the ordering within each pair doesn't matter, since each of us is speaking to the general set of issues that define the topic and writing with a keen awareness of the other's position. It really is true, then, that each essay is meant to stand on its own logical merits. The alert reader will readily see the engagement between the pairs of essays and gain a cumulative sense of the mounting disagreements between two major worldview alternatives. In fact, some topics—such as the amalgamation of Greek and Judeo-Christian elements in the Western God concept or the role of chance in science and theology—will be developed over several chapters because of their relevance at different stages of the debate. After working through the whole debate, one may go back and read just the essays by Peterson, thereby getting a kind of treatise on a theistic interpretation of science and evolution, or just the essays by Ruse for a complete treatise on his atheistic interpretation. In all that we present, in science or philosophy, we strive for accessibility of style, without technicality, so that all interested readers may benefit.

A final note: we are sincerely dedicated to a moderate and respectful tone in undertaking the task of debating two diametrically opposed philosophical positions. Feelings between the two writers could not be more pleasant. This debate is not personal at all. It's not about one-upmanship. Frankly, we dislike the unpleasant air of animosity that characterizes some debates in this area, regardless of whatever intellectual merits they may or may not have. Plain and simple, this is about the interplay of ideas, our reasons for holding two different positions. We trust that the positive spirit of this debate may serve as something of a model for all readers.

And now, with our program laid out before you, let us turn to the task at hand.

1

Autobiographical Reflections

A Life Observed

Michael Peterson

"Life can only be understood backwards; but it must be lived forwards." Applying Sören Kierkegaard's principle in the current context means reflecting on my past involvement in science–religion discussions and contemplating the trajectory for my involvement in the future. Ideas that shaped my thinking, people who influenced me, roads taken as well as those not taken—all factor into my approach to the issues. I'm fortunate to have an academic background in essential areas that impinge on the issues pertaining to the relationship between science and religion. I trust that sketching my own journey is helpful to readers who want to explore this important topic.

Formative Experiences

Early in my teens, entirely of my own volition, I read Plato's *Republic* and Aristotle's *Nicomachean Ethics*, an exercise that awakened in me strong interest in big-picture thinking as well as the close analysis of ideas. Perhaps coming from a broken home provided a certain motivation for me to try to understand life and the world, and these classical sources pointed me in the direction of philosophy. Through high school, I was always academically inclined, loved science, and aspired to a career in medicine. Midway through high school, I began dating Rebecca Shannon, the daughter of the Methodist minister in my hometown. Being exposed to Christian belief stirred me to ask many questions about the reasonableness of Christianity. In conversations with Becky and her family, I eventually found myself accepting Christian belief as credible and embracing faith. During our college years, Becky and I were married, and I remain to this day deeply in love with her.

In 1968, while taking a philosophy course in college, I began to think in terms of the relation of philosophy and Christian faith. A possible career in philosophy rather than medicine began to look attractive, although I continued taking advanced science electives as possible. At this point in time, however, no philosophers I knew of were working on any philosophical topics expressly related to theistic or Christian belief. Yet I kept plugging along in a broad undergraduate major in philosophy while continuing to explore possible graduate programs. My appreciation for Aristotle, particularly in his analytical and empirical approach, led me to the works of Aquinas, which are a philosophical model of both critical thinking and systematic synthesis applied to the claims of Christianity. Thomas Reid soon appeared on my radar, and I began to think in terms of doing graduate work on Reid's realist epistemology.

Plans developed to work with Roderick Chisholm at Brown University because he saw early on the resurging interest in Reid. We confirmed our mutual interest in several phone chats during my senior year, and we agreed to continue our conversation at the American Philosophical Association meeting that same year. Long story short, Rod broke the news to me that the university had just announced severe funding cuts for incoming grad students in the philosophy department. Since I could not afford to go on without funding, I rethought my direction for grad study and settled on philosophy of science with Edward Madden at the State University of New York at Buffalo, where funding was abundant. With Madden's invitation, I began to move in that direction.

Interestingly, a rebirth of realism, both epistemological and ontological, was occurring in philosophy of science as well, and Ed Madden was on the ground floor. He was the consummate professional, model, and mentor and liked to do dissertation guidance in his home where his wife, Marian, would make lunch and tea. Ed's contributions to the history and philosophy of science are highly regarded—such as his *Theories of Scientific Method* and the Harvard Source Book Series in the History of the Sciences. In addition to his work in the history and philosophy of science, Ed made regular contributions to the literature in American philosophy and was also well published on the problem of evil as one taking a strong atheist position. Many times after Ed and I had finished a session talking about the dissertation—on the topic of causality, law, and explanation in science—Ed would want to discuss the problem of evil and its negative bearing on the rational status of theism. Although Ed and I differed a great deal with regard to the assessment of theism, we became close friends.

Dissertation completed and doctorate in hand for a few years, I moved in 1978 to a faculty position at Asbury College. Over the next couple of years, Ed and I corresponded frequently and talked occasionally by phone. In a phone call in 1980, Ed announced that he had taken early retirement and wanted to explore relocating near me so that we could be closer and once again conduct our conversations in person. I was thrilled. Ed and Marian soon thereafter purchased a home in my area, and we had almost two decades of friendly interaction before declining health forced them to move to Vermont to live with one of their adult sons.

Witnessing God Make a Comeback

Time magazine reported in 1980 that God was "making a comeback" in a curious sector of the intellectual community. After many decades of being banished from professional philosophy as a serious topic of discussion by the prevailing positivism, God had begun to show surprising signs of life in the crisp scholarly circles of analytic philosophers. There were no surprises for me here because in 1978 I was a founding member—actually, the youngest founding member—of the Society of Christian Philosophers, an organization reflecting the renewal of interest in the engagement between philosophy and Christian faith. In the preceding years, a handful of us who were professional philosophers and also Christians had decided that the time was right to launch this organization. The society has grown tremendously over the years and continues as a robust movement.

There was so much talent in the ranks of the society that I soon became convinced that it needed its own first-rate academic journal—and I began trying to persuade its first president, William P. Alston, of the feasibility of this dream. Alston, a famous philosopher of language who had recently returned to faith, agreed that there should be a journal and soon thereafter accepted a commission as its first editor. I was commissioned as managing editor. *Faith and Philosophy: Journal of the Society of Christian Philosophers* first saw the light of day in 1984. From the beginning, the journal has encouraged dialogue with those who do not share our commitment either to theism or to Christianity, and this has helped usher in a new tone all around in discussions and debates related to these subjects. The philosophy of religion, once thought otiose, was beginning to thrive again.

Eventually, various atheist philosophers began calling for a counterpart to *Faith and Philosophy*. Editorials and articles in the magazine *Free Inquiry*, published by the Council for Secular Humanism, began to reflect serious puzzlement at the renaissance of theistic and Christian belief within a profession where topics related to God had been stereotyped as meaningless and without intellectual merit. One atheist philosopher in *Free Inquiry* opined that he was disturbed by the "uncommonly large number of bright believers" in professional philosophy. An editorial in that magazine in the late 1990s called *Faith and Philosophy* an "outstanding journal" and announced that the council would begin sponsoring its own journal as a counterpart. *Philo*, the name of Hume's protagonist, would be the title of this new academic publication. A smile always crosses my face when I remember being asked to travel to the headquarters of *Philo* to consult about the intellectual standards and practical realities of scholarly journal publication. I had enjoyable and productive talks with Austin Dacey, the journal's first managing editor—and I have been happy since that time to see *Philo* rolling along.

The new era in the philosophy of religion is based on the understanding that theism indeed has substantial intellectual content—that meaningful assertions and denials can be made about it and that its major implications can be drawn out and analyzed. Bertrand Russell's insistence that there is no knowledge beyond scientific knowledge was shown to limit the human intellectual search, the kinds of questions we may ask, and the kinds of knowledge we may seek. Extreme empiricism supported an intellectual imperialism that itself has been rejected as inadequate. Religion as a worthy subject of rational discussion and debate has returned with capable philosophers representing it.

As the field of philosophy of religion was experiencing renewal, it occurred to me that there was no current introductory textbook discussing classical and contemporary topics and arguments. John Hick's little anthology *The Existence of God* was badly out of date. So, I proposed *Reason and Religious Belief* to Oxford University Press and, later, a coordinated anthology, *Philosophy of Religion*. My coauthors and I continue to take pride that these texts—which both reflected and helped shape the resurgence in philosophy of religion—have been widely used for decades (Peterson et al. 2012, 2014).

Undoubtedly, my lifelong friendship with Ed Madden was a major reason that I made a specialty of the problem of evil, a feature of every atheist perspective that must be carefully addressed by the theist. John Hick, who was kind and encouraging to me when I was a young philosopher, initiated several exchanges with me on issues in the problem of evil. I remain dedicated to being active in this area—and I'm sure that my past involvement with the topic will be visible as I discuss its relation to evolution later in this book.

Considering Intellectual Journeys to God

My sense of great privilege in being a small part of the theistic and Christian renewal in philosophy never wanes. Watching this movement grow made it clearer to me that philosophical questions about religious belief are important not solely on intellectual terms but also because they can become the basis for living one's life. After all, we make our choices and orient ourselves in the world within a framework of what we believe is true and reasonable about ultimate reality or valuable and worthy of our commitment and devotion. A change in belief can indeed mean a change in life direction. From this perspective, I have a strong interest in the intellectual journeys that have led people to belief in God. The journeys of four prominent intellectuals have particularly impacted my own journey, and each one actually has a definite bearing on the science–religion debate.

In *Surprised by Joy*, the famous author C. S. Lewis describes his search for truth as a progression in thinking, from atheistic materialism through certain forms of idealism, then to theism, and eventually Christianity. A number of important thinkers influenced the direction of his thought. On digesting the intellectually persuasive and insightful writings of G. K. Chesterton, Lewis remarked that "a young man who wishes to remain a sound atheist cannot be too careful of his reading" (Lewis 1955, 191). While teaching at Oxford, Lewis's personal contact with such thinkers as J. R. R. Tolkien and Dorothy L. Sayers meant even more sustained exposure to the intellectual power of theistic and Christian ideas. At Oxford, Lewis questioned, argued, studied, read, and ultimately reasoned his way to God, thus ending a fifteen-year search for reality and meaning. Lewis describes his intellectual process as a matter of discerning which worldview is most adequate—and many readers find his arguments so persuasive because he spent so many years convinced of the worldviews he critiques. No worldview is more of a target for Lewis than philosophical naturalism and its attempted alliance with science. I continue this theme in my parts of the chapters to come.

Albert Camus's religious and intellectual quest will come as a shock to those who know him as a textbook atheistic existentialist. Camus reflected in his writings what he had learned from Jean Paul Sartre: if modern science has completely described reality, then God is dead and humans are desperately alone, without hope or meaning. Out of the blue, I was visited in the mid-1990s by the Reverend Howard Mumma, the summer minister of the American Church in Paris during the last decade of Camus's life. Mumma, then quite elderly, recounted to me the story of how Camus had started attending that church and had formed a close friendship with him. Mumma was riveting as he told of many private conversations in which the great French novelist expressed deep dissatisfaction with the whole philosophy of atheistic existentialism. "I am searching for something the world is not giving me," Camus once said to Mumma. Camus expressed to Mumma interest in committing to Christian faith and being baptized, but these plans were cut short when a car crash took Camus's life in 1960. Reverend Mumma revealed that he had kept his relationship with Camus confidential for almost forty years but thought it was now time to make it public. Because of my connection with *Faith and Philosophy*, Mumma hoped I could help him publish this account of Camus's odyssey before it died with him. A friend of mine who owned a book-editing agency gladly assisted in preparing the manuscript; *Albert Camus and the Minister* tells the whole story (Mumma 2000).

In 2007, Antony Flew published *There Is a God: How the World's Most Notorious Atheist Changed His Mind*, which retraces the reasoning process that led him from atheism to something like deism, which affirms an infinite Intelligence behind the universe (Flew 2007). Flew had transitioned from extreme empiricism, which embraced science as the paragon of knowledge, to the realization that philosophical reflection on science—on the very existence of physical nature and on the fact that it obeys precise laws—demanded a better explanation than the materialism he had embraced all of his career. Although Flew never accepted a historical religion, there is a direction in his later thought toward a general theism and even an interest in Christianity. The striking turnaround of this influential analytic philosopher was vigorously debated, with some commentators contending that he had lost mental capacity and should not be taken seriously. I cannot take up that controversy here but will note that the lines of reasoning in Flew's book are logical entities to be dealt with on their own terms and that versions of them—such as the fine-tuning argument—will appear in the following chapters.

Furthermore, Tony Flew and his wife, Annis, had several times visited their friends Ed and Marian Madden, who resided in the college town where I taught. Ed must have told Flew of the journal *Faith and Philosophy* because sometime in the late 1990s a handwritten letter from Flew came across my desk expressing strong interest in the journal and remitting a check for a two-year subscription. My letter of reply stated that we would be pleased to provide a lifetime complimentary subscription in honor of his important contributions to philosophy. Some years later, in 2005, I chatted briefly with Flew at a conference in Oxford, and he expressed appreciation for the journal and its commitment to engage subjects in philosophy of religion with analytic rigor. So, the announcement of Flew's change of mind did not come as a total surprise to me because I had my own vantage point on his journey.

Francis Collins, the former director of the Human Genome Project and current head of the National Institutes of Health, the nation's largest scientific organization, found himself as a scientist on a journey from atheism to religious faith. During Collins's career as a physician, his encounters with sick and dying patients who expressed strong religious faith impressed him greatly and disturbed his confident atheism. While earning a Ph.D. in physical chemistry at Yale, Collins had concluded that "no thinking scientist could seriously entertain the possibility of God without committing some sort of intellectual suicide" (Collins 2006, 16). Nonetheless, Collins decided to embark on an intellectual exploration to confirm his atheism, thinking that science would disprove God and show religious faith untenable. In *The Language of God*, Collins explains how he eventually abandoned atheism and embraced Christianity as providing a more adequate understanding of life and the world, including the world of science. The geneticist who headed up the project of deciphering the human instruction book affirms that science and faith are far from being incompatible and instead form a "richly satisfying harmony." In the chapters to follow, I develop the theme that science and faith not only are compatible but also resonate at deep levels.

Christianity is not only a worldview; it is also a way of life. In this light, I am impressed by how cordial and irenic Collins has been in debates with New Atheists Richard Dawkins and Christopher Hitchens. When Collins learned that Hitchens had been diagnosed with esophageal cancer, he called to offer help: "As NIH director I approve many government-funded research grants, and I know about some rather cutting-edge approaches based on cancer genomics" (Yancey 2014, 41). Over the ensuing months, Collins spent hours with the Hitchens family discussing options for treatment. Shortly before he died, Hitchens wrote appreciatively in a *Vanity Fair* piece that Collins had been "kind enough to visit me in his own time and to discuss all sorts of novel treatments, only recently imaginable, that might apply to my case." In that column, he called Collins "one of the greatest living Americans" and "our most selfless Christian physician" (Hitchens 2010, 163).

Engaging Science and Religion

My participation in the science–religion discussion may have been predictable given my training in the philosophy of science and deep involvement in the philosophy of religion. I felt strongly that *Reason and Religious Belief* should be the first text to include a chapter on science and religion as a bona fide topic within the field of philosophy of religion. At least one other textbook in the field, I'm happy to say, has since seen fit to do this as well. My trajectory toward engagement with science–religion issues continued when I designed a model course on the subject, which won a modest Templeton award. One strength of a distinctively philosophical approach to the question of the science–religion relationship lies in the fact that philosophy is an inherently interdisciplinary, integrative, and holistic activity. Additionally, philosophy's purview includes attention to fundamental questions, the careful analysis of concepts, and the logical evaluation of arguments and counterarguments. Philosophy is the proper intellectual venue for worldview comparison and engagement. One of my goals is to reflect these philosophical benefits for the science–religion discussion.

In 2009, I was fortunate to participate in a workshop on "Evolution and Human Uniqueness" in Venice, Italy, an invitation-only affair supported by generous Templeton funding. Simon Conway Morris, Franz de Waal, Wentzel van Huyssteen, and Michael Ruse were also among the two dozen participants who came together at the Venetian Institute of Science, Letters, and the Arts.

Michael and I began a friendship in the best city on earth in which to discuss science and religion—or anything else, for that matter. We spoke then of someday writing a book together that would be at once fun, helpful, and important. It took some time to work the project into our professional schedules, but that day has finally come. I trust that our readers will find this book to exhibit the positive attributes we have tried to build into it.

A public debate on the question "Do Science and Faith Conflict?" seemed to us an auspicious way to launch our writing of the book. In the fall of 2013, Michael Ruse and I had an invigorating interchange, which is now readily available for viewing on the Internet (Peterson and Ruse 2013). Energy from that debate flows into this book, which expands the number of topics and goes into finer detail. The public debate was great fun, stayed on the issues, and was totally devoid of snarkiness and sarcasm, which, unfortunately, find their way into some exchanges in this area. My strategy in the public debate was to elaborate and defend theism as a compelling interpretation of science and evolution, occasionally referring to Christian belief to provide additional information and nuance. I continue that *modus operandi* in the rest of my contributions in this book.

I approach the current project as a "friendly theist"—and I mean this at two levels. Michael Ruse and I are personal friends, he an atheist and I a theist. I certainly admire Michael's great kindness toward other persons and his strong social conscience. As a professional, I also admire his numerous substantial contributions to the philosophy of evolutionary biology and related subjects. At another level, my intellectual posture really is technically that of a friendly theist, meaning a theist who thinks that some atheists can be rationally justified in believing that the theistic God does not exist. It all depends on the grounds that a given atheist has for atheism and the weight assigned to those grounds. I understand all of those grounds for atheism, assess them differently, and disagree; I also have additional grounds for theistic belief. By extension, I think that one can rationally hold the position that science and religion are in serious tension, perhaps even incompatible, and that this can be construed as a ground for atheism. Once again, I am aware of all of those lines of reasoning as well but wholeheartedly disagree. In the following pages, I seek to rebut those reasons and show that theism comports much better with science than does atheism. My approach is philosophical, making careful conceptual distinctions and appealing to what I consider the best reasons for the positions I hold.

My dialogue partner has made clear in various venues that he is what I would call a "friendly atheist," thinking that some religious believers can be entirely rational in their belief and even that there could be ways of making science and religion compatible. For him, it depends on what grounds one has for his or her position and what implication one draws for science—and all of these matters are up for evaluation in the ensuing debate. The project unfolding before us, then, reflects a genuine respect for each other and a mutual desire to find truth through the interplay of ideas. Argument and counterargument, a clarification here and a distinction there, all make for a thorough debate that stays on message and presents the reader with two different visions of science and religion and of the world in which they occur.

Apologia Pro Vita Sua

Michael Ruse

In 1981 I was an expert witness for the American Civil Liberties Union (ACLU) in a court case in Little Rock, Arkansas (Ruse 1988a). The case was about the constitutionality of a new law mandating the "balanced treatment," in the science classrooms of the state, of rival hypotheses about organic origins— Darwinian evolutionary theory and so-called creation science (aka Genesis taken literally). As it happens, the law was ruled an unconstitutional violation of the First Amendment separation of church and state, and I like to think that my testimony, as a historian and philosopher of science, helped the cause. In the course of my cross-examination, the prosecutor asked me repeatedly about my own religious convictions until finally I blurted out, "Surely you can see, Mr. Williams, that I am not an expert witness on my own religious beliefs." I am still rather proud of that response, something demonstrating that a good joke is worth a thousand arguments, because the court broke up in laughter and the judge made us move on.

Early Years

However, it wasn't really a joke then, and it isn't really a joke now. I was born in England at the beginning of World War II (1940) and raised a Quaker, although for the first thirteen years of my life I went to state schools, and in those days that meant one got a good dose of basic, Church-of-England-style, religious instruction. For that reason, given that the Religious Society of Friends is not a *sola scriptura* branch of Protestantism (focusing more on the actions of the Holy Ghost and on the Inner Light, "that of God in every person"), I know more about the Bible than might be expected from one of my religious denomination. I think it fair to say that until I was about twenty or a bit later, I was a fairly committed Christian, although hardly particularly sophisticated. In my early years, we lived in the English Midlands (just outside Birmingham). I was an enthusiastic member of "Junior Young Friends" and would go off to holiday camps and join in discussions and the like with fervor. Indeed, my main memories are of being told to let others get in a word. I do cherish those experiences, and one thing my family has always taken as sacred is the encouragement of conversation around the dinner table—based on the absolute refusal to put any limits on the range of topics being discussed and equally absolute insistence that everyone has a voice.

In my teens I went to a Quaker boarding school and, as I remember, felt quite comfortable going to meeting. Yet I do remember religion being rather less vital and more part of the culture. I went to school with boys whose families' Quaker connections reached back into the seventeenth century, and they would have considered any undue display of enthusiasm rather vulgar. I suppose I accepted the argument from design—I know my father did because, when we were kids on camping holidays in Wales, he was always drawing our attention to sunsets over the Irish Sea and expressing the sentiment that they could not be pure chance. I don't think I was generally a literalist; I do remember being told that Adam and Eve were symbolic for humankind and finding the fact interesting rather than shocking, although like all Quakers I was pretty literalistic about the Sermon on the Mount and remember years later being scandalized at learning that it was put together by followers of Peter rather than being an account of an actual sermon given one Sunday afternoon on the shores of Galilee. I certainly didn't know much about the science–religion relationship, mainly because I didn't know much about the pertinent science. Like most reasonably bright children in England in the 1950s, I was force-fed math, physics, and chemistry and carefully shielded from the contaminating influences of biology. This last subject, along with Spanish, geography, and woodwork, was for "late developers." In other words, it was not really an A-stream subject. I guess I must have known something about evolution, but I was totally ignorant of its causes. The late Ernst Mayr, one of the towering figures of twentieth-century evolutionary biology, used to say that German-born as he was, he knew nothing of natural selection and was a Lamarckian (inheritance of acquired characteristics) until he was twenty-seven, around 1930. I can testify that I was a Lamarckian until I was twenty-seven, in 1967.

Loss of Faith and Finding Darwin

Two important pertinent things happened in my twenties. First, my faith faded away and has never returned. It would be easy and slick to say that this was a function of the fact that I had rather backed into doing an undergraduate degree in philosophy—"backed into" because I started off doing mathematics and on the second day at college realized that, although I was a good high school mathematician, I was no university mathematician, and the only way I could get out of doing nothing but mathematics was to pick up philosophy courses. (There was no real logic to this except that the professor of philosophy was keen on mathematics and so had set up this exit process so he could get students versed in mathematics.) I remember that the topic of the first class I took was Descartes's *Meditations*. Descartes starts with his systematic doubt, asking whether we can know if we are awake or asleep. Within twenty minutes I was hooked. I had been thinking about these things all of my life—and the Humean question of whether there is anything behind me when I am not looking—and here were grown-ups taking these sorts of questions seriously. Of course, an immediate passion is not necessarily lasting. I used to be desperately fond of baked beans, and don't ask me about some of my personal relationships—they were fun while they lasted, however! I do think my lifelong devotion to philosophy—I do a lot of other things besides philosophy, especially history, but ultimately I cannot imagine a life where philosophy is not the central passion—is a function of my Quaker childhood. We were encouraged to argue and to think things through for ourselves. It was not easy defending pacifism in the years after World War II, but we Junior Young Friends were expected to do so. But I don't think philosophy had much to do with my loss of belief. It may sound selfish, but that was more to do with the discovery that petitionary prayer was going nowhere and that I was simply speaking into the void and not *to* someone. I have never been impressed with "God hears your prayers but He gives you what you need, not what you want." I want what I want. No answers, so stop wasting my time.

With my loss of belief came a reluctance to join in public (or private) acts of worship. I have never been tempted toward the Unitarians, for instance, and frankly, although I love many of them individually, I think the whole organization is a bit daft. Erasmus Darwin, Charles Darwin's grandfather (and an evolutionist), used to say that Unitarianism is a feather bed to catch a falling Christian—and I feel a bit the same way. I do wonder whether I would still go to Quaker meeting had I married a co-religionist—as it happens, although both of my two wives have been people of driving moral concern, neither has been in the slightest sense religious, and the same is true of my five children. I suspect I might be at least (what Quakers call) an attender if not a full member, especially since today, unlike my youth when we were all firmly Christocentric, it seems that a lot of Quakers have little more belief than I. On reflection, however, I am not sure I could have stood fifty more years of the pontificating of what were known semiaffectionately as "Weighty Friends"—a term referring less to girth and more to a sense of self-importance. One of the pitfalls of not having a trained clergy is that you are exposed to an awful lot of bad philosophy and theology. For all this, I do nevertheless cherish many of the values of Quakerism. For fifty years as a college professor I have tried (in an entirely secular sense) to recognize the Inner Light in each and every one of my students, especially those who are not particularly loveable. I am no longer a total pacifist and would almost certainly have joined up to fight in World War II. I hope I would have had the guts to refuse to go to Vietnam, although I would have felt dreadful turning my back on those who did.

The second important event in my twenties was that I discovered evolution and Charles Darwin's contribution to the subject. As with philosophy, it was all somewhat serendipitous. I had moved to Canada after my first degree, and such were the opportunities in those days that by 1965 I was teaching at the newly founded University of Guelph in southern Ontario. I needed a doctoral degree and was faced with the need to find a dissertation project. I wanted to work on the philosophy of science. Today I might be tempted to try moral philosophy, but back then the area was all rather dry, analytic metaethics; I did not want to work on formal problems divorced from real science—at the time the rage was to discuss the implications of such statements as "all emeralds are green before time *t* and blue after time *t*"; and I didn't think I was up to the intricacies of modern physics. The ideal topic was philosophical issues to do with evolutionary biology. There was some literature, but it was not very good, and people felt vaguely guilty that no one much was working on the topic. In other words, you would not get official disapproval for turning to the subject as one might if, for instance, one wanted to work on some kind of pop or unorthodox thinker like the Maharishi Mahesh Yogi, the propagator of transcendental meditation (then popular because of its endorsement by the Beatles).

It was love at first sight—or at first gene, as one might say. The concept of evolution excited me; the idea of natural selection was so clever that it had to be true, and the formal material working out the dynamics of heredity was a piece of cake to someone with my training. Moreover, the philosophical problems, for instance, puzzling through why teleological thinking is allowed in biology but not in the physical sciences, were challenging but soluble. It was a wonderful experience and led to my first book, with the overly ambitious title *The Philosophy of Biology* (1973). And there were new directions. The most influential book in my field in the 1960s was Thomas Kuhn's *Structure of Scientific Revolutions* (1962). Among other things, Kuhn argued that if philosophers are to understand science and its changes, then they must get to know the history of science as well as the historians. Like a number of others who heard this call—interestingly, although perhaps expectedly, including several of that small group like me turning to philosophical issues in biology—I took up the history of science, of the Darwinian revolution in particular, even spending my first sabbatical at Cambridge in England, working in the archives. This led to my second book, *The Darwinian Revolution: Science Red in Tooth and Claw* (1979a). The book had been started as a refutation of Kuhn's theory of theory change. Literally, the night before I sent it to the publisher, I dropped the final philosophical chapter as just too much. Many have been the criticisms (praise too), but never once has anyone said, "Mike. Great book, but it really needs a chapter on Kuhn!"

Creationism

Biologists have the concept of "preadaptation," meaning a feature produced for one reason that then finds a different role. It turns out that by the mid-1970s I was well on my way to being preadapted to fighting creationists. I knew the philosophy, I knew the history, and, as it happens, many of the arguments of the biblical literalists have been faced and answered by evolutionists, if not by our generation then by previous ones. I started to get involved in debates with creationists; inevitably there was another book, *Darwinism Defended: A Guide to the Evolution Controversies* (1982); and finally came the call to Arkansas. It was now the 1980s, I was in my forties, and again there were two significant events. First, thanks to my engagement with creationists, I was brought more and more into contact with liberal Christians, often clergy, also fighting the good fight. Perhaps because of my childhood, I felt comfortable with and welcomed by these people who accepted my nonbelief as genuine and sincere and who were comfortable in return. I became an enthusiastic member of the Institute for Religion in an Age of Science and for many years would go to the annual meeting on Star Island, one of the Isles of Shoals off the coast of New Hampshire. Although I had given up Christianity, because of my Quaker childhood I could never hate Christianity—I saw the fight against creationism as much a fight for believers as for nonbelievers—and increasingly I became interested in trying to resolve the tensions between science and religion. In Arkansas, the standard position by the ACLU was what Ian Barbour (1988) has called the "independence" position, something associated with the theological stance known as "neo-orthodoxy" (going back to Karl Barth and represented in the United States by the University of Chicago professor and ordained Baptist minister Langdon Gilkey [1959], also one of the Arkansas ACLU witnesses). I still feel empathetic to this position—science and religion do not necessarily conflict because they talk of different things—although I now see that it requires a fairly sophisticated handling and does not necessarily exclude other approaches. You will see much of this in the chapters that follow.

Second, significant for me in my forties was the growing realization that, although Darwinism was never a religion substitute for me, it might be the basis of a religion alternative. If we really are the products of a long, slow process of evolution through natural selection, rather than the miraculous creation of a good God on the sixth day, then it really should matter both for epistemology (theory of knowledge) and for ethics (theory of morality). I worked on this along lines that I think can be found in Darwin himself, arguing that our brains and subsequent thought and behavior are molded in the struggle for existence, for survival and reproduction, and that this at once and always influences how we think and behave. Another book! In fact, *Taking Darwin Seriously: A Naturalistic Approach to Philosophy*, published in 1986, has a rather delicious history. At first, it got a rough reception from the philosophical community. Thanks to the founders of analytic philosophy, especially Bertrand Russell and Ludwig Wittgenstein, any attempt to use Darwinism in philosophy was considered not only wrong but also unsavory. There are reasons for this attitude, not the least being anti-Americanism, expressed in a distaste for the distinctively American philosophy of pragmatism, which did take Darwin seriously. Over the years, however, pragmatism has become more acceptable and so has Darwinism. I find now that I am almost orthodox!

The point is that I not only had nonbelief but also had a world philosophy, a kind of empiricism that I like to describe as David Hume brought up to date by Charles Darwin. I really thought that as I got older, because of the fear of death and the unknown, I would be tempted back into belief. I find that this is not so. I am pretty atheistic about the main tenets of Christianity—other religions too—but generally, speaking perhaps more technically than emotionally, I am more agnostic or, as I like to say (because so often "agnostic" means not interested, and I am very interested), skeptical. I find the world quite wonderful and its existence a total puzzle. I feel privileged to be alive and doubly privileged that I have had a life that meant I could explore it and be related to other humans and, above all, to have been a teacher and able to share this with others. Please don't think that this is a way of getting God in through the back door. I don't think that there is a fifty–fifty chance that in a few years I am going to be playing a harp or shoveling coal. I really don't know whether there is more or whether there is overall meaning. I am just wary of believing that there might be because I would like this. Philosophers have talked of the "tedium" of immortality, suggesting that even if it is available, it might not be such a good thing. I will take it, so long as I can have a new Mozart opera every evening, fish and chips at the intermission, and no student papers to mark when I get home. What I dread is that God might give me what I need rather than what I want.

Accommodationism

In 2000, to avoid compulsory retirement, my family and I moved south to Florida. The main intellectual movement has been more an intensification than a change of focus. Now, when I am not directly pursuing my passion for things

Darwinian, I work almost entirely on the science–religion relationship, trying to articulate important aspects and presenting my ideas at various levels, professional and public (most recently, Ruse 2015). I should say that when I talk of "religion," I usually mean the Christian religion. This, of course, reflects my background and interests, and I am aware that I run the charge of being unduly Eurocentric. I can mount some defense, starting with the fact that my work on Darwin (not to mention creationism) forces a focus on Christianity rather than on other religions. Also, much that I have to say extends to the other Abrahamic religions—Judaism and Islam—so generally what I have to say applies to what comes under the broader title "theism." Elsewhere recently I have also been looking at neopaganism as well as Eastern religions (Ruse 2013). Be all of this as it may, my work in the past decade and a half is in line with a general trend among philosophers, theologians, and others to an increased interest in and work on the science–religion interface. I suspect much of the growth has been a result of the arrival of the John Templeton Foundation, with large resources dedicated to the whole area of science and religion. However, although I have certainly had support from the foundation, and although I had respect and a certain fondness for Sir John himself, I have generally tended to keep some distance. I like to be my own man, aided admittedly by the gift from William and Lucyle Werkmeister that endows my professorship.

My ongoing and increased interest in the science–religion relationship comes first from the continued existence of creationism as a factor in society, especially a factor threatening education in society. Far from going away, creationism has morphed into the more sophisticated intelligent design theory and still is a grave threat to science education and understanding generally. I am not a Mother Teresa, but given my Quaker background, trying to do things that are morally worthwhile has always been a major motivating factor in my life, and I do derive great satisfaction from fighting creationism. This sense of duty was intensified by moving to America and becoming a citizen. I feel that if I am to be effective in this battle, then I must show that I am committed to the society and its culture. I am not just a Brit doing a job on Yanks. There are days, however, when the religious aura of Florida really has me wondering whether there might be an ontological argument for the necessary existence of Beelzebub. It is all so different from what I learned as a child.

Not much more than ten years ago, a second factor in my continued engagement with the science–religion interface would have surprised me greatly. I and others who believe in the possibility of good relations between science and religion have been attacked by extremists in the religious field. We expect that. I did not much care for the treatment of me in Ben Stein's movie, *Expelled*, but really it was water off a duck's back. What we did not expect is that we would be attacked, often bitterly, by those on the side of nonbelief. I thought

I had a good relationship with people like Richard Dawkins. Imagine my surprise when, on opening Dawkins's smash-hit best seller the *God Delusion* (2006), I am identified with Neville Chamberlain, the pusillanimous appeaser of Munich. Because I have argued that one can believe in evolution and still be a Christian, I (like others) am an object of scorn. We are what is known as "accommodationists," although as a sometime Quaker (a term that was first used in abuse and was then worn with pride) I am less than perturbed by the use of this term and have in fact taken to using it without comment to describe myself.

I am a philosopher, not a sociologist, so I am not so much concerned about the causes behind this attack—a classic case of what Freud called the "narcissism of small differences" given how close my thinking really is to someone like Dawkins. He too rejects Christianity, yet he too admits that you cannot absolutely, for all time, never say die, Scout's honor, assert that there is nothing beyond the grave. I am concerned with trying to articulate a position on the science–religion front that can withstand the assaults of the nonbelievers—the so-called New Atheists—as much as the fanatics on the side of belief. And, as you will by now expect, the books have poured forth, including in the past decade a trio on the subject: *Can a Darwinian Be a Christian? The Relationship between Science and Religion* (2001); *The Evolution–Creation Struggle* (2005); and *Science and Spirituality: Making Room for Faith in the Age of Science* (2010). *Atheism: What Everyone Needs to Know* (2015) also has a hand in all of this.

So I am here and ready to go at it again! I spoke at the beginning of not really knowing what I believe. In an important sense this is true because I feel very much that I am still on a voyage of discovery and that I could learn lots of new things that might yet make me change my mind. To this end, I love to have a good opponent with whom I can argue and try out my ideas, while of course showing that no person of intelligence or moral sensitivity or spiritual worth could possibly accept his ideas, and I hope I won't let down either him or you.

2

Science

Thinking about Science

Michael Ruse

One of the most irritating things about professional philosophers is that they seem obsessed with language. You ask an interesting question, and their response is, "It depends what you mean by . . ." Often this is a bit of breathing space to give them time to think of an answer. Every college professor knows that the immediate response to a tricky question is, "I am glad you asked that question." Whether or not you have an answer, the person who asked the question feels good! But, back to the philosophers (and as one of that ilk), let me say that often getting the terms right is important. How often, for example, have people argued about the existence of God although they are at complete cross-purposes? The person denying is denying someone who looks a bit like me—aged, in bad need of a haircut, and (this does not apply to me, at least not at the moment) dressed in a bedsheet. The person affirming is talking about something completely different—an ethereal entity, the "ground of our being" or some such thing. It is the same with "science." Since this is the crucial notion in our discussion, let us begin there.

What Is Science?

Start at the most elementary level. What is "science"? Elementary, but difficult to answer. Rushing in as a fool where angels fear to tread, let me follow the great English philosopher John Locke and say that science is an attempt to understand the world of experience, meaning now the world of the senses and also the world within us, of sentience. What is understanding? The Greek philosopher Aristotle (at the beginning of his *Metaphysics*) is pretty good here: "Understanding is knowledge about certain principles and causes." Then he goes on to say,

> that of knowing all things must belong to him who has in the highest degree universal knowledge; for he knows in a sense all the instances that fall under the universal. And these things, the most universal, are on the whole the hardest for men to know; for they are farthest from the senses. And the most exact of the sciences are those which deal most with first principles; for those which involve

fewer principles are more exact than those which involve additional principles, e.g., arithmetic than geometry. (Barnes 1984)

Let us concern ourselves less with how Aristotle might unpack this passage and more with how we, with our modern science, might unpack the passage. Note first the emphasis on the universal. Science is not a question of describing one darn thing after another. Somehow we have got to bring things beneath universals, or what scientists refer to as "laws of nature." "The rock is falling through the air." This is not a scientific statement as such, although it might be something explained by science. "The distance traveled by a falling body is directly proportional to the square of the time it takes to fall." This is a law of nature, and note that it tells you that this rock and any other rock will follow the same rule. Already we are on our way to grasping the nature of science. I myself would say that the most important thing is bringing phenomena—physical phenomena (and, somewhat artificially, I extend this here to mental phenomena)—beneath the rule of law, unbroken regularities.

Note, however, and this is also very important, that Aristotle doesn't think we have a bunch of separate laws, each going its own way. Laws come packaged in systems, and for Aristotle and for most modern thinkers, this means that laws are parts of "axiom systems," such as you find in geometry—first principles or axioms and then everything following deductively from them. This is not so much a question of familiarity—Aristotle hints that the axioms may be relatively unknown—but of how things fit together in the system. The classic case of a scientific axiom system—often known as a "hypothetico-deductive system"—is that of Newtonian mechanics. You start with Newton's three laws of motion—the first, for example, being that all bodies are in a state of uniform motion or at rest unless acted on by a force—and with his law of gravitational attraction, and then from these laws you deduce other laws, for instance, Kepler's laws of planetary motion—the best known being that planets describe ellipses with the sun at one focus—and Galileo's laws of terrestrial motion, one of which we encountered just prior when talking of falling rocks.

There is one more thing, something toward which talk of Newton's law of gravitational attraction points us. Aristotle again: "But the science which investigates causes is also instructive, in a higher degree, for the people who instruct us are those who tell the causes of each thing." Somehow we want to go beyond just describing things to saying why things work. We want to know the underlying causes. Hence, the best science has causes built into its first principles. In Newton's case, we know why things work as they do because (as his law of gravitational attraction states) every body attracts every other body with a force proportional to the masses of the bodies and inversely proportional to the square of the distance between them. There is this attraction between all bodies that makes everything do as it does.

No one thinks that science fits this model exactly. Indeed, no one thinks that scientists set out deliberately to fit this model exactly. For a start, rarely are scientists concerned to build full systems, all laid out carefully. Usually scientists work on some little area of experience—one species, for example, or one island and its ecology—and run up little systems, often idealized, and see whether reality fits the systems (usually called "models") that they have built. But even if you are working with just one species or island, the aim is generality. For instance, there is a famous formula about the rate at which islands emptied of their inhabitants will repopulate—a formula dependent, among other things, on distance from the mainland—and this formula is general, for all islands (including land islands, as in the middle of deserts), and then applied to the particular. If you destroyed all of the life on Prince Edward Island in Canada, then it would repopulate at a rate dependent on the distance of that island from the mainland (MacArthur and Wilson 1967).

Metaphor

Thus far, I have been talking more at the formal level. Now I want to flesh things out a bit, as it were. Note that although Michael Peterson does not deny anything I say here, neither does he stress the points I am about to make. I know (and I do not say this in a critical way) this points to a different reading of science between the two of us. Whereas I see science as a human construction, with its feet in the culture of its day, he sees science more as a disinterested reflection of objective reality. His realism and my antirealism play out in various chapters in this debate about science and religion—and it is a difference you should think about.

You don't do science just by putting on a white coat on a Monday morning and walking into the lab and looking at the world. You have questions, you have problems, you have ideas, you have hypotheses. In one of the most famous passages in his correspondence, Charles Darwin put his finger on things precisely:

> How profoundly ignorant B. must be of the very soul of observation! About thirty years ago there was much talk that geologists ought only to observe and not theorise; and I well remember some one saying that at this rate a man might as well go into a gravel-pit and count the pebbles and describe the colours. How odd it is that anyone should not see that all observation must be for or against some view if it is to be of any service! (Darwin 1985–, Charles Darwin to Henry Fawcett, 18 Sept [1861] Letter 3257)

But how do you generate the ideas, the hypotheses, that you will use to do your science? Thomas Kuhn talked of scientists working within what he called "paradigms," kinds of conceptual frameworks that set the picture and the limits and that gave strong heuristic hints about how to move forward (1962). He subsequently stressed that the key to paradigm thinking is metaphorical thinking (Kuhn 1977, 1993). We look at the world, or parts of it, through the lens of something with which we are familiar, spurring us to ask questions and (with luck) to find answers. We do this all of the time and not just in science (Lakoff and Johnson 1980). Think of the metaphor of up and down, as in "Rise up and shine!" "He was looking awfully downcast." "Stand up, stand up for Jesus." "A man never stands so tall as when he kneels to help a child." (I can forgive the Shriners much—even those silly hats—for that one.) At once we have thoughts that go with the metaphor, such as being strong and fresh and not wilted or diseased and so forth. In science, however, metaphor really comes into its own, and the practice is drenched (metaphor!) in them: force, work, attraction, genetic code, natural selection, plate tectonics, Oedipus complex, and more. Cutting to the quick, what I want to point out—and I am saying nothing that wouldn't be said at this point by any other historian or philosopher of science—is that modern science is characterized by one dominant metaphor— what students of the subject call the "root" metaphor:

> No Christian could ultimately escape the implications of the fact that Aristotle's cosmos knew no Jehovah. Christianity taught him to see it as a divine artifact, rather than as a self-contained organism. The universe was subject to God's laws; its regularities and harmonies were divinely planned, its uniformity was a result of providential design. The ultimate mystery resided in God rather than in Nature, which could thus, by successive steps, be seen not as a self-sufficient Whole, but as a divinely organized machine in which was transacted the unique drama of the Fall and Redemption. If an omnipresent God was all spirit, it was the more easy to think of the physical universe as all matter; the intelligences, spirits and Forms of Aristotle were first debased, and then abandoned as unnecessary in a universe which contained nothing but God, human souls and matter. (Hall 1954, xvi–xvii)

Although written many years ago, historians of the Scientific Revolution—that great transformation of our understanding of the natural world that began with Copernicus at the beginning of the sixteenth century and ended with Isaac Newton at the end of the seventeenth century—agree that this passage stands the test of time. From the time of the Greeks, the world was seen in organic terms. We see it (or parts of it) as if it were an organism, as if it were living. Then, above all, we had a change of metaphors—from the world seen as an organism, or at least in terms of living beings, to the world seen as a machine, designed and created by God, but nevertheless a clockwork-like system bound by unchanging and never-ending laws.

What Is Naturalism?

The worm in the bud was that with God taken out of the system, in the language of Descartes, the physical world is pure *res extensa*, extended material, whereas God is pure *res cogitans*, thinking material. Increasingly from the viewpoint of science, God was seen as irrelevant. It was not that the scientists were atheists—they were not—but that they could—they should—ignore God and get on with the job. In the words of another of the great historians of the Scientific Revolution, God became a "retired engineer" (Dijksterhuis 1961). You might wonder how this could be so. The defining mark of the Aristotelian organic model is that you can ask about purposes or ends, what Aristotle called "final causes" and what in the eighteenth century became known as "teleological" questions. Just as you can ask, say, about the purpose of the funny plates down the back of the dinosaur stegosaurus (they are probably for heat regulation), so you can ask about the purpose or end of a stream or a mountain. Surely, even if you replace the organic model or metaphor by the machine model or metaphor, you can still ask about purposes. Automobiles have parts with purposes no less than dinosaurs. And what this seems to imply is that God is still in the business. You cannot think of a steering wheel without thinking of a designer and a user. So intention seems to cross over the Scientific Revolution. The point, however, was that in the physical world—I will talk later about the organic world—the metaphor was refined, as one might say, so that all of the focus was on blind laws operating endlessly without meaning (Ruse 2003). Final causes, said Francis Bacon, the philosopher of the Scientific Revolution, are like vestal virgins, decorative but sterile. God was put out to pasture.

This kind of metaphysics of science, as we might call it, has come to be known as "naturalism." In a way, this is unfortunate, because naturalism is somewhat of a weasel word. It means so many different things to so many different people. When I was a kid, often naturalism referred to people who took their clothes off—nudists! I am sure that there are scientists who are nudists, but generally I am not suggesting that the first thing a scientist does on entering a lab is to strip naked. Apart from anything else, what would they do with all of those white coats? By naturalism here I mean going only with nature, that is, understanding only in terms of unbroken law, without any interventions from outside nature, that is to say without any "supernatural" phenomena intervening. In an important sense, this is simply a methodological principle. It is simply a strategy of not appealing to causes that are not natural;

in other words, no supernatural causes, or, as they are usually known, no miracles, meaning no breaks in or suspensions of the regular causes of nature. A scientist, let us say a medical scientist, might be a sincere Christian, but if a patient suddenly is cured of a bad cancer, it is not acceptable qua scientist to say that it was a miracle—that Jesus heard our prayers and fiddled around with the cancer cells.

For the purposes of doing science, you are, if you like, an atheist. I am sure that this will come up again, but for the record I don't see anything at all irreligious about this. When I am teaching the philosophy of religion, I ask—I beg—my religious students to write essays attacking God. As I tell them, if God is going to strike anyone dead, it will be your teacher and not you. But, as I also tell them, God isn't about to strike anyone dead. He knows and approves of what I am up to. To understand something, especially if you believe it strongly, push the other side as hard as you can. And that is what the "methodological naturalist" is doing: pushing and pushing the rule of law and finding that it pays incredible rewards. It's a "heads I win, tails you lose" situation for the believer. The more you find out about the workings of the natural world, the more amazing it and (to you as a believer) God who created it will seem.

Are you denying the very possibility of miracles? In a logical sense, you can hardly do that. The molecules of the cancer cells could be rearranged. What you are denying as a methodological naturalist is that it is ever going to happen. Is this a statement of faith, and if so, is the scientist really any different from the Christian who has faith that Jesus will forgive even the worst sinner among us? The scientist will say no and probably talk in terms of some kind of pragmatic justification. For the moment, let us just take note of this question and recognize that it is one that will have to be addressed before this book is finished. Rather, here, let us turn to another pressing question that needs an answer. Contrasting with "methodological naturalism" is "metaphysical naturalism," where one claims that what you see or get is all you can see or get. There is no God, of Christianity or anything else. God does not exist. Nature is all. Obviously, the metaphysical naturalist is going to be a methodological naturalist. The question here is whether the methodological naturalist is going to be a metaphysical naturalist. Many people think—and this includes some Christians (who for this reason, therefore, are usually critical of naturalism)—that there is a link or at least a steep and slippery path. The Nobel Laureate in physics Steven Weinberg has said, "The more the universe seems comprehensible, the more it also seems pointless" (Weinberg 1977, chap. 8). In other words, what you are saying is that the success of modern science pushes out religion.

As you can imagine from what I said in the previous chapter, I am uncomfortable with this. Of course, modern science pushes out some claims made in the name of religion. You cannot hold to modern geology, including paleontology, and to a universal flood that supposedly Noah and family uniquely survived. The sun cannot have stopped for Joshua. And there is more, including some pushing out that we shall see causes more trouble for more Christians than one might anticipate. But I am not sure that modern science as such, based as it is on the machine metaphor, makes all religious claims immediately untenable. Indeed, I would say that because modern science is based on the machine metaphor it cannot completely negate religion. Note that I am not now giving up on metaphysical naturalism (meaning atheism). I am saying that I don't think that science on its own does the job.

Here, incidentally, may be a point where there are implications from the different ways that Peterson and I view the nature of science. I feel a need to justify the potential place of religion in this age of science, and as you will see, metaphor is the key to my thinking at this point. I don't think—and I am trying not to put words in his mouth—Peterson feels this need in exactly the way I do. Although he claims not to be an independence theorist about the science–religion relationship, he does assert their different explanatory roles. Theism, for him, is a philosophical frame for science, whereas science can weigh in on religious claims about accessible empirical facts. As I see it, for him, the challenge is in how the two types of explanation—governed as I say by different metaphors—can be harmoniously related.

I do think my position superior because clearly there have been (and still are) times when religious people want to encroach, I think illicitly, on the domain of science—making claims about universal floods, for instance. Then one has got to show, as I am trying to show, why there are times when religion can legitimately make claims. Obviously, I am starting with the presumption that normally it is science that tells us about reality and exceptions must be justified. Perhaps that is the difference between us, because Peterson starts with no presumption that religion needs special justification before the bar of science. Further, what would he see as the conditions when religion can speak to the same subject as science and yet not be encroaching on science? You might want to ask whether he gives an adequate answer to this question.

The Limits of Metaphor

To return to the main thread of my argument, to see why I am saying what I say, start with a point that Kuhn always stressed about paradigms/metaphors, namely that they work in large part because they rule out questions. It is not that the questions are not legitimate but that the metaphor discourages you from wasting your time by asking them. I say my wife is a beautiful rose. You know that she is fresh and lovely, something that appeals to people. If you are joking a bit, you know that she is a little bit prickly. What you don't know, what you are not even thinking about, is whether she is good at mathematics or whether she is a New Atheist. Those questions are not being asked—their truths are not being considered—because the metaphor is not about them. They are outside the domain of discussion.

Now, what about the root metaphor of modern science, the metaphor of the machine? The physical world is seen as if it were a machine, a large clockwork. Of course, it is now more complex than when it came in during the sixteenth and seventeenth centuries, what with such things as electricity and quantum mechanics, but the basic metaphor is the same. So this then raises the question of what kinds of things the machine metaphor leaves out. If the world is a machine, what questions are simply not being asked? I don't think there is or could be a definitive list, and, in a way, any such a list is true throughout history. If, for instance, someone discovered something really amazing about roses—such as that grasping them increased one's perceptual powers incredibly—then this would have implications if I called my love a rose, implications that are not there at the moment.

Now let me offer the following four areas not touched by the machine metaphor, recognizing that they are not set in stone for all time. First, there is what is sometimes known as the fundamental question: Why is there something rather than nothing? Why does anything exist at all? Some people say that this is not a genuine question, but I don't think this at all. It is, however, a question that is not answered by science because it is a question that is not asked by science. You can, of course, ask from where came the materials of the machine—the steel of the automobile came from a mine in Wales perhaps—but ultimately the existence of the materials is taken for granted. It is like the recipe: first, take your hare. Second, and you would expect this, given earlier discussion, science doesn't tell you about the foundation of morality. At least, science might tell you about how a moral sense evolved, but it doesn't justify morality. Why should I love my neighbor as myself? No answer from science. With my guillotine, should I chop off the head of the murderer? Science doesn't tell you. I am a bit run down, so should I use my treadmill to get in better shape? No answer from science. Science can be of value in achieving ends. I need to get to the hospital to help deliver a baby: use an automobile built by the knowledge given by science. But whether you have an obligation to get to the hospital is another matter.

Third is the matter of sentience. I personally don't think you can solve the body–mind problem, and I am beginning to doubt whether we will ever solve the body–mind problem. Giving an account of how the brain works can be tremendously insightful and tell you how brain motions affect the way we think. But I see no bridge between the material brain and the thinking mind. Descartes said they are two different independent substances, and they certainly seem that way. But then how do they connect? The point is that the machine metaphor of the brain as a computer tells you how the hardware works and perhaps even what that means for the software. But it doesn't interpret the results of the software. You have marks on a screen but no meaning. Fourth, and finally, ultimate meaning. Now you might think that the machine metaphor does lead to meaning, in the sense of purpose. Guillotines are for chopping off heads and treadmills are for getting in shape. This is true. But, as we have seen, the point about the machine metaphor in science is that people felt that there was no point to asking about ends, and so such language was dropped. The machine metaphor extends only to things moving around eternally as governed by unbroken law. The watch is not there to tell time, just to keep going around and around and around and . . . There are no ultimate purposes in modern science.

There are four questions that I claim that science does not answer because science does not, and by its very nature could not, ask: Why is there something rather than nothing? What is the justification of morality? What is sentience? What is the ultimate meaning of it all? They seem to me to be genuine questions, and that means that they could have answers. I don't have them. Does this mean that my position is inadequate? My position is certainly incomplete. I say simply that I have no answer. I am an agnostic or a skeptic in some sense. Is there an answer? Perhaps. As the great biologist J. B. S. Haldane used to say, "My own suspicion is that the universe is not only queerer than we suppose, but queerer than we *can* suppose" (Haldane 1927, 286). Or perhaps not. Either way, I don't think that my skepticism—note incidentally that this is skepticism about the answers to these questions, not about God—rules out others attempting to give answers. It is just that they cannot be scientific answers, at least not scientific answers in terms of modern mechanical science.

This is why ultimately, as I said in the previous chapter, I don't see why science and religion cannot coexist. At least I don't see why from the viewpoint of science. If religious persons offer answers and these answers are not scientific answers (or quasi-scientific answers), then I don't see how a scientist can lay a finger on them. Of course, as we know full well, religious people do want to have a go at answering the questions and claim they can give answers. In the Christian context—and I would take it in a theistic context generally—why is there something rather than nothing? Because a God, a necessary being, decided out of goodness to create the world and its inhabitants. What are the foundations of morality? God's will. He decides what we should do and what we should not do. What is sentience? Being made in the image of God. Being given the power of reason and of moral understanding. What is the purpose of it all? To do what God wants and, as a reward, to enjoy eternal bliss with Him.

Just so we understand each other terminologically, then, let me say or resay where I stand on naturalism. I think science is by its very nature methodologically naturalistic, taking God-talk out of the equation and refusing to allow miracles. It justifies this pragmatically, by its success. I think metaphysical naturalism is the claim that God does not exist. I don't think a methodological naturalist has to be a metaphysical naturalist, although I do think a metaphysical naturalist will be a methodological naturalist. I am a metaphysical naturalist, but as you will see, I argue this on theological and philosophical grounds. I therefore differ from Michael Peterson not only in thinking that God does not exist but also in thinking that science offers no support for God's existence.

Note that I am not denying the logical possibility of miracles. I am asserting that modern science does not allow the possibility of miracles. Miracle claims lie outside science and must be based on faith or some such thing. Hence, I have no time for those who try to justify miracles naturally, for instance, by claiming that because, back at the time of Jesus, women did not have high status, we should take as especially significant (and truth conferring) the fact that it is women who report on the empty tomb. The gospel writers would not have made this up. I think you are, as Stephen Jay Gould used to say of evolutionists who make up fairy tales, indulging in what the author Rudyard Kipling called "just so" stories—the elephant has a long nose because the crocodile pulled it. If you deny the worth of pragmatic arguments, then let me ask my Christian friends like Michael Peterson why they reject (as they obviously do) the historical authenticity of Joseph Smith's discovery of the golden plates. It seems to me that sauce for the Mormon goose is sauce for the Christian gander.

Mine is the better position, but if only because we have much yet to discuss; no victory laps yet, please. Note what I have allowed and what I have not allowed. I am saying that science cannot rule out the religious person offering answers to some important questions. It does not follow that the person of science has to accept the religious person's answers. On philosophical or theological or other grounds, one might reject them. For this reason, because science has no answers and the person of religion claims to have answers, it does not follow that in some sense the religious position with respect to the world is better or stronger. Bad or incorrect answers—if such they be—are never better or stronger. It is just that the science–religion relationship is more complex than simply one of conflict or indeed of unqualified independence. These are things to bear in mind as now we plunge into the nature and meaning of evolution and its significance for religious belief, specifically Darwinism and its significance for theism generally and Christianity specifically.

The Harmony of Science and Religion

Michael Peterson

As a theist, I find it difficult to believe that anyone could be more positive toward science than I am. Theism is the belief that there is a supreme personal being, God, having neither beginning nor end, who is omnipotent, omniscient, and perfectly good and who created, sustains, and interacts with the universe and all it contains. On this view, the physical universe has the status of a creation of an infinite rational being and is therefore itself intelligible to finite rational beings. Science, then, is a legitimate means of learning about the created universe.

Such a clear religious affirmation of science is difficult to hear in today's culture as polarizing voices proclaim the "warfare" between science and religion. In the United States, the conflict particularly revolves around the theory of evolution as a key feature of contemporary science. Some, such as Stephen Jay Gould, have sought peace in the supposed war by insisting on compartmentalization. My dialogue partner, Michael Ruse, advocates accommodationism. Agreeing with John Hedley Brooke, a noted historian of science, that the science–religion relationship is "rich and complex" (Brooke 2014, 6), I argue here that certain clarifications regarding the nature and scope of these two important human activities reveal not merely their compatibility—that is, no incompatibility—but also their close ties. This sets the stage for discussing the following.

Where the Conflict Really Lies

Although there have been political, cultural, and intellectual disagreements between science and religion, conflict is not inherent to their relationship. Many controversies trace to the "demarcation problem" of stating what is and is not properly science—and of clarifying boundaries between these two intellectual activities. Michael Ruse distinguishes them as operating by different metaphors that shape the types of questions they can raise and types of answers they can countenance. I prefer to clarify the boundary between science and theology by distinguishing their respective aims, objects, and methods. Theology explains God's purposes in the world, not the natural world per se, and its essential task is the rational presentation of an understanding of God arising from scripture, tradition, and the experience of the believing community. Thus, science and theology cannot do each other's business, but they are not unrelated, as the accommodationist holds, or hermetically sealed from each other, as those advocating compartmentalization maintain.

Ruse takes science, with its machine metaphor, as the best way of knowing the world, thus elevating science according to his worldview commitments. He thinks that science can negate incorrect factual claims made by religion—a point on which we agree—because such claims venture into the realm of the machine metaphor. Furthermore, he links his metaphor theory to a social constructivist view of knowledge, which is inherently antirealist. By contrast, I'm an epistemological realist generally and in regard to science specifically. Hence, an interesting irony emerges: science may deal only with the realm of facts, but the very concept of "fact" is problematic for antirealism in a way it is not for realism. This point will play out as we proceed.

If we transition from speaking of religion broadly to focusing on theism specifically, we can see how theology and science are related although they have different missions. For example, theology provides a large scale understanding of the reality and intelligibility of the world in which science occurs. Science, on the other hand, can obviously speak to factual claims that are sometimes intertwined with theological claims. Another example is that science and theology can provide different types of explanation of the same phenomenon, largely mechanical (how) and purposive (why), respectively. Scientific and theological explanations can be complementary—having a common reference but explaining different aspects of it. Thus, the two explanations need not be rivals or mutually exclusive and together offer a fuller understanding. A painting may be described entirely in terms of the distribution of the chemicals used to create it or entirely in terms of the aims of the artist. But neither description alone is complete; both explanations together provide a more complete understanding of the painting (Berry 1991, 9). I affirm science but resist the typical naturalist elevation of science as the exclusive or best type of explanation.

As we proceed, I will not be defending religion in general, which is at best a vague abstraction. Each religious tradition must engage science with its own intellectual resources—and, frankly, the results will vary greatly. As a theist, however, I do appreciate and affirm the desire for the divine that seems endemic to the human race. Nevertheless, for the intellectual heavy lifting that must be done in the rest of this book, I'm representing theism. Theism, technically, is not a living religion but does form the common conceptual core of the three great Abrahamic religions—Judaism, Christianity, and Islam. Theism projects a worldview framework that contains important information about God and his relation to the world that has considerable philosophical potency for the discussion at hand.

Atheism—either the refusal to affirm or the outright denial that God exists—does not explain much of anything. In modern secular culture, atheism typically finds fuller intellectual expression in philosophical naturalism. Naturalism is the position that the physical realm alone is real, that nature operates by causal laws, that nature is causally closed to outside influence, that all genuine knowledge is empirical, and that human beings are nothing but complex animals (Clark 2007). New Atheists such as Richard Dawkins and Daniel Dennett combine a naturalist worldview with science in their attacks on religion. My friend Michael Ruse, although more moderate in tone toward religion and more nuanced conceptually about its claims, works out his own synthesis of naturalism and science, particularly evolutionary science, as his total worldview package. His position includes accommodationism toward religious explanations of certain big questions, skepticism about those explanations, and explicit reasons to reject theism. Ruse thinks that his evolutionary naturalism does, whereas theism does not, offer a satisfactory interpretation of all we know.

To the contrary, I will argue as we go that theism is the basis for a philosophically more adequate worldview. Speaking to the larger conversation, I'll show that the absolutist atheist position of someone like Dawkins fails to show that science conflicts with theistic belief. Addressing Michael Ruse's position, I argue that it still gives undue priority to scientific knowledge because of his commitment to naturalism and therefore cannot give credence to religious explanations anyway. Not only is there is no science–theism conflict, but also theistic explanations have no less credibility than scientific ones have.

The real conflict is a worldview conflict between theism and naturalism and crucially involves how the opposing positions respond to science, including evolutionary science. Every worldview, religious or secular, offers a philosophical explanation of the major phenomena of life and the world—fundamental reality itself, knowledge, the status of humanity, the ground of morality, and so forth. Clearly, both theism and naturalism generate important implications for the topics covered in this debate. However, since basic theism does not provide a complete picture of God's nature and purposes, I sometimes draw additional information from orthodox Christianity or the central beliefs that all Christians share in common, as summarized in the Nicene Creed. This understanding of Christian faith is often called "classical orthodoxy" or "ecumenical Christianity" (Oden 2002).

The choice between competing worldviews should be guided by an assessment of their comparative explanatory power. My basic argument throughout this debate is that theism "explains" important phenomena (such as mind or morality) better than naturalism does. The kind of explanation involved is philosophical and may be understood by introducing the idea of antecedent probability as follows. To assert that theism explains a certain phenomenon better than naturalism is to say that the probability of that particular phenomenon occurring is much higher on the assumption that theism is true than on the assumption that naturalism is true. We can helpfully represent this comparative judgment in symbolic format. Where T is theism, N is naturalism, and X is the phenomenon in question,

$$P(X/T) > P(X/N).$$

Although it's difficult to make precise judgments of probability about the topics we are considering, the idea of making sensible comparative judgments of probability is reasonable and will prove enlightening. Regarding every important phenomenon discussed in this book, I raise the question of whether that particular phenomenon is more probable given theism or given naturalism.

The kind of probability I'm dealing with pertains to the closeness or naturalness of the conceptual connections between a stated philosophical worldview and the phenomenon in question. The idea of closeness in conceptual connections here gives our worldview comparison an epistemic dimension and leads to the notion of "epistemic surprise." The conceptual content of a given worldview may make the existence of a given phenomenon more or less epistemically surprising. I'll be arguing that assuming the truth of theism makes mind, morality, and many other features of reality much less epistemically surprising than naturalism does. Conversely, I'll contend that, on the assumption that naturalism is true, these same phenomena are surprising indeed. This is one way in which science supports theism: science itself is one of those important phenomena that make better sense on the assumption that theism is true.

Some call this "inference to the best explanation." C. S. Peirce coined the term "abduction" to label this process, which goes roughly as follows: *The interesting or important phenomenon X exists; if hypothesis H were true, X would be likely; hence, there is some reason to think that H is true.* When comparing rival worldviews, we may say that X is more likely (or is less epistemically surprising) on one hypothesis than on the other. Regarding mind or morality or other important phenomena, this will be my recurring theme: that theism explains each major feature of the world better than naturalism does and that theism makes the occurrence of that feature, and all we know about it, more likely.

In the history of science, there is no more impressive example of inference to the best explanation than Charles Darwin's postulating in the *Origin* that natural selection accounts for a wide array of data—adaptation, extinction, geographical distribution, vestigial structures—that were problematic for all other theories, including special creation. Although our unfolding debate is not about rival scientific explanations, it is very much about comparing philosophically how well two opposing worldviews explain major aspects of reality about which science adds important detail. Before launching into discussion about such matters, let's first address some major concerns about how the enterprise of science affects the debate between naturalism and theism.

Does the Method of Science Support Naturalism?

Science is one of the most impressive knowledge-gathering projects in human history, providing an astounding amount of information about the world and promising much more. The method of science is at the heart of this success. However, the *scientific method* is not a single procedure but a number of practices in which scientists engage—from observing to experimenting, from creative theorizing to constructing models. The key is the intentional rigor of scientists in tying hypotheses to empirical experience. Hypotheses are accepted when they are considered to explain and predict better than alternatives and to connect well with prevailing theories. Science is an important reflection of the human drive to understand the physical universe, how it is structured and how it works.

The explanatory work of science is anchored in its ability to identify causes of the phenomena under study. As modern science ceased to refer to supernatural activity and teleology in fulfilling its explanatory mission, we were left with a world of natural causes—in Aristotelian terms, efficient rather than final causes. As Ruse notes, *methodological naturalism* is the common term for the procedure of seeking natural causes for natural phenomena. To do its work, science must assume that there are physically necessary connections between causes and their effects—and that these connections can be codified as scientific laws. Scientific explanation, then, brings empirical phenomena under known laws. Theism readily affirms all legitimate avenues of knowledge, including empirical knowledge of the regularities of the world.

Interestingly, Alvin Plantinga argues that methodological naturalism unfairly tilts the scales against religion and theism and is purely a creature of Enlightenment rationalist elitism (Plantinga 2011, 168–78). The overblown rationalism of modernity looks to the interaction of human reason with an orderly nature as the basis for all explanation, setting the stage for the reductionistic rejection of other legitimate types of explanation. But the ideal that the method (as well as the content) of science should be religiously neutral in generating explanations of natural phenomena is not inherently antireligious. Maintaining that claims about theology, values, and purposes cannot enter into scientific explanations hardly excludes such claims from entering into metaphysical explanations. This is why people with different background beliefs about religion or values can all engage in science and rally around the scientific method but can then construe science according to their own larger philosophical perspectives.

The New Atheists and other scientific critics of religion believe that methodological naturalism supports *metaphysical naturalism* and puts serious pressure on theism. Ironically, proponents of creation science and intelligent design theory agree and therefore criticize and reject mainline science for ruling out God or scripture or teleology. To counteract what they perceive as the naturalistic bias of science, these religious movements promote alternative versions of scientific investigation to block evolutionary conclusions or propose their own supernatural explanations. Yet both of these groups, secular and religious, are mistaken that methodological and metaphysical naturalism are linked.

I ask the hard-liners: what important or compelling linkage could there possibly be between methodological naturalism and metaphysical naturalism? Methodological naturalism clearly does not *entail* metaphysical naturalism. And there is no need to *assume* metaphysical naturalism to make methodological naturalism work as a mode of inquiry. Sidney Hook typifies the many thinkers who are determined to argue, nevertheless, that methodological naturalism somehow makes metaphysical naturalism the most reasonable position:

> [T]here is only one reliable method of reaching the truth about the nature of things . . . this reliable method comes to full fruition in the methods of science. . . . Naturalism as a philosophy not only accepts this method but also the broad generalizations which are established by the use of it; *viz*, that the occurrence of all qualities or events depends upon the organization of a material system in space-time, and that their emergence, development and disappearance are determined by changes in such organization. (Hook 1961, 185–86)

What we have here is the epistemological exaggeration of science—the claim that empirical science is the sole arbiter of truth—used to pave the way for the metaphysical inflation of science—the claim that only the empirical is real. These subtle moves allow naturalism to masquerade as science, both in broader culture and in academia, and thereby gain credibility in its crusade against religion.

Michael Ruse is not far from Hook, indicating that his metaphysical naturalism strongly inclines him toward methodological naturalism as the best way of knowing the natural world. Further, stating that the natural world is the only reality rules out the supernatural. So, theology, with its explanations and target subjects, immediately starts from a disadvantaged position relative to science. I will engage this theme extensively as I tackle the issues of the book, including those issues that Ruse allows religion to address.

Historically and currently, a great many methodological naturalists are theists. The early chemist Robert Boyle was a Christian and methodological naturalist; Francis Collins, who directed the Human Genome Project and was appointed head of the National Institutes of Health in 2009, is a contemporary Christian who strongly advocates methodological naturalism. As the Christian philosopher of science Ernan McMullin states,

> But, of course, methodological naturalism does not restrict our study of nature; it just lays down which sort of study qualifies as *scientific*. If someone wants to pursue another approach to nature—and there are many others—the methodological naturalist has no reason to object. Scientists *have* to proceed in this way; the methodology of natural science gives no purchase on the claim that a particular event or type of event is to be explained by invoking God's creative action directly. (McMullin 1991, 56)

The intellectually sophisticated theist who affirms the integrity of the natural creation and its operations sees no problem in bracketing God, miracles, and final causes while seeking empirical explanations of how nature works.

In this light, Ruse's feeling that religion should be justified in an age of science emanates more from naturalist precommitments, as I see it, than from scientific standards. Although I'm not trying to insulate religious claims categorically from any appropriate scientific scrutiny, I must alert the reader that naturalists commit various fallacies depending on how they involve science in their rejection of religion. However, identifying bad arguments against religion is hardly to justify or defend or endorse any religion whatever. Each religion will have to make its own case—and they will not all be equal in this regard.

It's actually a fair request that theism be reasonably articulated in connection to science, but not in the way Ruse thinks. For the process to be fair, at least two conditions must be met in this context. First, any evaluation of religion by science must be decoupled from bias toward naturalism. Second, we must expand our idea of what kind of support science could offer to religion— and, again, here I mean theism. And remember: atheistic naturalism must make its own case in relation to science. The theist bears no special burden of proof here. What we need is a level playing field on which both worldviews give their explanations of how they relate to science—and to a number of other important phenomena as well.

When naturalists of various stripes involve science in their presentation—coopting science or claiming to speak from a rigorous scientific mind-set—they put a logic in motion that sets up one kind of competition or another between science and religion. Unfortunately, perceiving competition and possible conflicts of various sorts is also endorsed by some religious advocates who seem unable to discern the difference between authentic science and atheistic claims made in the name of science. We have seen creationists reject carbon-12 dating to support their Young Earth position; we have witnessed intelligent design proponents insist that teleological explanation must be returned to biology to make room for God in science; and the list goes on. Although Ruse does not hold a total warfare viewpoint, he does recognize that science can check factual claims made by religion.

The history of science makes the stereotype of competition and conflict somewhat understandable from both sides. As modern science defined itself and mechanical explanations became successful, God and teleology were progressively eliminated from its explanatory framework. The revolution Newton began in physics Darwin completed in biology—that is, to solidify the scientific conception of the world as operating entirely by laws. Conflicts and misunderstandings occurred as science established its mode of explanation via efficient causes, whereas theology and metaphysics dealt largely with final causes. To the extent that competition occurred between science and religion, religion retreated as science advanced.

Stephen Jay Gould sought to make peace by designating science and religion to be "nonoverlapping magisteria"—two separate domains of authority with absolutely no commerce between them (Gould 1997). Science deals with the realm of facts accessed by empirical inquiry; theology deals with the realm of value and meaning accessed through church authority. The element of truth in Gould's point is that we must understand the integrity of these two important disciplines and locate them accurately on the intellectual map—largely by understanding their respective objects, aims, and methods (Peterson et al. 2012, 297). This would allow for scientists who hold firm belief in God but understand that science as a discipline is simply neutral about God's existence and involvement in the world. The element of error in Gould's approach is that it implicitly interprets the science–religion relationship in terms of dichotomies—how/why, fact/value, objective/subjective—and envisions no bridges between the two sides.

Michael Ruse also allows for the possibility of peace between science and religion under certain conditions. Although science cannot surrender empirical questions to religion, religion is permitted to answer certain nonempirical questions. Despite the honesty and humility in Ruse's skepticism about religious answers, a skeptical stance has its own vulnerability—because the problems are still there, and both naturalism and theism must take their shot at them. Ruse's position is still better than the totalizing naturalist positions claiming that science allows no other dimension of reality or modality of knowing. In the end, however, all naturalistically driven approaches to the relation of science and religion—warfare, independence, accommodation with skepticism, scientific imperialism—fail to provide an adequate basis for a comprehensive, unified worldview.

Theism actually provides a basis for appreciating all different aspects of reality and putting them in a helpful philosophical perspective. Theism implies that all truth is God's truth, wherever it may be found—and that there are many kinds of truth and methods for seeking truth about the multifaceted reality that is a divine creation. Science, theology, mathematics, and ethics merely begin the list. To speak of different kinds of truth—as well as different methods for accessing them—is not to compartmentalize them but to recognize the multifarious nature of a single but complex reality. Aquinas provides the master principle: the truths of reason—including those of science—cannot contradict the truths of faith because God is the author of both (Aquinas 1975 *SCG* I, chaps. 7–8). Theism further implies that created reality is a unified whole and that all truths about it form a consistent and coherent whole. In practice, we may sometimes struggle with exactly *how* various truths fit together, but the theist knows that, in principle, all truths do fit together.

Specifically, theological and metaphysical truths relate to scientific truths in special ways. On the one hand, theological and metaphysical truths offer principles that frame up the kind of world in which science operates. But science is only one avenue of access to the created world; there are other avenues of access that theism also affirms, such as history and ethics. A theistic worldview puts all of these kinds of truth in perspective. On the other hand, as Aquinas held, science offers correction to invalid biblical interpretation as well as enlightenment about the workings of the world that are intertwined with theological commitments. Science is then clearly relevant to religious claims regarding a universal flood or the sun standing still, but literary and cultural studies of the ancient biblical texts that contain such claims would also be relevant to determining their basic message (Wright 2011). Theology, of course, would still be in the business of clarifying the themes and enduring meaning of any biblical texts that may utilize symbolism or myth in the classic sense. My position, quite emphatically, is that the essential relation of science and theism is not one of either conflict or independence; it is actually a particular kind of integration within a total worldview.

Do the Laws of Science Exclude Miracles?

A miracle, for current purposes, is a violation of the laws of nature by a supernatural force or being resulting in an event that would not have occurred through natural processes (Peterson et al. 2012, 207–9). Michael Ruse and other critics claim that the laws of science pose a problem for belief in miracles, but classical theism implies the possibility of miracle. Ruse in particular grants that miracles are not logically impossible and that science per se cannot disprove that a miracle occurred, but the problem he raises is that the belief in miracles must be held by faith. Ruse's problem with miracles has two sources. First, his naturalism includes the metaphysical idea that nature is a causally closed system, not open to supernatural activity. Second, there is the epistemological thesis that miracles cannot be justified empirically by citing natural events. This leads to the dichotomy between rational belief (presumably only scientific belief) and faith. Belief in miracles must, then, be pure faith.

Any philosophical discussion of miracles must include commentary on David Hume, whose thought Michael Ruse employs at various points in our discussion. Hume argues that rationality requires that we proportion our belief to the evidence—and then states that the overwhelming weight of human experience favors the uninterrupted regularity of nature:

> A miracle is a violation of the laws of nature; and as a firm and unalterable experience has established these laws, the proof against a miracle, from the very nature of the fact, is as entire as any argument from experience could possibly be imagined. (Hume [1748] 2000, 86)

Statistically, the probability that an event is a miracle is always significantly smaller than the probability that it was produced by lawlike processes. Hence, the Humean line is that it's always more rational to believe that a miracle did not occur.

Hume's attack on miracles applies broadly but specifically targets testimony to miracle. Yet the narrower attack on testimony regarding a miracle is hardly problem-free. An improbable event can be supported by sufficiently strong testimonial evidence. I would be rational in believing that the improbable event of John winning the lottery (entered by several million people) occurred based on a public statement by lottery officials who employed a reputable accounting agency, since it is unlikely that the announcement would have been made falsely. However, Hume adds the caveat that the chances that persons are deceived or trying to deceive about extraordinary events are always greater than the chances that they are correctly reporting. Reasons for incorrect reporting include gullibility, lack of education, insufficient observers, attempted fraud, and so forth. Since miracles are often falsely reported, even by well-intentioned people, healthy caution or even skepticism about such reports is indeed advisable.

As a theist, I have no obligation whatsoever to defend just any report to miracle. And I understand that discussing various miraculous biblical stories requires attention to science as well as to the genre of literature where the accounts occur, the ancient cultural context, and so forth. Although this is not the place for full-scale examination of such matters, the interested reader may pursue them in other scholarly sources (e.g., Wright 2014). My point here is that theism implies that God created and sustains the lawlike behavior of nature and that he intervenes relatively rarely, but that miracles are both possible and possible to believe rationally. Therefore, the Humean-type argument that miracle reports must be rejected on rational grounds is badly flawed.

One mistake in the Humean argument is the assumption of a universal standard of rational belief—an overblown Enlightenment idea. Contemporary epistemology tells us that what is rational for a given person to believe depends on that person's total set of background beliefs, or noetic structure. This makes Hume's assessment of miracle claims too restrictive, since it appeals only to the shared human experience of regularity in nature. Yet each person assessing a miracle claim will have his or her own fuller set of background beliefs, which will include a lot more than simply the knowledge of nature's regularities—and these background beliefs will differ among people.

Theism is part of the background beliefs for a theist—and theism includes the idea that God can intervene in natural processes. Where M is a putative miracle, L is belief in the common human experience of the lawful behavior of nature, and T is theism, the theist would generally conclude that $P(M/L \ \& \ T)$ is not prohibitively low. Of course, there is no obligation for the theist to assign any given miracle report a high probability, since a final judgment must await further investigation and reflection. Where N is philosophical naturalism, the naturalist would say that $P(M/L \ \& \ N)$ is exactly zero. It's difficult to specify what the honest skeptic would say about this without knowing his other background beliefs—whether he is genuinely open to some form of supernaturalism, whether he considers some experience of or testimony to miracle to be convincing, and so forth. But the argument from the human experience of the regularity of nature is insufficient to show the irrationality of ever believing that a miracle occurred.

For Christians, God has already miraculously intervened in the natural world in important ways—most notably, in the Incarnation and Resurrection—and may intervene for good reasons in the future. So, the Christian belief in the lawlike regularity of nature is qualified by belief in the power and the purposes of God. A classically Christian interpretation of miracles completely agrees that science must either assume lawlike operation in nature or cease to be science. But it disagrees with both the hard-line position that science shows that nature cannot accept miracles and Michael Ruse's position that miracles lie beyond rational belief. Let us explore this further.

First, any statement of scientific law carries an implied *ceteris paribus* clause—that "all things being equal," a specific cause brings about its usual effect. A scientific law (stating causal connections) holds when initial conditions—pertaining to the relevant natural objects and their properties and powers—are held constant in each case. However, a claim to miracle is a claim that a supernatural agent was involved in bringing about an event that would not have been generated by the workings of nature. Thus, in a miraculous event, the initial conditions really don't hold—"all things are not equal" (*non ceteris paribus*)—which means that the law is technically not broken.

Second, science—which speaks to regular, repeatable empirical events—is not the only discipline that determines whether a belief is rational. History—as that discipline which studies the arena of collective human thought and action—rests on the fact that there are intentional agents with the power to violate initial conditions and bring about unique events that would not have occurred in the regular workings of nature. We form rational beliefs about human actions in history or even in common life by gauging the quality and credibility of testimony, considering other sources and documentation, and explaining them largely by reference to agent intentions—Julius Caesar crossing the Rubicon because of his political ambition or Jonas Salk developing a vaccine because he wanted to eliminate polio. But we don't think that our beliefs are irrational if they are about actions of finite personal agents that weren't produced by regular natural processes. We speak of human actions—which bring about singular events that would not otherwise have occurred in the regular workings of nature—as making sense in light of the beliefs, values, motives, choices, powers, and opportunities of those involved.

The discussion of miracle is very much about what we can rationally believe as historical fact and explain in terms of the purposes of an omnipotent agent. For an orthodox Christian, the authenticity of reports of miraculous divine activity are also judged by the believing community according to its consensus about the character and purposes of God. This consensus is drawn from the biblical canon, based on Christian history, and reflected in the theological framework of universal theological orthodoxy (Wright 2011). In this light, any claim to miracle would be evaluated in terms of whether it is a significant indicator of God's love and goodness as understood within this context. Happily, this sane approach rules out alleged miracles that are trivial, bizarre, self-serving to the one reporting, meant as manipulative pressure, or contrary to the core understanding of God's nature. For me, as a Christian believer standing within historical orthodoxy, such miracle claims as that of an angel revealing golden plates to Joseph Smith get no traction. Not all miracle claims, past or present, are equal, and all must be considered on a case-by-case basis.

Consider the Resurrection of Jesus, which is central to Christian orthodoxy, in the context of our science discussion. Christianity makes an astounding historical claim—that God in the person of Jesus overcame death. This is the paramount example about which science cannot say that natural law has not been or cannot be broken, although it can rightly insist that its specific method must always look for lawlike regularities. The religious scholar Bart Ehrman argues the Humean line, already refuted, that a historian can never say that a miracle occurred because a miracle is "highly improbable" (Ehrman 2000, 50). Although a miracle is improbable on the exclusive background belief that nature is regular, final judgment must be made on the basis of all background beliefs and relevant evidence. If one has some degree of openness to supernaturalism and understands that rationally explicable events can be unique as well as regular, then he or she might evaluate the evidence as pointing to a miracle. Considering that no corpse was ever produced, that gospel accounts converge on the central resurrection story, and that people usually do not choose to die horrible deaths, as the disciples did, to defend claims they know to be false, he or she would be entirely rational in believing in the historicity of the Resurrection. It's a rational belief about a unique event based on reasoning that is perfectly natural to history or common sense or even forensic science (Davis 1984).

Many thoughtful people have, of course, weighed various natural reasons against the Resurrection (the stolen-body hypothesis, conspiracy hypothesis, etc.) and still reasonably concluded that Jesus was raised from the dead. The noted New Testament expert N. T. Wright evaluates the evidence and focuses on the fact that some powerful, transformative event was necessary to convince and motivate the disciples so powerfully. Wright concludes, "That is why, as an historian, I cannot explain the rise of early Christianity unless Jesus rose again, leaving an empty tomb behind him" (Wright 1993, 26). Ironically, critics who disallow natural explanations for believing in the Resurrection readily give credence to one or more natural explanations against it. Reasonable people can differ over the Resurrection and other miracle claims, but it is intellectually unfair to settle such issues in advance by appealing to naturalist assumptions about reality or insisting on science as the bar of all rationality. Beyond the issue of intervention miracles, other modes of divine action in the world await discussion in later chapters.

Theism as the Worldview Home of Science

Science as an intellectual enterprise does not conflict with theism, although science combined with naturalist philosophy by hard-liners or moderates conflicts with or illicitly shifts the burden of proof to theism. Let's now reverse the question of how theism fares in light of science and ask instead how science fares in light of theism. Since we are comparing worldviews, we must also ask how science fares in light of naturalism. In what kind of world does the very fact of science make the best sense—a world described by theism or by naturalism? My argument is that theism as a worldview explains the enterprise of science better than naturalism does. Remember that we are not speaking here of generating a scientific explanation because science cannot explain itself; it is philosophical explanation that is needed, or, we might say, metascientific explanation.

Edwin Burtt has shown that the enterprise of science requires metaphysical interpretation because it rests on assumptions that it cannot establish by its own methods and because its findings raise philosophical questions not answerable on its own terms (Burtt 1948). Science must make two assumptions: (1) that the physical universe has a coherent rational structure, manifested in its behavior according to regular laws; and (2) that human beings have the rational capacity for understanding the physical universe. Note the compatibility, the conceptual fit, between rational universe and rational inquirers.

Theism implies that the universe exists by the will of an omnipotent God and has intelligible order because of his supreme wisdom and intelligence. This supports the first assumption above. For the universe to come into being and persist as an organized physical system, it must be characterized by a coherent set of physical values and laws. For a rational, orderly universe to come from a rational creator makes preeminently good sense. By contrast, naturalism maintains that physical nature itself is ultimate, all there is; there is no rational deity above nature. Consequently, the intelligibility we ascribe to nature is something brute and inexplicable. Michael Ruse does not share my ontological realism about science, a realism which affirms that reality is mind independent and inherently intelligible—a position supported by my theistic position.

The second assumption, which has epistemological importance, likewise receives stronger support from a theistic position. Theism implies that a rational God might create rational creatures that have the ability to investigate his creation and to form true beliefs about it. Naturalism, on the other hand, does not imply that it is likely that rational creatures will arise at all, although naturalists exert substantial energy trying to explain the improbable appearance and function of mind in the universe. It is much more likely that finite minds would come to be in a universe described by theism than in one described by naturalism. Furthermore, as a theist, I take our minds to be well suited to know truth about the universe—a point I revisit in Chapter 7 on rationality.

Ruse, on the other hand, embraces epistemological antirealism—the position that knowledge is socially constructed. Controlling metaphors for him are essentially human cognitive projections onto a reality that we cannot actually know. I would counter that the recognition of shared organizing ideas—models, metaphors, paradigms, and the like—that suggest questions and directions for answers in scientific inquiry need not be taken in an antirealist direction. For one thing, all metaphors must ultimately be "cashed out" in more literal terms—such that the general machine metaphor in science must be reflected in specific, literally stated scientific laws about how physical reality works. For another thing, the success of science, as Hilary Putnam has argued, becomes a "miracle" if subjective constructs apply to the objective reality we inhabit (Putnam 1975, 73).

Ruse's belief that methodological naturalism is justified pragmatically by its success is curious in this regard and at best must be seen as a brand of instrumentalism regarding the usefulness—but not the objective truth—of scientific theories. Although scientific realism is often caricatured as the notion that we have pristine and perfect truth, it is actually the idea that we are gaining increasingly accurate and complete knowledge of reality, refining and improving it as we go (Harré 1994). My earlier points were that science must assume—and historically has assumed—that reality is inherently rational and knowable and that we are rational beings who can investigate and know it with reasonable reliability. All of this means that the phenomenon of science itself (S) is more probable on theism (T) than on naturalism (N), or

$$P(S/T) > P(S/N).$$

Science is explained better by theism because of the close conceptual connections between theistic commitments and the conditions that make science possible.

Theism makes the existence and nature of science less epistemically surprising than naturalism does by readily supplying and reinforcing the assumptions on which science rests. On the assumption that naturalism is true, the existence of science is unlikely—indeed, it is epistemically extremely surprising. This is a philosophical argument for theism from science, not a scientific argument for theism. I agree with Ruse that there is no support for theism from within the business of normal science; but I must stress that neither is there any support whatsoever for atheism. Science nevertheless supports theism in the following important way: the very existence and nature of science make far better sense on theism than on naturalism. This is certainly a justification of theism in light of science.

Although the logic of theism provides a general philosophical framework for science, it was specifically Christian belief that historically supplied even a richer understanding of nature out of which science emerged. The doctrine of "creation out of nothing" (*creatio ex nihilo*) implies that the natural world is real, rational, and good—displacing the ancient Greek view that matter is less real, irrational, and of no intrinsic value and that immaterial Forms are the proper objects of science. E. L. Mascall explains that science flourished as it adopted methods appropriate to the investigation of a created nature:

> A world which is created by the Christian God will be both contingent and orderly. It will embody regularities and patterns, since its Maker is rational, but the particular regularities and patterns which it will embody cannot be predicted *a priori*, since he is free; they can be discovered only by examination. The world, as Christian theism conceives it, is thus an ideal field for the application of scientific method, with its twin techniques of observation and experiment. (Mascall 1956, 132)

It is no wonder that pioneer scientists—such as Copernicus, Kepler, and Galileo—saw their scientific work as an expression of their Christian calling to understand God and his world. The nuclear physicist C. F. von Weizsäcker says, "In this sense, I call modern science a legacy of Christianity" (von Weizsäcker 1964, 163).

Contrary to the New Atheists, there is no convincing case that the enterprise of science conflicts with theism. Contrary to Michael Ruse, there is no good reason to think that theistic explanations are adequately accommodated if they simply stay off scientific turf. In the end, there is an underlying conflict of worldviews, theism and naturalism, and how they respond to science. However, there is a compelling case that theism—and specifically Christian theism—provides a favorable worldview context in which science makes best sense. The comparison of worldview frameworks on this exact point shows that theism has greater explanatory power than naturalism. Naturalism must generate an incredible "just so" story—about an orderly physical universe inexplicably coming into existence and being intelligible to mind—as the best account of why science as a human enterprise has traction. As the debate between theism and naturalism proceeds, I will contend that important findings of science—regarding cosmic and biological origins, mind, morality, and other key phenomena—raise fundamental philosophical questions that are answered in a more credible way by theistic and Christian worldview commitments.

3

Cosmic Origins

A Theistic Understanding of the Universe

Michael Peterson

Cosmological science plays heavily into the science–religion debate. In the past hundred years, science has provided a breathtaking explanation of the origin and early conditions of the universe. All religions offer explanations of the beginning of the universe as well. Theism implies that the universe was purposed by God and has its existence according to his wisdom and will. Many atheistic naturalists claim that the advances of science in the study of cosmic origins now render a theistic position false or unnecessary. Theists contend that these scientific findings raise serious questions about the universe that science itself cannot answer. As Michael Ruse has already agreed, there are philosophical questions beyond the reach of science. My argument here is that theism makes better philosophical sense of what we know scientifically about the origin and structure of the universe than naturalism does. I further point out that Ruse's skepticism about religious explanation and rejection of theistic explanation avoids facing inadequacies of the explanation implied by his basic naturalist position.

The Beginning According to Science

The Big Bang occurred about 13.75 billion years ago, when all matter and energy was compressed into an infinitesimally small point called "the singularity." Within 10^{-43} seconds after this cataclysmic explosion, rapid expansion took place, and the incredibly hot infant universe began to evolve. A modest asymmetry of matter and antimatter allowed matter to emerge—photons, neutrinos, electrons, and quarks formed and became the first building blocks of physical reality. Cooling allowed protons and neutrons to form, which were needed for the structure of hydrogen and helium atoms. Gravity drew hydrogen atoms into denser and hotter clouds, forming giant stars, which became nuclear cookeries for heavier elements—iron, carbon, nickel, sulfur, oxygen—which would later scatter into the universe as the stars exploded as supernovas.

Great clouds of swirling chemical compounds coalesced, ushering in an epoch of planetary development. Solar systems formed, with their planets, moons, asteroids, and comets. Galaxies came together—estimates are in the hundreds of billions—providing larger structures for many billions of solar systems. On one planet, Earth, revolving around a relatively small sun, conditions of temperature, radiation, and chemical composition were conducive to the emergence of life—the subject of the next chapter.

Interestingly, Big Bang theory was not always the dominant cosmological model. Albert Einstein and many other reputable scientists were attracted to steady-state theory, a cosmological model that maintained that the universe is static, infinite in age, and relatively constant in appearance. However, in the early 1930s, the Jesuit priest and mathematician Georges Lemaître began discussions with Einstein to persuade him that his own theory of general relativity actually predicted the Big Bang, giving it strong theoretical support.

Experimental support for the Big Bang came in 1929, when Edwin Hubble discovered the "red shift" phenomenon caused by stars and galaxies moving away from us. Sir Arthur Eddington argued in the journal *Nature* that the discovery of expansion is not evidence of a beginning (Eddington 1931). Lemaître replied in the same journal,

> If the world has begun with a single quantum, the notions of space and time would altogether fail to have any meaning at the beginning; they would only begin to have a sensible meaning when the original quantum had been divided into a sufficient number of quanta. If this suggestion is correct, the beginning of the world happened a little before the beginning of space and time. (Lemaître 1931)

When attending a talk by Lemaître in 1933, Einstein became convinced, declaring, "This is the most beautiful and satisfactory explanation of creation to which I have ever listened."

Resistance nonetheless continued in the scientific community. Fred Hoyle stated that the Big Bang is "an irrational process that cannot be described in scientific terms" (Hoyle 1975a, 658). In the late 1940s, Hoyle, along with Thomas Gold and Hermann Bondi, advanced a formal steady-state model, which accounted for the expansion of the universe by positing the continual creation of new matter to keep the density of the universe constant. Interestingly, Hoyle vigorously voiced his opposition to an absolute beginning of the universe in the Big Bang. He once wrote,

> This most peculiar situation is taken by many astronomers to represent the origin of the universe. The universe is supposed to have begun at this particular time. From where? The usual answer, surely an unsatisfactory one, is: from nothing! (Hoyle 1975b, 165)

Hoyle further rejected the idea of some people that there is a supernatural cause of the universe—in other words, that "a 'something' outside physics can then be introduced at $t = 0$." It is significant that steady-state theory never secured a single piece of experimental confirmation; its appeal was purely that it offered Hoyle and others metaphysical solace from having to refer the universe to an ultimate divine source.

Yet the 1965 Bell Labs discovery of microwave background radiation added more major evidence for the Big Bang. Mounting experimental evidence—such as the increasing rate of expansion of the cosmos—eventually made steady-state theory obsolete. Interestingly, Georges Lemaître, a Christian believer, possessed the intellectual framework to able to contemplate the possibility of an initial point at which the universe came into being, that there was once "a day without yesterday" (Farrell 2005). In effect, the idea that there was once a Big Bang beginning amounted to the "historicization" of the universe as our total physical environment, now replete with a whole story of how things have changed over time. This new understanding of the cosmos eventually overturned all old ideas that it was eternal or uncaused. Much more remains to be discussed about the history and import of different cosmological models and the reasons for them. But one thing is clear: the idea of a beginning from nothing was radical and revolutionary, changing forever how we think about the physical universe and how we reflect philosophically on it.

A Metaphysical Explanation of the Cosmos

Does Big Bang theory settle the question of origins? Stephen Hawking announces in *The Grand Design* that Big Bang science replaces religious accounts of cosmic origins. Hawking states,

> Because there is a law such as gravity, the Universe can and will create itself from nothing. . . . Spontaneous creation is the reason there is something rather than nothing, why the Universe exists, why we exist. It is not necessary to invoke God to light the blue touch paper and set the universe going. (Hawking and Mlodinow 2010, 180)

Given quantum gravity, God is no longer necessary. Hawking, who admits to an atheist perspective, treats scientific and religious explanations as competitive, such that his theory preempts reference to God as an explanation of the beginning of the universe. If space permitted, we could review all of the different scientific attempts—the oscillating model and others—to avoid looking outside of nature for the cause of the natural universe.

Hawking's futile attempt to give an exclusively scientific explanation of how the universe originated is confused at best and obscurantist at worst, but it is a last defense for those who insist on a purely naturalistic account of reality. However, as I argued in the previous chapter, science and religion answer different kinds of questions—science answers "how" questions, whereas religion answers "why" questions—and those answers converge on the same unified reality. Hawking's awkward language about the universe creating itself is best viewed as a mechanical explanation of "how" things developed—a *quantum fluctuation*, the spontaneous but short-lived appearance of subatomic particles from a vacuum. His idea that the universe "creates itself from nothing" is most charitably interpreted as referring to "nothing" as far as science can determine; but it is still not really *nothing*, not absolute nothing—not zero, zip, nada, as we say in the vernacular. It is actually "something" called quantum gravity. After all, something (in this case, the universe) cannot preexist itself to cause itself to exist. Otherwise, we could express Hawking's claim even less charitably: that nothing created everything! Actually, Hawking merely pushes the question of origins back one step: why is there quantum gravity and all of the relevant laws of physics? Surely, Hawking would not answer that the laws of physics create themselves! From within science, there is no answer to this question. We are now in the territory of metaphysics where theism and naturalism are major competitors.

The physicist Paul Davies, a recipient of the Faraday Prize, contemplates the only two remaining options now that we know the universe had a beginning and cannot exist by its own internal necessity:

> "What caused the big bang?" . . . One might consider some supernatural force, some agency beyond space and time as being responsible for the big bang, or one might prefer to regard the big bang as an event without a cause. It seems to me that we don't have too much choice. Either . . . something outside of the physical world . . . or . . . an event without a cause. (Davies 1995, 8–9)

The intractable problem is that claiming that the Big Bang is an event without a cause is both scientifically untenable and metaphysically absurd. Therefore, if the universe began to exist, we are driven to the second alternative: a supernatural cause beyond space and time is the external ground of all finite existence. Of course, now we are speaking of a kind causality beyond what science studies—an idea we must now probe more deeply.

Over many centuries, philosophers and theologians have developed various lines of reasoning for the existence of a transcendent cause of the universe. Their theistic explanation of the universe is that God is the cause in the sense that he exercises the power to bring something into being. What is typically known as the cosmological argument is actually not one argument but a family of different argument strategies (Peterson et al. 2012, 185–93). Let us briefly consider two insightful versions of the argument—one triggering on the fact that the universe had an actual temporal beginning and the other utilizing the important idea of the contingency of the universe.

The first argument is often termed the kalām cosmological argument, inspired by the medieval Islamic tradition of rational theology, typified by Ibn Rushd (Averroës) in the twelfth century (Peterson et al. 2014, 161–69). In historical context, the argument was connected to reasoning that protected God's power and sovereignty by denying the efficacy of creaturely (secondary) causes and that rejected the doctrine of creation out of nothing. I have no sympathy whatsoever with these other connections but think that an important line of reasoning can be extracted and considered on its own merits. For current purposes, a brief formulation goes as follows:

1. Everything that begins to exist has a cause of its existence.
2. The universe began to exist.
3. Therefore, the universe has a cause of its existence.

Let's take stock of where we are: we know that the universe did not create itself, contrary to Hawking's proposal, and that the concept of an uncaused event is incoherent, as Davies maintains. Hence, the temporal beginning of the universe begins a line of reasoning that ends up facing us with the real prospect of a cause of the universe from beyond the universe. This is not the simplistic view that the Big Bang is confirmation of the creation story in Genesis, but it is a profound metaphysical insight into what it means for the universe to have a beginning in time, whatever the details of that beginning turn out to be (Peterson et al. 2012, 86–89). Of course, the cause beyond the universe must be of such a nature that it does not itself require a cause, as though it could be caught in a regress of causes.

A Deeper Metaphysical Understanding of the Cosmos

Staying on the subject of cosmological metaphysics, there is an even more penetrating insight into what's behind the universe that is based on an atemporal consideration–the cosmological argument from contingency that is based on Aquinas's Third Way. Aquinas states, "We find in nature things that are possible to be and not to be, since they are found to be generated and corrupted, and consequently, they are possible to be and not to be" (Aquinas 1981, *ST* I, Q. 2, Art. 3). In other words, the things spoken of are ontologically contingent or nonnecessary—they need not exist. At the heart of Aquinas's point, we find a key metaphysical principle:

(P1)   Contingent being requires necessary being.

Alternatively stated,

(P2)   If a contingent being exists, then a necessary being exists.

Or,

(P3)   Either a necessary being exists or nothing exists.

Now, if the universe can reasonably be taken as contingent, then its existence must ultimately depend on a necessary (noncontingent) being. Since our prior discussion of the Big Bang philosophically rules out the universe existing by its own necessity and exposes its contingent nature, we need not repeat those points. Thus, the universe depends for its existence on a necessary being. Theism affirms that God is that necessary being. In the words of Aquinas, "Therefore we cannot but postulate the existence of some being having of itself its own necessity, and not receiving it from another, but rather causing in others their necessity. This all men speak of as God" (Aquinas 1981, *ST* I, Q. 2, Art. 3).

What kind of necessity does God have? God's necessity is certainly not logical necessity, as if the denial of "God exists" is a contradiction, as Descartes's version of the ontological proof contends. With this idea in mind, J. N. Findlay tried to articulate the negative analogue of this sort of ontological argument—an ontological disproof of God's existence (Findlay 1948). Relying on the strict Humean distinction between "matters of fact" (which are logically contingent) and "relations of ideas" (which are logically necessary), Findlay argued that all existence is contingent. Hence, the theistic concept of God as a necessarily existing being is incoherent, meaning that God's existence is impossible. Without trying to defend the ontological argument, it is still worth observing that what is at issue here is whether the idea of ontological necessity is meaningful. Mainline theism asserts God's unique mode of being in contrast to all contingent being. God's necessity is metaphysical, or what John Hick and Richard Swinburne call "factual necessity" (Hick 1961, 16; Swinburne 2004, 44). This is the idea of a sheer, ultimate, unconditioned reality, without beginning or end. The medieval scholastics spoke of "being from itself" (*ens a se*) in contrast to "being from another" (*ens ab alio*). For Aquinas, God's "aseity" (self-existence) means that God does not derive his existence from any other being but rather exists purely in and through himself (Aquinas 1981, *ST* I, Q. 3, Art. 3; *2012,*

2012, *DQP*, Q. 7, Art. 2). The Thomistic doctrine here is that God's essence is pure existence—that he cannot not exist, whereas creaturely realities can not exist (Aquinas 1981, *ST* I, Q. 13, Art. 11). Along with most scholastics, Aquinas saw God's declaration of his true name to Moses as I AM WHO I AM in Exodus 3:14 to be God's revelation of himself as pure Being (Aquinas 1981, *ST* I, Q. 2, Art. 3).

Empiricist critics on this point typically conflate logical and ontological sets of modals, mistakenly correlating the distinction between necessary and contingent truth with the distinction between necessary and contingent being. What the cosmological argument does is to discover *a posteriori* a being that anchors all other beings, a necessary and self-existent being on which all else is ontologically dependent. The cosmological reasoning here is straightforward: if anything exists, something must exist as the Fundamental Fact; a universe exists; therefore, there must be a Fundamental Fact. For theists, this Fact is God.

Moreover, I aver that some critics misunderstand Aquinas's point in trying to pin a "quantifier shift" fallacy on his argument. They interpret Aquinas as concluding from the statement "Everything has some time at which it does not exist" that "There is some time at which everything does not exist" by shifting "everything" to a different position in the second statement. However, this critique analyzes Aquinas's point solely in terms of predicate logic and the concept of sheer possibility, whereas it actually carries a richer metaphysical meaning rooted in Aristotelian thought. Aristotle's hylomorphic analysis of material objects is that they are "possible" in the sense that they have an inherent tendency to go out of existence, to cease existence, a proclivity to "be corrupted," which must manifest itself given sufficient time. Otherwise, it makes no sense to say that these objects are corruptible. Thus, if "everything" were contingent in the relevant Aristotelian sense, there would be some time in the past, particularly given infinite time, when nothing existed, in which case nothing would now exist. Aquinas's insight is that the intrinsic metaphysical instability of finite things must be counteracted by something ontologically noncontingent—that is, ontologically necessary. "That," Aquinas says of this noncontingent being, "all persons call God."

Naturalists reject God as the Fundamental Fact but, wittingly or unwittingly, embrace a different Fundamental Fact: nature. The ancient materialist Lucretius poetically wrote that reality is "material atoms eternally combining and recombining in the void" (Lucretius 2001). Ernest Nagel declared the "existential and causal primacy of matter in the executive order of the universe" (Nagel 1954, 8). Carl Sagan boldly declared, "The cosmos is all there is, all there ever was, and all there ever will be" (Sagan 1980, 4). The ultimacy of the physical is the common theme for naturalists and materialists. Naturalists accept nature metaphysically as a brute fact, an unexplained given, a chance happening that need not have occurred. My friend Michael Ruse is in this camp. His skepticism toward religious explanations generally and rejection of theistic explanation specifically can't escape the fact that there still must be some metaphysical account of the universe that science studies. And it does nothing to display the credibility of his naturalist explanation.

What we have in this debate is an inescapable choice between two candidates for Fundamental Fact—God or nature. For theism, God is ontologically fundamental and nature is derivative, a creature; for naturalism, nature is ontologically fundamental. The critical question is, which worldview—committed to which Fundamental Fact—makes better sense of the existence of the universe?

Once all of the science is done, once it has reached its limit, the question of why the universe exists is still meaningful. Leibniz famously expressed what he called the "first question" (Leibniz 1973a, 136; 1973b, sec 7, sec 7, 139):

Why is there something rather than nothing?

The early Wittgenstein tried to silence the question by placing it beyond the scope of empirical discourse (Wittgenstein 1998, props. 6.44, 7), but the question remains meaningful and pressing since the death of positivism and the revival of substantive metaphysics in our day. It's the primordial metaphysical question, not beyond the scope of philosophy, and it's still a question about the facts—not about particular empirical facts but about what Ultimate Fact best explains the totality of all other facts.

Is God or nature the better choice for the Ultimate? In keeping with their idea of a scientific mind-set, most naturalists cite Ockham's razor as the reason for positing the brute, unexplained existence of physical nature as the simpler hypothesis. But a quick review of philosophy of science reminds us that simplicity is not the sole criterion of theory choice if there are significant differences in explanatory power between rival theories. Sometimes a more complicated theory, which posits more entities, both is true and explains relevant data better than simpler theories. Theistic cosmological reasoning identifies God as the proper basis for adequately explaining nature and everything else. God as fundamental reality is conceptually more credible to explain and shed light on all else.

As the medieval philosophers said, out of nothing, nothing comes (*ex nihil, nihil fit*). Genuine, absolute, literal "nothing" produces nothing. The Christian doctrine of "creation out of nothing" (*creatio ex nihilo*) indicates that God has the power to bestow being—the power of exnihilation, of bringing something into being and keeping it from lapsing into nothingness. Understanding God as possessing the power of exnihilation corrects fallacious images of God as the first cause in a long causal series. The kind of causality God exercises to create the universe is not like any other form of causality we know. As Aquinas observed, the dependency of the universe on God remains regardless of whether the universe had an actual beginning in time because even an eternal universe would still be ontologically contingent and still need to be continually exnihilated. Although Big Bang theory is highly confirmed, theists should not marry their position to any scientific theory. The salient theistic point is that the universe—whatever the exact mechanical details of its origin turn out to be according to science—must still rely for its existence on the will and power of God (Peterson et al. 2012, 89–93).

Michael Ruse and other critics often criticize the kinds of metaphysical arguments we have been considering on grounds that they are creatures of classical Greek thought and result in a picture of an Absolute Being—involving necessity and immutability—that is inconsistent with the Judeo-Christian idea of a God who has pathos and relationality toward creatures. I side with the Christian opinion that ancient Greek reason arrived at certain attributes of the divine—such as unchangeability, power, and intelligence—which are qualified, reinterpreted, and elevated in the Christian conception of deity (Peterson et al. 2012, chap. 5). God's general revelation of himself to human reason is thus put in context by the special revelation of himself in the Judeo-Christian scriptures, which are foundational to historical orthodox theology. God's ontological necessity in standard theism, therefore, is not like the necessity that the Greeks imputed to mathematical and other abstract objects, but it is actually related in Aquinas's work to Aristotle's idea of a metaphysically necessary absolute. The Christian God can thus be unchangeable in his essential nature—a point correlating with Greek immutability—while being able to interact with and respond in personal ways to his creation—something the Greek thought could not countenance. This theme will surface again in subsequent chapters.

The Fine-Tuned Universe

Modern science tells us that the fundamental physical constants that characterize the universe fall within a narrow range that makes it conducive to life. Since the 1970s, astrophysicists, nuclear physicists, cosmologists, and other scientists have been talking about the "fine-tuned" structure of the universe. The distinguished Princeton physicist Freeman Dyson remarks,

> There are so many . . . lucky accidents in physics. Without such accidents, water could not exist as liquid, chains of carbon atoms could not form complex organic molecules, and hydrogen atoms could not form breakable bridges between molecules. (Dyson 1979, 251)

Dyson surmises that the universe, in some sense, "knew we were coming" (Dyson 1979, 250).

Brandon Carter, an astrophysicist and cosmologist, introduced the term "anthropic principle" to make the point that, if any of the fundamental physical values of the universe were significantly different, intelligent carbon-based life would not be possible (Carter 1974). B. J. Carr and M. J. Rees state their version of the principle:

> The possibility of life as we know it evolving in the Universe depends on the values of a few basic physical constants—and is in some respects remarkably sensitive to their numerical values. (Carr and Rees 1979, 612)

This is one statement of the weak anthropic principle, which is my interest, not the strong version, which asserts that the universe must have values leading to life.

Scientists have identified fifteen or so constants required for the emergence of intelligent life. Consider just three of them:

- If the strong nuclear force had been stronger or weaker by even 2%, life would be impossible.
- If gravity had been stronger or weaker by one part in 10^{40}, life-sustaining stars could not exist.
- If the electromagnetic force were slightly stronger or weaker, life would be impossible, because it would alter the ability of atoms to share their electrons (e.g., hydrogen and oxygen make water or H_2O and carbon combines with other elements to form complex organic molecules).

In *The Accidental Universe*, Paul Davies writes, "Extraordinary physical coincidences and apparently accidental cooperation . . . offer compelling evidence that something is 'going on'" (Davies 1982, 90, 110). Davies has made the very convincing case that we have hit the "cosmic jackpot" in the way the laws of physics create the conditions that are just right for life (Davies 2007).

The impressive list of precise physical values for the universe does not constitute a "scientific proof" for a Supermind or God because the question regarding something beyond the universe investigated by science is not itself a scientific question. Science can reveal that the conformity of the universe to a particular coherent set of laws makes it life permitting, but these laws are taken as "givens" by which science explains the behavior of the physical system and all it contains. Yet the unexplained givens of science themselves require metaphysical explanation. Why would the universe be fine-tuned for life? Theism and naturalism are understandably at odds over the explanation of fine-tuning. If theism makes better sense of fine-tuning, then we have another reason to prefer theism to naturalism. The fine-tuning argument, involving the anthropic principle, is actually a particular version of teleological argument. Other much less viable versions of the teleological argument include William Paley's analogical argument from design and William Dembski's intelligent design argument, both of which are discussed later.

The fine-tuning argument in focus here involves two main parts. The first part of the argument recognizes the significant improbability that the physical parameters of the universe would fall within the narrow life-permitting range. Employing classical probability theory, if we assume that a large number of possible values are equiprobable, it follows that it is highly improbable that any single constant would have the value it does. For instance, the cosmological constant—which governs whether matter tends to attract or repel other matter—must be precise or the universe will either explode or implode. The probability of the cosmological constant being fine-tuned for life is estimated to be one part in 10^{120} (1 followed by 120 zeroes!).

Furthermore, if the probability is low that any single physical constant be what it is, then the probability is staggeringly low that all of the constants required for life would occur together in a coherent, interrelated system as they in fact do. This is because the probability calculus requires that we multiply all of the small individual probabilities, which yields an incredibly low probability. The eminent cosmologist Donald Page has estimated that the probability of all the initial conditions coming within the life-permitting range would be one part of $10^{10(124)}$—a number virtually beyond comprehension. Calculations differ, depending on the exact statement of initial values, but the main point remains that the ratio of universes with life-permitting values to the whole range of possible universes is exceedingly small (cited in Thompsen 1985, 73). As Michael Turner, an astrophysicist at the University of Chicago and Fermilab, has remarked, "The precision is as if one could throw a dart across the entire universe and hit a bull's eye one millimeter in diameter on the other side" (quoted in Weinberg 1994). This kind of consideration—about the preeminent rationality of nature—is one of the major reasons that moved Antony Flew along in his intellectual journey from atheism to the recognition of a Supreme Mind (Flew 2007, chaps. 4 and 5).

The second part of the argument—which is also persuasive for many, including Flew—is that theism explains the highly improbable fine-tuning of the universe for intelligent life far better than naturalism does. After all, the naturalist asserts that the universe came into existence purely by chance and has the structural features it does by chance. Chance reigns supreme. Thus, we have no more reason to think that the physical parameters of the universe will fall within the life-permitting range than within any other range. This is part of the background thinking of Michael Ruse and others who reject the fine-tuning explanation as persuasive and yet embrace the implications of their default naturalist explanation. The theistic position that the universe comes from a supremely intelligent being strongly resonates with the Hebrew idea that God's Wisdom created (Prov. 8:22) and the Christian idea that God's Word created everything that was made (John 1:1–4).

Comparing worldviews again, the probability of a universe fine-tuned for intelligent life (F) coming to be if theism (T) is true is much higher than if naturalism (N) is true. Or,

$$P(F/T) > P(F/N).$$

Framed in terms of antecedent probability, independently of knowing whether fine-tuning is true, the rational degree of belief we would assign to fine-tuning being true if we assume theism is true is much higher than if we assume naturalism is true. There is a close conceptual connection between the idea of an intelligent creator and the idea of a universe with constants precisely balanced to permit life. There is no similar conceptual connection between the idea that nature is an inexplicable surd and yet enjoys amazingly coincidental balances. Thus, the evidence of fine-tuning strongly supports theism over naturalism (Peterson et al. 2012, 94–97).

Naturalist Objections

Atheistic naturalists have attempted various rebuttals of the fine-tuning argument, four of which I briefly evaluate here. First, some say that the argument reflects biological elitism by presuming that all forms of intelligent life must be like our own, whereas other forms of intelligent life might exist even if the physical constants of our universe were different. As Robin Collins points out in response, the argument "merely presupposes that intelligent life requires some degree of stable, reproducible organized complexity" (Collins 1999, 56–57). Intelligent life forms consisting solely of hydrogen gas are fictions like those seen on *Star Trek* but lack sufficient chemical stability and complexity to be credible realities.

Second, naturalists argue that, for all we know, there is a more fundamental law that determines that the parameters of physics have their current life-permitting values. Yet this alleged fundamental law is presumably contingent and not necessary, making it reasonable to ask why such a law exists to determine fine-tuning. The problem is just backed up a step: how probable is it that we would have exactly this fundamental law that generated a set of fine-tuned physical laws from a large number of possible fundamental laws? Such a fundamental law is not improbable given theism, but is quite improbable given naturalism and its claim that the universe exists purely by random chance.

A third naturalist ploy is to turn the appeal to God as the explanation of fine-tuned complexity against itself. Would not God also be complex and therefore require explanation as well? George Smith writes,

> If the universe is wonderfully designed, surely God is even more wonderfully designed. He must, therefore, have had a designer even more wonderful than He is. If *God* did not require a designer, then there is no reason why such a relatively less wonderful thing as the universe needed one. (Smith 1980, 56)

The obvious theistic reply is to remind Smith and other naturalists that every worldview must have a fundamental, unexplained being that is the basis for explaining everything else. Naturalism and theism are on equal footing in this respect—and theism bears no special burden as though atheism is somehow the presumed default. Organized complexity is a contingent fact. The theistic God is a better explanation of this fact than the primeval randomness posited by naturalism. The regress of asking for explanations is appropriately stopped once one has reached a credible self-existent reality. That credible reality is God, not nature.

The fourth naturalist maneuver advances an alternative cosmological theory—the many-universe hypothesis—to neutralize the probability calculations of the fine-tuning argument. As the theory goes, a large number or even an infinite number of universes may exist, all unknowable from our universe and all with different fundamental physical laws. The majority of these universes would not have life-admitting values, but some small proportion of the universes would have these values. The atheistic physicist Victor Stegner argues that, with a large number of universes, it would no longer be highly improbable that one or more universes would be fine-tuned for life. As Stegner contends, the argument that fine-tuning is probable on theism and improbable on naturalism becomes more difficult to make (Stegner 2014). Multiverse proponents offer various models for how these universes came to exist—oscillating vacuum fluctuation models and oscillating Big Bang models—which the reader can research later in more detail.

It is difficult to assign the multiple-universe hypothesis much credibility. The hypothesis is highly speculative and does not emerge from anything for which we have evidence. In the science–religion debate, the mistaken reasoning for the hypothesis—a common fallacy known as an argument from ignorance—goes as follows: "for all we know" there might be other universes (or "we don't know that there aren't" multiple universes); therefore, we will take it that there are other universes. However, the key point is that, for any cosmological model the naturalist picks, there must be the generation of universes such that some universes will be fine-tuned for life—and yet it is difficult to know what law or mechanism could possibly create and coordinate different sets of coherent physical laws that make for different sequential or parallel universes. Even a random generator would still be a type of order system, which would then need explanation. Surely, a mechanism for producing universes, where some will be fine-tuned, is still more probable on theism than on naturalism.

Beauty, Elegance, Intelligibility

Other phenomena related to fine-tuning also make better sense on a theistic view of reality. For one thing, beauty—as manifested in elegance, simplicity, and symmetry—in both nature and theories has impressed many top scientists. The physicist Steven Weinberg states, "The physicist's sense of beauty is . . . supposed to serve a purpose—it is supposed to help the physicist select ideas that help us explain nature" (Weinberg 1993, 133). David Papineau, a philosopher of science and metaphysical naturalist, says that the general constitution of the universe displays a "physical simplicity," which leads us to believe that "this kind of simplicity will *for that reason* be a reliable route to the truth" (Papineau 1993, 166).

According to naturalism, beauty in nature results from sheer dumb luck. Not surprisingly, naturalism has no meaningful account of why beauty in theories is a guide to truth. Theism, by contrast, implies that nature—in all its beauty, simplicity, and elegance—is the creation of an intelligent creator and that likewise the creator has given human beings the power of understanding nature and of appreciating these qualities. Comparing probabilities again, where B is all that we have been saying about beauty in the universe,

$$P(B/T) > P(B/N).$$

The deep aesthetic structure of the universe—and its resonance with mind—is more probable on theism than on naturalism.

Mathematics is a key to the general intelligibility and discoverability of the universe—related again to fine-tuning. Eugene Wigner, one of the principal founders of quantum mechanics, wrote a famous article entitled "The Unreasonable Effectiveness of Mathematics in the Natural Sciences" (Wigner 1960). The fact that pure mathematicians can develop formal mathematical systems for their own purposes, being largely concerned with the consistency and limitations of the systems themselves, and then those systems can be found fruitful in the physical sciences suggests a profound isomorphism between mathematics and physical reality. Newton, for example, used mathematical calculations from Kepler and Galileo to deduce his laws of motion and gravitation, which predicted the paths of known planets and even of some unknown planets.

Roger Penrose, an Oxford mathematician and physicist, dismisses claims that our good theories—he actually says, our "superb theories"—just happen to fit the world, stating, "There must be, instead, some deep underlying reason for the accord between mathematics and physics" (Penrose 1989, 556–57). Once again, naturalism has no good explanation for the fit between mathematics and the physical universe, whereas theism affirms both a rational creator and the rationality of creation. Michael Ruse's view of the social construction of scientific knowledge assumes an epistemological antirealism that makes it difficult to imagine any credible account of the relation between theory and the world. The intrinsic rationality of mathematics and its applicability to the world are more probable on theism than on naturalism. Or, where M is the rationality of mathematics and its applicability to the world, $P(M/T) > P(M/N)$.

In reflecting on the rich rational structure of the universe, science reaches an appropriate limit. Science takes the physical constants of nature as given, but science cannot explain why these auspicious constants are given in the first place. On the metaphysical level, theism provides a better explanation of the existence of fundamental constants than naturalism does. In the family of teleological arguments, the fine-tuning argument for a transcendent intelligence points to a bona fide metaphysical explanation of the universe. It is not a God-of-the-gaps argument that competes with scientific explanation and can eventually be overturned by advancing science. Neither is it a convenient post hoc argument to get the results we want. And it certainly does not imply that God meticulously plans detailed outcomes in the contingent world—a point we will explore more fully in later chapters as chance, free will, and evil are discussed. What the argument does show is that naturalists cannot adequately understand nature at a metaphysical level because they take it as ultimate; theists know that only something transcendent to nature can make complete and full sense of nature.

In the Beginning

Michael Ruse

Charles Darwin's discussion of (what we might call) prehistory in the *Origin of Species* (1859) was atypically truncated for the topic, deliberately so because he did not want to get bogged down in areas on which he was not directly qualified to comment and also because he was not convinced that what he had to say applied to the time and events before flourishing organisms appeared on the earth. Until 1859, the year of *Origin*, it was more or less automatically assumed by those writing on the topic, whether or not evolutionists, that it was appropriate (if not mandatory) to talk of the origin of life and, extending the discussion backward, of the origin of the universe itself. Thus, for instance, the publisher Robert Chambers, the anonymous author of *Vestiges of the Natural History of Creation* (1844), had all sorts of speculations about the spontaneous generation of life from nonlife and a detailed treatment of the so-called "nebular hypothesis," a speculation from the eighteenth century proposed by (among others) Immanuel Kant and Pierre-Simon Laplace that saw solar objects as forming naturally out of clouds of gases. Moreover, many assumed that one theory had more or less to fit all. In the 1850s, Darwin's fellow Englishman and evolutionist Herbert Spencer was confident that one law of change applied universally. To this end, he adopted a criterion of progress that involved division and specialization or, as he called it, a move from the homogeneous to the heterogeneous:

> Now we propose in the first place to show, that this law of organic progress is the law of all progress. Whether it be in the development of the Earth, in the development of Life upon its surface, in the development of Society, of Government, of Manufactures, of Commerce, of Language, Literature, Science, Art, this same evolution of the simple into the complex, through successive differentiations, holds throughout. From the earliest traceable cosmical changes down to the latest results of civilization, we shall find that the transformation of the homogeneous into the heterogeneous is that in which Progress essentially consists. (Spencer 1857, 2–3)

For Spencer, everything obeys this law, making for a certain inevitability to the process. Causes just keep multiplying effects, and this leads to ever-greater complexity. Apparently, this all occurs in waves. Something disturbs the natural balance and forces work to reachieve the balance, but when this occurs we have moved a stage higher: an overall process of "dynamic equilibrium."

The Big Bang Theory

Today we can share the sentiment that a full discussion of origins is naturally going to direct us back to the earliest history of the universe, although currently I doubt that anyone would feel a strong compulsion to insist that the forces forming the universe necessarily must be those also forming organisms. And so it is. There is no secret that, compared to a hundred years ago, our knowledge of the origins of the universe is simply orders of magnitude greater. There is no secret that we are still ignorant of much—and perhaps a hundred years hence our knowledge will be more orders of magnitude greater. In the first part of the twentieth century, there were two rival theories. Both tried to take account of findings by the American astronomer Edwin Hubble that apparently the universe is expanding. One, the "steady-state" theory, supposed that new matter is constantly being created and that, although the universe is getting bigger overall, one has a uniformity where the past is much like the present. The other, the Big Bang, supposed that the universe has a directional history and that at some point in the past it exploded into being from a virtually spatially dimensionless point.

Evidence kept accumulating in favor of the second hypothesis, and since the 1960s, thanks to the discovery of cosmic microwave background radiation that it alone predicts, it has been the generally accepted theory of the origin of the universe. It has been possible to fill in a great many details, and again, I think it fair to say and important to stress (lest we get diverted), by and large there is general agreement to their truth. There is no quarrel between Michael Peterson and me on this. The Bang occurred just under 14 billion years ago, and it was in the first few seconds that huge amounts of activity occurred. Subatomic particles formed very rapidly and were followed by hydrogen and deuterium. Temperatures were huge, and expansion was phenomenal, but in a short time things settled down, and new elements were being formed and the development of the universe as we know it was underway.

Of course, a hypothesis like this gives rise to all sorts of further questions, most obviously about what, if anything, was around before the Big Bang, what caused it, and whether it was unique. Are there other Big Bangs and, if so, did they cause—are they still causing—other universes, what have been labeled "multiverses"? I stress that these are empirical questions, and it is not at all to disparage how far we have traveled to say that nothing much, if at all, is yet settled. For our purposes, it is enough to say that some people seem to think that there was nothing. Everything sprang into existence at the beginning of our Big Bang, and that is it. Others seem to think that we have one system that keeps exploding and expanding and then stops and reverses until finally you get the "Big Crunch" and everything starts all over again. Yet a third group thinks that perhaps our universe or some universe gives rise every now and then to a Big Bang in a new dimension, and so you are getting constantly created multiverses. As you can imagine, you get all sorts of variations on these themes, although do note that all of this thinking goes on within the confines of the mechanical model—the machine metaphor—meaning that everything is grounded in a basic strategy of methodological naturalism.

Religious Implications?

So what has any of this to do with the Christian religion or indeed with any religion positing a Creator God? At one level, I want to say, "nothing much at all." I see no reason why you should not go on doing the science without bringing God into the discussion. Stay with methodological naturalism and keep going. The fact that you don't have all of the answers yet is no good reason to give up now. It is hardly undue optimism to say that the progress made in the past hundred years bodes well for possible progress in the next hundred years. At another level, we start to raise some interesting and important questions. Let's start by clearing out of the way two perhaps obvious but bad reactions. As you will see, Ruse and Peterson have little disagreement on the first and little agreement on the second.

The first is to argue that the Big Bang is confirmation for the Creation story of Genesis. God created the world in an instant, and science backs up this scenario. However, for all that, something along these lines was embraced by Pope Pius XII; moves like this are always dangerous. You may worry because, even if the Big Bang is true, you are going to have to stretch the Genesis story. For a start, everything happened a lot farther back in time than anyone supposed because the universe and the earth are much older than many religious believers realize. For a second, one doubts that there was much light around at first, at least not of the day-and-night kind. For a third, there was no water or firmament above, below, or in the middle of the water. We can, however, glide over these sorts of issues. Christians have long been in the business of interpreting things allegorically, and the point is that in both the Big Bang story and the Genesis story we have a beginning. The problem, rather, is that if the science changes or is modified, then you may well find that you have committed to something that is not religion-friendly. In this case, if pre–Big Bang stories gain traction, you are worse off than before. You need an infinite number of books before Genesis telling you all about the earlier creations!

A second bad reaction or inference is to say that the Big Bang and what follows shows that nothing could be pure chance. For the world to work as well as it does, making a home for life, the constants of the universe—the determinants of the laws—had to be "fine-tuned" and that means design. Invoking what is known as the "anthropic principle"—a claim about the necessities of existence—it is argued that, had certain crucial factors been other than they are—for instance, if the strong nuclear force were 2% stronger than it is—stars would be different from what they currently are, and it is highly unlikely that life could have got started (Barrow and Tipler 1986). In this particular case, with a different nuclear force, diprotons would never be stable (this is a form of helium that in this universe is generally unstable), and deuterium and regular helium would not be formed.

Unlike Peterson, I confess that at its best—and it is rarely in such a state—I find this argument singularly unconvincing. This is because you are arguing from a given datum of one, admittedly one more than you usually find in philosophical arguments, but still. Think of a number, double it, and the answer is a half. How can anyone really know what the world could or could not have been like? If there is anything to multiverses, perhaps our universe is simply the one that functions and has no more significance than that there is one lottery ticket winner of millions. And in any case, some serious physicists doubt that the world is so fine-tuned. The Nobel Prize winner Steven Weinberg (1999) points out that there is often a lot more wiggle room in chemical reactions than appears on first sight. For instance, the natural production of the carbon atom is often highlighted as literally miraculous, but in fact, when you break down the steps involved in its production, far from there being one crucial energy level that is uniquely needed for the production of carbon, there is a range of possible energies that would do the job.

Much more interesting is the possible role of God once you have a natural story of origins, like the Big Bang theory. As a Christian, however allegorically you may want to interpret Genesis, you want to say that God is the Creator. This puts us in the neighborhood of the causal form of the cosmological argument. But doesn't this put God in the causal chain of things, and doesn't this at once open you up to the objection of the first-year student of philosophy, not to mention Richard Dawkins? What caused God? If God had a cause, then He is not God. And if God didn't need a cause, then why bother with God in the first place? You are invoking God in the chain of causation, arguing that you need Him; otherwise, you are stuck with an infinite regress. But are you not making "the entirely unwarranted assumption that God himself is immune to the regress" (Dawkins 2006, 77)? And to this you might add that the naturalist doesn't really care if you have a regress. So be it.

One hesitates to disagree with Richard Dawkins, but fairness demands that we tackle what Christians actually believe rather than a parody of such belief. Agreed, it is true that many Christians have wanted to prove the existence of God by a causal argument ("cosmological argument") of the ilk being sketched here. "Everything has a cause. The world is a thing. Therefore, the world had a cause, call it God." But note also that many Christians, often the more sophisticated ones, either think the argument secondary or don't much care for it at all. Aquinas, who on this topic is always abstracted in readers in the philosophy of religion, thought that anything arrived at by reason only supplemented that found first by faith. And there is a strong strain of Protestant thought that doesn't like any of this argumentation to God—so-called "natural theology." It is argued that if God's existence can be proven, then it gelds the real significance of faith, something requiring (in the words of the nineteenth-century Danish thinker Sören Kierkegaard) a leap into the absurd. In the twentieth century, the great Swiss theologian Karl Barth thought in a similar way.

The Fundamental Question

This is not to say that there is no argument going on, but that it is not a simple scientific-type argument of the kind just presented. The great theologians like Anselm and Aquinas knew all about the regress, but they were not bothered because this was not their topic. Rather, they were trying to speak to what has been called (by Martin Heidegger 1959) the Fundamental Question of Metaphysics: "Why is there something rather than nothing?" They are certainly concerned about origins, but they are concerned about the present too! People like Anselm and Aquinas knew nothing about the Big Bang, but had they known, they would have been moved and excited. If you had told them that there was something before the Big Bang, they would probably have been even more moved and excited. They would certainly not have been threatened. Nor would they have thought that their own work had come to an end. Any story of origins, any story of existence, still raises the issue of why there is anything there in the first place. And this is where and why they think they can and must invoke the Christian God. He and He alone gives the answer. He created out of love to make the world, a place for His creatures, above all humans, whom He may love and who in return can worship Him.

As you will know from the previous chapter, I am in considerable sympathy with the theologians here. I don't think science can give you an answer to the question of why there is something rather than nothing. The machine metaphor makes the question unanswerable. You may object that Anselm and Aquinas were writing before the machine metaphor triumphed, but on the one hand, we are living today when the machine metaphor has triumphed, and on the other hand, I am not sure that the organic metaphor in this respect does any better. Remember that hare that the cookbook ordered. Where the hare comes from is another matter. This said, of course, the question now is why you should go with my skepticism—I don't know the answer—rather than the theologians' affirmation of God—a divine creator was responsible.

There are some who would say that they have little time for anyone in this debate. Far from being fundamental, they deny that the question is a genuine question at all. This was the inevitably influential opinion of the early-twentieth-century Austrian British philosopher Ludwig Wittgenstein:

> To say "I wonder at such and such being the case" has only sense if I can imagine it not to be the case. In this sense one can wonder at, say, the existence of a house when one sees it and has not visited it for a long time and has imagined it had been pulled down in the meantime. But it is nonsense to say that I wonder at the existence of the world, because I cannot imagine it not existing. I could of course wonder at the world around me being as it is. If for instance I had this experience while looking into the blue sky, I could wonder at the sky being blue as opposed to the case when it's clouded. But that's not what I mean. I am wondering at the sky being *whatever it is*. (Wittgenstein 1965, 8–9)

To that, I can only say that perhaps I have an overextended imagination, but I can certainly imagine nothing existing at all. Just nothing. Not empty space. Not Michael Ruse. Just nothing.

Why Skepticism?

Suppose you do allow that it is a genuine question—something on which, incidentally, Ruse and Peterson agree. Surely the Christian's answer is more satisfying in a way than the skeptic's answer. I agree entirely. But it does not mean that it is satisfactory. To answer this, we must dig into that God that the Christian supposes (Ruse 2015). One thing is clear. God is not just a First Cause operating like other causes, a contingent being, an original link in the chain. God's causation in a way is orthogonal to the causal chain. As Peterson says, God brings the whole business into being and keeps it in existence. This means that God is, in some sense, necessary. He *must* exist. He cannot not exist. To ask about what made or caused God is as silly as asking what made the law of noncontradiction. The law always held and God always existed without cause. What kind of being is this? How can we make sense of it? By doing what we have just done, by turning to those things that we think necessary, like the claims of logic—the law of noncontradiction and so forth.

But does God, can God, have this kind of necessity? There are suggestions that this is indeed so. The ontological argument of Anselm derives God's existence from the contradiction of assuming Him nonexistent. But generally people pull back from this. Logical necessity, like the claim that something cannot simultaneously be of one kind and not of that kind, does seem something that holds of statements, not things. So the usual characterization of God is as a factually necessary being. Actually, Anselm himself gives the classic explication: "The supreme Substance, then, does not exist through any efficient agent, and does not derive existence from any matter, and was not aided in being brought into existence by any external causes. Nevertheless, it by no means exists through nothing, or derives existence from nothing; since, through itself and from itself, it is what it is" (Anselm 1903, 48–49, *Monologium* 6).

David Hume would have nothing of this, thinking it just empty words. Perhaps he has a point, but before we give it to him, let us push a little further. Plato has been mentioned, and it does seem that we are toying with a conception of God that owes much to the theory of forms, especially to the Form of the Good. This being so, one thinks immediately of why one might take any of this seriously because, as Plato stressed, whatever may be the case in the world of logic, we have already one apparent realm of existence where objects exist in eternal necessity. I refer to mathematics. Many people, including virtually all professional mathematicians, think that mathematics is about necessarily existing objects—the right-angled triangle, for instance—and what we try to do is ferret out their properties.

However, against this there are those who argue that this is a conceptual mistake. You don't have a three-four-five triangle drawn in the dust on the floor and then an eternal triangle that guarantees that one angle of the dust triangle is a right angle. You have three lines drawn in the dust and the relations between them. To say more is to fall into the same fallacy as to conclude when someone says that no one runs faster than Achilles that Achilles, therefore, is only the second-fastest runner. "No one" is a placeholder and not a thing. The same is true of mathematics. On top of this, and even more worrisome, is that even if you allow the objects of mathematics, you have still got to get to God. Most mathematicians don't feel that they are compelled to make the move. And even if you do get to God, you must ask yourself whether this is really the God that you want.

It is true that this being necessarily exists, is therefore eternal, and hence is outside space and time. This would make Augustine happy. He wrote in his *Confessions*,

> Thou precedest all things past, by the sublimity of an ever-present eternity; and
> surpassest all future because they are future, and when they come, they shall be

past; but Thou art the same, and Thy years fail not. Thy years neither come nor go; whereas ours both come and go, that they all may come. Thy years stand together, because they do stand; nor are departing thrust out by coming years, for they pass not away; but ours shall all be, when they shall no more be. Thy years are one day; and Thy day is not daily, but To-day, seeing Thy To-day gives not place unto to-morrow, for neither doth it replace yesterday. Thy To-day, is Eternity. (Augustine 1998, Bk. XI)

One God or Two?

But is this really the God of Christianity? It certainly doesn't seem much like the God of the Bible. Although there are claims about God being unchanging, these seem to refer more to God's moral nature and His love for humankind. More generally, the God of both the Old Testament and the New Testament seems much more like a person than like a mathematical object. God takes action, He has feelings, He can change His mind (or at least is open to the possibility), He (especially in the Old Testament) plays favorites and encourages humans to do the same (think of the story of Jacob and Esau), and so much more. It is hard to see how God could have emotions unless He is part of the space-time continuum. This is a fact that, perhaps to their credit—and then again perhaps not—the great theologians recognized. I think most of us would want to say that although He may not have been willing to lift a finger to help her, God lay next to Anne Frank in Bergen-Belsen as she lay dying in the spring of 1945. Not so Anselm: "For when thou beholdest us in our wretchedness, we experience the effect of compassion, but thou dost not experience the feeling" (Anselm 1903, 13). Likewise, Aquinas: "To sorrow, therefore, over the misery of others does not belong to God" (Aquinas 1981, *ST* I, Q. 21, Art. 3).

I am not drawing attention to anything new. Christianity was not something handed to humankind on a plate the day after the Ascension. Starting with Peter and Paul and going on through the early Church Fathers and on to the great philosopher-theologians, believers have been working out both the fundamentals and the details of their faith. And right from the beginning they have been torn by the two influences of Jerusalem, the God of the Bible, and Athens, the God of the philosophers. Unfortunately, for all of their individual virtues, when put together, the two conceptions of God do not mesh well. The God of the Bible is the God of the Jews, and He is a person. Protestants, who tend to make the Bible all definitive—*sola scriptura*—stress this repeatedly. Thus, the Anglican philosopher Richard Swinburne states, "That God is a person, yet without a body, seems the most elementary claim of theism" (Swinburne 1977, 99). Not only Jewish, but also Christian. We humans are persons. We are made in His image. It is this personhood that makes for this connection and is the reason why God was prepared to suffer for our sins. To the contrary, the god of the philosophers is simply not one of the chaps. He is not a person. He is a necessary being, eternal, unchanging, outside time and space, without or beyond emotions. He is, we are told, thanks to Aquinas's theory of analogy, loving in some sense, a father in some sense, but only dimly or tenuously in any human sense that we might understand and grasp.

These two gods are not the same being, and it is no use pretending that they are. This is why Peterson must struggle with the charge that Christianity has incommensurable visions right at its heart. It is hard to employ a concept to do important intellectual work in the science–religion area if it is internally incoherent. Of course, there have been attempts to patch this up. Popular in some quarters today is so-called "process theology," owing much to the Anglo-American philosopher Alfred North Whitehead. This theology sees God as having given up some of His powers, so He is no longer the God of the classical theologian-philosophers. He is in some sense working alongside human beings to achieve the desired end of eternal salvation. But for all, there is some (tenuous) biblical evidence for this position—usually resting on the notion of "kenosis" where God supposedly emptied Himself—and although for obvious reasons it appeals to those who take evolution seriously, here we can skim past this and related attempts. As noted in the preface, my coauthor and I agree, if only on one thing, namely, that we want to debate traditional positions. We both agree that attempts like these tend to fail and, in any case, from an orthodox Christian perspective, are deeply heretical.

So here we come full circle back to the position I endorse. I agree that study of the world, including study of origins, raises questions about ultimate causation and meaning. I don't think these are pseudoquestions. I agree that science cannot answer them. I agree that the Christian (or the theist generally) can try to answer them, and you will find at certain points in our exchange that Michael Peterson is well aware of these specific issues and speaks to them. I agree that *prima facie* the Christian answer is more satisfying than a retreat (if such it be) into skepticism. The only trouble is that, on philosophical and theological grounds, the Christian answer does not work. That, I am afraid, is definitive.

4

Origin of Life

It's All Purely Natural

Michael Ruse

Start with the known facts. We saw that the universe itself dates back almost 14 billion years. The age of our solar system, including our planet Earth, is about 4.5 billion years. Initially, the earth was hot, far too hot for life, but it started to cool. The fossil remains of the earliest life forms are to be found in Australia and are around 3.5 billion years old. However, in Greenland there are deposits of about 3.8 billion years old that are suggestive of photosynthesis. What we can say is that life began here on earth soon after it was possible for life to survive. We will have more to say later about the history of life here on earth once it had begun, but it spoils no secrets to say the pattern makes good sense. You don't find elephantlike creatures coming suddenly 3 billion years ago and then nothing but microbes for another 2 billion years. Rather, life builds up from simple forms and then gets more and more sophisticated and complex as the years go by.

Once again, I don't think there is much disagreement here between Ruse and Peterson on the science. But before we rush off to examine the implications of this science, we are now far enough into the discussion that it is worth taking a moment to reflect on the nature of our exchange. People arguing about the science–religion relationship, and the evolution–creationism relationship, might differ on the science itself. An evolutionist and a creationist are going to differ on the historical authenticity of Adam and Eve. By and large, these are not issues that divide Ruse and Peterson. We are both well up on modern science and we both accept its findings with (I think it fair to say) joy and awe. For instance, when molecular biologists recently discovered that humans and fruit flies have the same genes and are assembled from the same building blocks—rather like the Lego principle—I accepted it and was stunned by the elegant simplicity (Ruse 2006). I am sure Peterson feels the same way.

This said, it is possible for two such as us to differ on some of the more contentious parts of science. Without putting words into people's mouths, as you will see, I accept natural selection whole-heartedly and see its action everywhere. There are many scientists who agree with me, but there are scientists who feel that perhaps other factors are as significant or more so. It is certainly open for someone like Peterson, perhaps because of his religious motivations, to follow alternative routes from mine, which will lead to differences. For example, multiverses, covered to some extent in the previous chapter, are a debated issue, and I know scientists who are Christians and who don't much care for them (Ellis 2011). By blocking multiverses, these thinkers shore up the anthropic argument for God's existence. I would challenge this, but I don't think, given the current state of play of science and the highly speculative nature of multiverse theories, that this strategy is illicit.

Peterson does see problems with multiverses but is not on a crusade. He is secure with established science because it is not, for him, all-dominating. He openly accepts the ontological possibility of miracles as a matter beyond or outside science. Arguing that the standardly accepted science is wrong or needs modifying—in the sense of tweaking, not wholesale rejection or revision like that proposed by creationists—is a strategy more attractive to those (like Unitarians and a Quaker like George Ellis) who think themselves wholly onside with the ubiquity of science, who would deny miracles, but who nevertheless want more than the nonbeliever would allow. What they are up to becomes more apparent when we turn to matters of meaning, something important to us all.

In the case of two people like me (a nonbeliever) and Peterson (a Christian theist), we accept all of the science but put different interpretations—perhaps theological but (particularly given our shared training) more likely philosophical—on this science. For us, that is enough. For Peterson and me, the science is not the source of our differences. It all lies at the level of interpretation. This happens a lot in our exchange over things like chance—a difference that plays through several chapters. I think I am right. Peterson thinks he is right. That is for you to decide. However, if you don't want to put all of the work on interpretation—if, most particularly, you don't want to be forced to give a more conservative interpretation of the kind Peterson happily endorses—but you want to get a different answer from nonbelievers like me, then the strategy just mentioned above (tweak the science) is probably the way to go. It is easier to do or at least opens itself more readily to different conclusions—the anthropic principle points to God; the anthropic principle does not point to God—if you put some of the burden on the differences in the science rather than putting all of the burden on different interpretations of the same science.

I am not saying one strategy is better than another. I have my opinion and express it. But I think it useful here to disentangle the levels at which our exchange is occurring. And with this, let us again pick up the thread of discussion.

Defining Life

What is life? Aristotle thought it was some kind of force, akin in some way to consciousness—or perhaps we might want to say that consciousness is one aspect of some life—pervasive through the organic world. It is characterized by movement and sensation. With the coming of the mechanical model, this kind of thinking was pushed aside and out of science, although around the turn of the century from the nineteenth to the twentieth, a kind of neo-Aristotelian philosophy made somewhat of a comeback. Vitalism, so called, was championed by the German biologist Hans Driesch (1908), who called the life force "entelechy" and by the French philosopher Henri Bergson (1907), who spoke of the "élan vital." The problem with such an approach, however, is that it didn't seem to do much, especially by way of explanation. If you kill a pig and cut it up—as my wife learned to do when she did an undergraduate major in animal and poultry science—you don't find a life force along with the heart and lungs and liver.

People working within the mechanical model, therefore, tend to go with some notion of "organization." A watch laid out in parts on the table and its sister assembled and functioning don't differ in "watch force." It is a matter of one being put together in a certain way and working and the other not so being. Likewise with organisms. The living pig is put together in a way that is no longer true of the dead pig. Of course, you may argue about the nature of this organization. The physical chemist James Lovelock (1979), when he produced his "Gaia hypothesis" that earth is an organism, argued that the mark of the living is feedback mechanisms, leading to balance or "homeostasis." I suspect that most biologists would say that homeostasis is only the precondition for what really matters, namely the ability to reproduce. Even here there will be borderline cases. Is a tornado living because it can reproduce? Or what about a virus, which needs a host to reproduce? But the basic idea seems clear and sound.

A Natural Solution?

What about the origin of life? As I noted at the beginning of the previous chapter, Darwin was careful in the *Origin* to stay firmly away from that can of worms. With people like Pasteur in France driving a stake through the heart of earlier views of "spontaneous generation," where organisms somehow just come to life thanks to magnetism or electricity or whatever, Darwin knew that silence is golden. He said just enough to acknowledge the issue:

> There is grandeur in this view of life, with its several powers, having been originally breathed into a few forms or into one; and that, whilst this planet has gone

cycling on according to the fixed law of gravity, from so simple a beginning endless forms most beautiful and most wonderful have been, and are being, evolved. (Darwin 1859, 421)

This does not mean he had no thoughts on the matter. To his great friend, the botanist Joseph Hooker, on February 1, 1871, he wrote that "it is often said that all the conditions for the first production of a living being are now present, which could ever have been present. But if (and oh what a big if) we could conceive in some warm little pond with all sort of ammonia and phosphoric salts,—light, heat, electricity present, that a protein compound was chemically formed, ready to undergo still more complex changes, at the present such matter would be instantly devoured, or absorbed, which would not have been the case before living creatures were formed . . ." (Darwin 1985–, 19, 53–4).

Whatever his thoughts about God—and more on this in a moment—Darwin believed firmly that the origin of life is law-bound, at the least methodologically naturalistic, although it seems fair also to say that he didn't think his own biological theory of natural selection was particularly relevant at this point. Or at least it is relevant only inasmuch as it was working on the moves made by chemical processes. It seems also fair to say that this seems to have been the attitude of subsequent thinkers on the topic, from then up to and including the present. This is a natural solution, but one that is more biochemical than biological, or at least only biological when the biochemistry has done its work.

A natural solution? Is this to take you on a journey into cloud-cuckoo land? Such seems to be the opinion of some big names in the philosophical community. The philosopher of science Karl Popper was of this opinion: "An impenetrable barrier to science and a residue to all attempts to reduce biology to chemistry and physics" (Popper 1974). More recently, writing of the claim that "life arose by naturalistic means," the noted Calvinist philosopher Alvin Plantinga declares, "This seems to me for the most part mere arrogant bluster; given our present state of knowledge, I believe it is vastly less probable, on our present evidence, than is its denial" (1991). This too was the position of Antony Flew. A long-time and prominent atheist, toward the end of his life Flew returned to the faith of his fathers, finding "improbable" the possibility of a natural origin of life: "I have been persuaded that it is simply out of the question that the first living matter evolved out of dead matter and then developed into an extraordinarily complicated creature" (quoted by Wavell and Iredale 2004). Even more recently, the atheist philosopher Thomas Nagel has joined the chorus, writing of the possibility that life could have emerged on earth purely through the actions of physics and chemistry: "My skepticism is not based on religious belief, or on a belief in any definite alternative. It is just a belief that the available scientific evidence, in spite of the consensus of scientific opinion, does not in this matter rationally require us to subordinate the incredulity of common sense. That is especially true with regard to the origin of life" (Nagel 2012, 7).

Can this truly be so? Modern thinking about the origin-of-life problem dates from the 1920s when, independently, the Russian biochemist Alexander Oparin and the British biologist J. B. S. Haldane proposed an updated version of Darwin's hypothesis, supposing that the early earth atmosphere was reducing (takes oxygen out) and that in such circumstances organic molecules could form in the atmosphere (from ammonia and thanks to the action of ultraviolet radiation), and then, falling into the oceans, making for what Haldane called a "pre-biotic soup," self-replicating molecule clusters could be formed and life would be underway (Farley 1977). In the early 1950s, a graduate student in Chicago, Stanley Miller, working in the laboratory of Nobelist Harold Urey, simulated what folk thought the early atmosphere would be like. He mixed a compound of the chemicals expected to be present and, having run an experiment where electrical discharges were administered on an ongoing basis, produced "amino acids," some of the essential molecules found in living beings. This was not the creation of life as such, but it seemed that one of the major steps along the way was now well established.

Would that it were all so easy. A handful of components is one thing. A fully functioning cell, the essential unit of the living organism, is another. It is like going from the watch spring to your time-telling Rolex. You start with the molecules carrying the genetic information, to be passed on from generation to generation. In (most) living things these are long chains of deoxyribonucleic acid (DNA), which in turn are transcribed along another kind of nucleic acid (ribonucleic acid, or RNA) that then uses the information to form the amino acids and to join them up in more ("polypeptide") chains. These make up and run the cell, which in turn must be enclosed in a bag or container made of other organic molecules. As it happens, like the amino acids, you can make the parts of the nucleic acid fairly readily. Joining them up is a huge problem. And even when you have done that, the chains are small and tend to be unstable. On top of that, there were growing doubts about whether people had got the original atmosphere right. Perhaps it was not so reducing after all. Moreover, there is the issue of the containers for the cells and how these can be strong enough to work but porous enough to pass information from within to without and so forth.

Some significant progress has been made (Bada and Lazcana 2009). It seems more and more clear that before we had a DNA/RNA world, we had a world with just RNA. It can (and in some organisms still does) carry the genetic information, and it does have the ability to self-replicate. Some exciting experiments have been performed where the molecules can be made to look after and replicate themselves. With respect to other questions, although there are no firm answers, there are promising strategies and hypotheses. Perhaps it was not the atmosphere that was the key to the start of life. With the coming of plate tectonics, we know all about deep-sea vents and how they spew out chemicals and, being very hot, provide sources of energy. Could it be that this is the place where the original action occurred? And in the case of other issues, there are at least avenues of research to be followed. Could it be that RNA was not the original macromolecule that carried the information? Were there other such molecules now lost that did the job? Apparently there are candidates, for instance, peptide nucleic acid and threose nucleic acid, although how and when these might have been formed is currently lost in the mists of time.

The task here is not to follow the science in detail. No one would deny that there are huge gaps in our knowledge, and it is almost as if with each new discovery or hypothesis the problems multiply. A recent survey by leading researchers is candid:

> Although there have been considerable advances in the understanding of chemical processes that may have taken place before the emergence of the first living entities, life's beginnings are still shrouded in mystery. Like vegetation in a mangrove swamp, the roots of universal phylogenetic trees are submerged in the muddy waters of the prebiotic broth, and how the transition from the non-living to the living took place is still unknown. (Bada and Lazcana 2009, 72)

At the same time, whether justified or not, there is significant optimism. It is felt that steps forward have been and are being made. Also, now we do have tools to tackle the problems. We are not just stabbing in the dark. These same researchers conclude, "We face major unsolved problems, but they are not completely shrouded in mystery, unsolvable, or unknowable" (Bada and Lazcana 2009, 74).

Impossible!

So what do we say to the naysayers, theists and atheists? One tries not to be sarcastic but would have considerably more confidence in their doubts and denials if they had made the slightest effort to look at the theoretical and empirical research being done today on origin-of-life issues. When people like the biologist Richard Dawkins make swingeing attacks on religion or when people like the physicists Steven Weinberg and Laurence Krauss make equally swingeing attacks on philosophy, people in those two disciplines rise up in anger. It is not so much that they object to being attacked. That comes with the territory. Rather, it is being attacked by outsiders who make no attempt to understand the subjects, simply show ignorance and derision, and end up with criticisms of the quality you might expect. We encountered some of this surrounding the causal argument in the previous chapter. But these things cut both ways. Philosophers and theologians have no less obligation to work at understanding that which they want to criticize. Trite and nasty statements from on high do not advance scholarship. This is irrespective of whether one is a religious believer.

This said, start with the atheists, Thomas Nagel, to take a prime example. First, note that there is nothing showing his atheism to be the source of his doubts about finding a chemical (hence, mechanical) solution to the origin-of-life problem. I do not know the religious beliefs of the leading researchers in this field, but given what one does know of the religious beliefs of elite scientists, it would be surprising to find that they are committed Christians, one and all. Francis Crick of double-helix fame was much interested in the problem, and he notoriously was a nonbeliever. One can say that one never finds these people in their work making a link between a faith-based conviction and the optimism that the origin-of-life problem will have a natural, mechanical solution.

Turn the question around. If you doubt that the origin of life can be given a mechanical solution, can you truly continue to be an atheist? Many have found Nagel's position, shall we say, discordant. In large part, this is because of history. Nagel does not want to give up on the problem or, indeed, on science generally. What he urges on us is a return to the earlier metaphor of the world as an organism. At some level, he sees the whole of nature as infused with life—consciousness being just the most visible end of the spectrum—and so for him the origin of life is in a way a nonproblem. There is no specific origin of life, except inasmuch as there might be an origin for everything. However, what this means is that Nagel is urging on us a return to an Aristotelian worldview, and although it is true that the great Christian philosophers laid on this the revelation of Genesis with its creation story, the fact is that what Nagel wants is something that has a long Christian tradition. It is indeed odd for an atheist to be so enthusiastic.

But is it impossible to be an Aristotelian about the physical world and an atheist? As you might suspect from what I said about metaphor earlier, truly I don't see the incompatibility. I think we should reject the organic metaphor as a whole because it isn't as good as the mechanical metaphor, but that is another matter. I don't see why you shouldn't think of the world in organic terms and yet be a skeptic about ultimate causes and meaning. As it happens, Aristotle believed in an unmoved mover, to which all things were directed. But this is not the Christian deity. Apart from anything else, Aristotle's unmoved mover spends all of its time contemplating its own perfection and has no knowledge whatsoever of us. This is not the God who died on the cross for our sins.

Miracles?

Turn now to the theist. First, what is the theist expected to believe about the origin of life? At one level, the answer is unambiguous. God did it. The Judeo-Christian scriptures contain the following passages:

> And God said, Let the earth bring forth grass, the herb yielding seed, and the fruit tree yielding fruit after his kind, whose seed is in itself, upon the earth: and it was so. (Gen. 1:11)
>
> And God made the beast of the earth after its kind, and cattle after their kind, and every thing that creepeth upon the earth after his kind: and God saw that it was good. (Gen. 1:25)
>
> So God created man in his own image, in the image of God created he him; male and female created he them. (Gen. 1:27)
>
> And the Lord God formed man of the dust of the ground, and breathed into his nostrils the breath of life; and man became a living soul. (Gen. 2:7)

Now I don't quote Genesis just to force the believer into accepting it literally. I am quite content to accept that the believer reads this metaphorically or allegorically. But the believer such as Peterson does think that in some important sense this is true, so the big question is what is meant by this "breath of life" talk.

Darwin is interesting and instructive. Remember how he introduces the origin of organisms in the *Origin*: "this view of life, with its several powers, having been originally breathed into a few forms or into one." This is biblical talk, and later editions were even more so. The second edition came in 1860: "in this view of life, with its several powers, having been originally breathed by the Creator into a few forms or into one." Darwin stayed with this second version through the sixth and final edition of 1872. Was he being honest, or was he just playing to the religious gallery? We know for sure that Darwin believed in a deity when he wrote and published the *Origin*. In a famous letter written in 1860 to his American friend Asa Gray, he wrote, "I cannot anyhow be contented to view this wonderful universe & especially the nature of man, & to conclude that everything is the result of brute force. I am inclined to look at everything as resulting from designed laws, with the details, whether good or bad, left to the working out of what we may call chance" (Darwin 1985-, 8, 224). It is true that by 1872 Darwin probably no longer believed in a deity, and one presumes he retained the words about the creator because removing them would cause comment. But around 1860 he certainly thought one could have God breathing in life and yet doing this through unbroken law.

Let us agree that Darwin was not contradicting himself. You can believe in a methodologically natural origin of life and in a deity. But is this the Christian deity? It is clear that by 1860, Darwin's deity was not the Christian deity but much more a deistic god who set things in motion and then stood back. To be fair, the main reason that Darwin rejected the Christian God was more theological—he hated the idea of eternal damnation for nonbelievers (like his own father)—but in his *Autobiography* he made it clear that he wanted nothing to do with miracles, biblical or otherwise. The question now is whether this is good enough for Christian theists or, more particularly, whether this *should* be good enough for Christian theists.

If theists want to argue for actual miraculous interventions by God to create life, then there are two ways of going about this. First, one might want to say on scientific or philosophical grounds that life simply could not have emerged through purely natural processes. Famously or notoriously, since the 1990s, this has been the position of advocates of intelligent design theory (IDT), who claim to have a scientific argument for a nonnatural intelligence behind life as we know it. They, the biochemist Michael Behe (1996) in particular, argue that some organic features—the bacterial flagellum and the blood-clotting cascade have been highlighted—simply cannot have origins that can be explained naturally. Such phenomena are "irreducibly complex" and hence must have a non-natural (presumably miraculous) origin. It is true that IDT has been embraced by creationists and it might be objected that this is not traditional Christianity (an opinion I endorse) and hence is of no relevance to us here. But Michael Behe (a practicing Catholic) in fact is an evolutionist of a kind, and Plantinga (Nagel, for that matter, too) has sidled up to IDT at this point, so it is fair to introduce it here. Unfortunately, however, irreducible complexity has not stood the test of time, and conventional biologists—notably the Catholic textbook-writer Kenneth Miller (1999) of Brown University—have shown in great detail that things like the bacterial flagellum and the blood-clotting cascade can readily be explained naturally. As a proof that we must invoke miracles for the start of life, that line of argument fails.

The second move for the theist is simply to appeal to faith, making neither scientific nor theological argument. The Bible says that God breathed life into things, and that is all there is to it. The theist might agree that this breathing does not necessarily mean a literal breath like an Aristotelian vital force and can refer to organization instead—which, of course, is the position of the intelligent design theorists. Yet something out of the regular order of nature—something nonnatural or supernatural—had to happen and did happen. End of argument. Or is it? If one claims to take science seriously, evolutionary science in particular, is one contradicting oneself if one appeals to miracles? One is getting close to doing so if one appeals to science for one's position. Someone like the nineteenth-century historian and philosopher of science William Whewell (1840) said that, with respect to origins, science says nothing but "points upwards," and this is more or less the position of the IDT supporter. But one is free in this case to urge people to keep trying. If one just appeals to the Bible and to faith, then I take it that one is altering the discourse. One is not appealing to science at all or interacting with the science and is simply saying that there are some things that science cannot and does not explain.

With my beliefs about the place and power of metaphor, have I not laid myself open to this objection? I have agreed that science cannot explain everything, so who am I to object when someone like Alvin Plantinga says that God created life miraculously and that is all there is to it? The situations are not quite parallel. My cases where science cannot explain are cases where, given its nature, science cannot *in principle* explain. However, the case of life's origin is one where science claims it can or will or can in principle explain. One is arguing for a solution in the future based on what we have now and the general success of science.

We now know (to take another complex issue of origins) how the eukaryotic cell, the cell with a nucleus, was formed symbiotically from prokaryotic cells, cells without a nucleus. So successes here bolster our belief in future successes. Theists have no such support of this nature. Theists simply opt for a different explanation because they are theists. Theists have simply taken themselves out of the discussion. Reason counts for naught. And that, of course, is the problem. For all they may say otherwise, religious people want to appeal to reason when it is on their side. My fellow philosopher Daniel Dennett (1995) has made this point well. A religious person with a heart problem goes to a cardiac surgeon, not a faith healer or a philosopher. They have no right to opt out or to keep our respect, when on other occasions, as it suits them, they let faith trump the evidentially reasonable. That is cheating. This is why I say theists as theists have every right to speak to the question: why is there something rather than nothing? Theists as theists have no right to speak to the question: what is the origin of life?

Where Do We Stand?

I have one final point before I conclude, picking up again on my discussion at the beginning of this chapter on the argumentative strategies open to Peterson and me. My suspicion is that Peterson will agree with just about everything I have argued in this chapter. He does not align himself with the intelligent design theorists who have God perform a miracle every time he wants a new life form. Yet Peterson will disagree fundamentally with my conclusion. Agreeing with Darwin at the time of the *Origin*, he will think that ultimately it all is part of and shows God's plan. All of that organization cannot be just chance; somehow it has God behind it. At one level, I can criticize Peterson by saying that this is all very well but shows a God who is an unmoved mover, not the God of the Bible. In other words, Peterson appears to be a deist, not a theist, meaning that he believes in a God who set things in motion but who does not then intervene, as opposed to a God who does at times get directly involved. To this Peterson can, for instance, respond that he is not now talking about the gospel events—which he accepts and which do make him a theist. And in return, I respond that although I have shown why I don't accept the significance of the gospel events—I deny the miraculous nature of the stories and, without that, I see no reason to take the whole message (of Jesus as God) as authentic—I do not yet have the tools to remove Peterson's God in his deistic mode. Just wait, because I think it runs into other troubles!

There Is Grandeur in This View of Life

Michael Peterson

Life is that special quality which distinguishes entities that possess it from entities that are lifeless, dead, inert. Biology as a science assumes life and then proceeds to study its development, structures, and processes. However, scientific work on the origin of life—abiogenesis research—inquires empirically into the actual beginning of life, which involves the transition from inorganic to organic. Questions about the origin of life inevitably take us to the interface of science and religion, facing us with the challenge of how to relate their respective explanations. How far can science take us in explaining the conditions of life's origin? Michael Ruse is confident that an entirely scientific explanation will be sufficient. However, I see that thought as governed by his underlying philosophical naturalism. In this chapter, I give scientific and theistic explanations their proper due, while arguing that all that we know or ever will know scientifically about life's origin makes better sense metaphysically on a theistic worldview than on a naturalistic worldview. As Ruse rightly notes, much of our debate pertains to philosophical interpretation, but some of it also regards frank scientific assessment of the state of the science.

The Biological and the Prebiological

Bios in classical Greek means "life"—physical life—and is the root of the term "biology." Aristotle—the first biologist in the Western tradition—identified the essence of life with "soul" (Greek: *psuché*) and assigned different kinds of souls to plants, animals, and humans. Complete explanation of any biological structure or function, for Aristotle, speaks to both the matter and the soul involved (as a hylomorphic unity) by invoking two types of cause—mechanical and purposive. Mechanical causation pertains to the material aspect, whereas the soul is the intrinsic purposive drive of a given biological entity.

Introductory textbooks in biology are written, of course, under the mechanical model in science. Rather than attempting to specify the essence of life, the typical biology text provides a list of characteristics that distinguish a living organism from nonliving things, such as the capacity to grow, the capacity to metabolize, the capacity to respond to stimuli, and the capacity to reproduce. Such traits denote physical capabilities of a living physical being—a biological organism—to act and react in certain ways under certain conditions. On the subject of life's origin, the typical undergraduate textbook—which Simon Conway Morris calls a "zoo of good intentions"—speaks of how easily organic compounds can be synthesized, conveying a sense that science is on the verge of solving the problem of life (Conway Morris 2003, 60). Michael Ruse's optimistic remarks on the subject are in this vein.

Religion defines and describes the existence of life in ways not captured by the mechanical model. Adherents of classical Hinduism, for example, generally accept the science of the Big Bang but maintain that the deeper meaning of the existence of the universe is that it is a manifestation of Brahman in a cyclical process of creating and destroying. Likewise, Hindus typically accept Darwinian evolution as the mechanism of how physical life develops and diversifies but assign all of this to the realm of *maya*, illusion. The essential energy of life, then, proceeds from True Reality, Brahman, the One: all individual living souls are ultimately rooted in Brahman, the Great Soul.

Theistic religions explain finite life as the work of an infinite supreme being. The scriptures of each theistic tradition contain concrete images of the creation of life. The Koran, for instance, states, "Allah has created every animal out of water" (24:45). Of course, the central message that God gives life can be articulated in conceptual language without the literary imagery of water. The Psalmist affirms that "the Lord is the maker of heaven, the earth, the sea, and all that is in them" (Ps. 146:5–6). Such passages convey the basic understanding that God is the ultimate source and sustainer of life and that without divine activity there would be no creaturely life.

The question of the origin of life—regarding the transition from a prebiotic to a biotic world—raises issues at the interface of science and religion. Are both science and religion speaking to the mechanical causes of life, in which case there is potential conflict between God and natural processes? Ruse is not accommodative to religion on the matter of life's origin, disallowing that teleological answers supplement or frame mechanical answers, because he thinks that the answer to this question is going to be entirely mechanical. In assessing theistic options, Ruse holds that the theist can either posit a kind of deistic God originating life through purely natural mechanisms or claim that something distinctively supernatural or miraculous occurred at the start. We will make a serious foray into these matters in this chapter and be alert to the implications that are generated for the worldview debate in subsequent chapters.

Origin-of-Life Research

How, when, and where did life first appear on earth? Science has made progress in pursuing such questions, but it has also encountered serious challenges. Although no brief treatment can do justice to many decades of scientific research, the following sketch provides a glimpse of both successes and failures. As mentioned, our goal in the debate is not to delve deeply into details of the science but, as always, to locate and interpret the science in light of the worldview conflict between theism and naturalism.

Progress in origin-of-life research accelerated in the early twentieth century as pure speculation transitioned to workable and testable research models. Oparin and Haldane were key, proposing that original life forms resulted from a slow, multistep process that began with the abiotic synthesis of organic compounds and the formation of a primordial soup. The fundamental idea of chemical evolution—that organic molecules were formed from certain simpler inorganic molecules through chemical reactions under certain conditions—provided a theoretical framework within which experimental study of the origin of life could be conducted. Biochemistry, genetics, molecular biology, cellular biology, and other disciplines now contribute to abiogenesis research.

Pursuit of the chemical evolution leading to life raises further questions about the timescale required, the primitive earth environment, the organic compounds on early earth, the catalyzing event resulting in their synthesis, and the initial mechanism of genetic replication. As we now know, life appeared early on the young earth—such as the microbial mat fossils found in Western Australia. It is clear that, shortly after conditions on earth were suitable, life didn't just struggle to get traction and then eke out a meager existence. It took off with exuberance, which is evidence that the earth is downright biophilic.

Finding fault with the chemical mix used in the 1952 Miller–Urey experiment, in which many essential amino acids required for life were produced, some researchers now believe that the atmosphere on early earth would have contained more carbon dioxide, nitrogen, and hydrogen sulfide. Others question the electric spark energy source, now theorizing that deep-ocean hydrothermal vents may have provided favorable conditions for the beginning of life. Details will remain controversial, but the point of all such research is to reduce the chemical gap between the nonliving and the living.

Efforts to close the gap get mixed reviews. Noteworthy advances have been made in our understanding of what chemical compounds and processes are required for life and reproducing some of them under laboratory conditions. For example, scientists have succeeded in forming small biomolecules such as amino acids and nucleic acid bases and getting them to combine into larger biomolecules such as proteins and lipids. However, serious challenges persist in the quest for the process whereby the abiotic parts develop into a whole living system. Stuart Kauffman, a noted theoretical biologist in abiogenesis, writes,

> Despite my valid insights in my own two books, and despite the fine work of many others, including the brilliance manifest in the past three decades of molecular biology, the core of life itself remains shrouded from view. We know chunks of molecular machinery, metabolic pathways, means of membrane biosynthesis—we know many of the parts and many of the processes. But what makes a cell alive is still not clear to us. The center is still mysterious. (Kauffman 2003, 48)

It is fair to say that no comprehensive scientific hypothesis of the step-by-step origin of life is even on the distant horizon.

One set of questions pertains to the ideas of self-organization and self-replication—concepts used by empirical scientists and needed by naturalists for the completion of their metaphysical vision. It remains unclear what sorts of interactions would bring about a semialive system, or precellular life. Molecular and supramolecular chemistry are now telling us of self-organizational properties occurring at the biochemical level, but these properties are not fully understood. Regarding the early system of self-copying, Francis Crick (who, along with James Watson, discovered the double-helix structure of the DNA molecule) postulated that RNA supplied the early genetic and metabolic machinery. Others have questioned the reproductive and metabolic effectiveness of RNA to serve as the precursor of cellular life. And so the debate goes.

Scientific opinions vary from one end of the spectrum to the other regarding prospects for a complete answer to the question of life's physical origin. In the 1970s, the Nobel Prize winner Jacques Monod represented the prevailing view that life, including human life, occurred completely by chance (Monod 1971, 167). In the same vein, Francis Crick stated, "Life seems almost a miracle, so many are the conditions necessary for it to get going" (Crick 1982, 38). Expressing the completely opposite opinion, Christian de Duve declared, "Life is a cosmic imperative!" (de Duve 1995, 300). With the same optimistic tone, Henderson James Cleaves of the Carnegie Institution for Science says, "Now making an artificial cell doesn't sound like science fiction any more. It's a reasonable pursuit" (cited in Zimmer 2009, 198). It is critical in this debate to understand that, on purely empirical grounds, it is impossible to discriminate definitively between these opposing opinions.

Perhaps the fairest assessment of the science is offered in 1998 by Leslie Orgel, a groundbreaking biochemist in this area:

> The problem of the origin of life on the earth has much in common with a well-constructed detective story. There is no shortage of clues pointing to the

way in which the crime, the contamination of the pristine environment of the early earth, was committed. On the contrary, there are far too many clues and far too many suspects. It would be hard to find two investigators who agree on even the broad outline of events. (Orgel 1998, 491)

In a *Nature* piece in 2006, Orgel reflects that, beyond the rudimentary time-line, "almost everything else about the origin of life remains obscure," particularly "the detailed steps that led from unconstrained abiotic chemistry to the organized complexity of biochemistry" (Orgel 2006). Acknowledging both successes and failures in this area, it is fair to say on scientific grounds that the obstacles are formidable and that the gap between nonlife and life remains wide.

The Mystery of Life

We speak of the mystery of life, but what kind of mystery is involved? Could there be different kinds of mystery? As far as science is concerned, a mystery is virtually always the challenge of developing an empirical explanation for some important but currently unexplained phenomenon. As far as religion is concerned, the ultimate source and meaning of things lies beyond the reach of science, a point on which Michael Ruse agrees. However, Ruse objects to religious explanations of life's origin, maintaining that religion has no right to speak to an area where science is having some empirical success. Yet the key lies in correctly understanding the role of religion—in this case theism—in relation to science. Ruse avoids the total conflict model with his accommodationism (the view that science can accommodate religion on questions it cannot itself answer) but perceives significant potential conflict with religion over the origin of life. Ruse exhibits the reductionist tendency—driven by his naturalistic worldview—to make the explanation of the origin of life exclusively mechanical. By contrast, I argue that theistic explanation contextualizes whatever physical processes can be given mechanical explanation by relating them to a larger framework that affirms the ultimate source of the amazing phenomenon of life.

As a theist who accepts methodological naturalism, I see no problem in principle with abiogenic research into the natural processes surrounding the appearance of life. This follows from the general theistic endorsement of science as an avenue of knowledge into God's world. Besides, the history of science is decorated with breakthrough discoveries previously unimagined—Copernicus overturned Ptolemy's astronomy, Einstein subsumed Newton's laws in a more complete system, and so on. When some person or group tries to limit scientific investigation, to dictate a point beyond which science cannot go, science has always had a peculiar way of going beyond that limit. In general, we should not draw a priori limits to empirical questions.

Of course, it is sometimes difficult to know where an empirical question ends and a metaphysical question begins. Interestingly, scientific questions related to beginnings (and endings as well) imply certain kinds of limits and invite a larger perspective on empirical inquiry. In the Big Bang, science reaches a limit: science can describe the initial conditions and physical laws present at the beginning of the universe, but it cannot explain why there are physical laws and why any material was present in the first place. Once again, reflection on the limits of science takes us into the arena of metaphysics and the need to interpret everything within a total worldview. Remember Stephen Hawking's failed attempt to show how the universe could create itself without God—an effort that is both conceptually confused about types of origins questions and biased by an atheist mind-set. Sound metaphysical reasoning shows that there must be a self-existent, transcendent being to provide ultimate explanation for the existence of the universe. As I argued earlier, theism tells us that this metaphysically necessary being is an omnipotent God.

Is there a comparable limit in origin-of-life research to the limit encountered in cosmological research that would also require metaphysical reflection? In origin-of-life research, most of the experimental successes are in prebiotic chemistry—laboratory creations of some of the building blocks of life. Major problems, however, concern how to use the building blocks to construct a living system, a cell, which is an immensely complex chemical factory. Realistically, it is difficult to predict future empirical advances or challenges. Yet the excessive exuberance of some scientists and philosophers regarding origin-of-life research goes beyond empirical findings and reflects an underlying commitment to metaphysical naturalism, as we see in Ruse's remarks. Metaphysical naturalism holds that all phenomena, including life, have a purely natural explanation because there is no supernatural. This worldview perspective colors attitudes toward the science. We might say that strong faith is exercised that science—given enough time, creativity, patience, and funding—will discover in practice what was always believed in principle. For those naturalists who speak of the occurrence of life as highly improbable, their confidence is that scientists can discover that fluky sequence of events—a kind of naturalist faith. Other naturalists who speak of life as an inherent inevitability, hardly a fluke, if the right ("earthlike") conditions occur anywhere in the universe, seem to subscribe to a kind of naturalist predestination.

Some religious groups on the other side allow their perspective to color their assessment of the science so that they ignore or underestimate its incremental successes. One serious problem with the strategy of trying to find difficulties or incompletions in abiogenesis research to make room for God as a mechanical cause is that it repeats the error of modernity of making God vulnerable to expulsion from the world when science finds a natural cause that does the same explanatory work. In *Science and Christian Belief*, Charles Alfred Coulson, an Oxford mathematician and theoretical chemist, writes,

> There is no "God of the gaps" to take over at those strategic places where science fails; and the reason is that gaps of this sort have the unpreventable habit of shrinking. (Coulson 1958, 20)

Another problem is that God-of-the-gaps thinking completely abdicates any theologically adequate account of both God's immanence and modes of divine action that are not reducible to efficient causality. Coulson continues, "Either God is in the whole of Nature, with no gaps, or He's not there at all" (Coulson 1958, 35). Coulson's statement, reminiscent of Aubrey Moore's words in the introduction of this book, begs for the theistic affirmation that God remains ontologically distinct from the world while generally working in it and through it. Such a God, who can give matter special properties and purpose, need not be a deistic God who is uninvolved in the world's continuing operations. I provide a fuller exposition of this idea in Chapter 5.

The crucial task is to identify the different kinds of legitimate questions being asked about the origin of life. Empirical questions about the natural causes of life are entirely appropriate and should be pursued, but honesty should prevail in assessing the viability of the scientific answers, which, of course, are part of the ongoing scientific quest. Yet metaphysical questions are also appropriate regarding why a natural world exists, why it contains delicately balanced natural processes that make life possible, and why the character of the universe permits such a thing as life. Naturalists and theists will differ drastically in addressing these metaphysical questions and, therefore, interpret abiogenic science from radically different perspectives.

God or Natural Process?

The transition from inorganic to organic is an event of incomparable significance. Further scientific understanding of the conditions making for this event will almost certainly come via the study of the molecular machinery at its foundation. Although some steps are being taken, many scientists are starting to admit that progress is extremely slow in determining the complete process. Since "life" is essentially a holistic phenomenon, the problem does not readily break down into a series of neatly compartmentalized smaller problems. If life is a reality that occurs when biochemical components go through a certain set of stages to a final outcome, then solving the problem of life scientifically faces the fundamental difficulty that emergent realities—in which the whole is greater than the sum of the parts—cannot be predicted from the collection of their parts. At a minimum, life is an emergent phenomenon or property that occurs when certain physical parts and processes are in a certain relation. Emergence conceived in this general way is a theme running through my portions in several of the remaining chapters. Ruse makes the category mistake of treating the phenomenon of life as if it is on the same level as one of its components.

Philosophical naturalists assume the primacy of matter, the causal closure principle, and the centrality of empirical knowledge—and are committed, therefore, to the ability of science to provide a complete mechanical explanation of life's origin. The general advance of science and some noteworthy successes in abiogenesis research are cited as additional support for thinking that we can eventually describe the originating process in completely empirical terms. However, difficulties in bridging the divide between the nonliving and living—in pinpointing exactly what occurred for the inorganic to cross the line to the organic—seem daunting. My question is, how, from a naturalist perspective, without some divine principle, energy, or activity, does life first occur?

Creative theories of purely natural origins have been offered by eager naturalists. After proposing in the 1960s that RNA was the pathway to cellular life, Francis Crick, a confirmed atheist, speculated further in the 1970s that life on earth must have arrived from outer space (Crick and Orgel 1973). In *Life Itself*, Crick expounded in 1982 the theory of "directed panspermia," which asserts that primordial life forms were intentionally sent to earth billions of years ago by alien beings with advanced intelligence (Crick 1982). The term *panspermia*, from Greek, literally means "seeds of life everywhere," suggesting that life is to be expected in the universe, which displays an impressive record of chemical evolution that is prerequisite to biological life. Interestingly, scientists at the National Aeronautics and Space Administration working on "exogenesis" have identified various prebiotic molecules—such as uracil, an RNA nucleobase, and xanthine—on meteorites and space dust. Carl Sagan plugged fairly high values into the Drake equation for calculating the probability of intelligent life on other planets and obtained wildly optimistic results, which he frequently touted.

Sagan's 1985 book *Contact* (made into the 1997 Jodie Foster film by that title), as well as researchers at the Search for Extraterrestrial Intelligence Institute, reflects that same optimism (Sagan 1985). Unfortunately, the appeal to alien life—which has attracted more than a few naturalists—does not answer but rather pushes back the question of life's origin: how did alien life arise—naturally by abiogenesis? Whatever their scientific value, exogenesis theories are typically advanced by thinkers who embrace philosophical naturalism and are, therefore, dedicated to avoiding the question of a transcendent and ultimate source of life.

Paradoxically, naturalists assert in other contexts that human life on earth is nothing special—and, by implication, hold that life in general is nothing special. It all results by pure chance, formed of common materials, on a small, unimpressive planet. This Copernican principle—sometimes called the mediocrity principle—is erroneously derived from the valid uniformity-of-nature principle on which science rests. Although science must assume uniformity in the laws of nature throughout the universe, it cannot make value judgments about life (including human life) being mediocre in the relevant sense. It is a ploy of naturalist philosophy to insist on mediocrity under the guise of science. Here's the other ploy to avoid the theistic question: if we are nonspecial creatures that appeared by chance, then there is no need to look for a transcendent source of human specialness. Copernicus, the great pioneering astronomer who was also a church canon, would be disappointed at this use of his good name.

Some religious groups—working off the same false dichotomies—reject abiogenesis research to assert that God is the cause of life. The Institute for Creation Research and Answers in Genesis insist on a literal interpretation of the Genesis account of the creation of life, thereby making science and religion mutually exclusive on this point (Numbers 2006). Of course, both organizations are products of the Protestant fundamentalist movement, which began in the early twentieth century and taught a literal interpretation of the Bible. In addition to reacting to Darwinian evolution, fundamentalism was a response to other modernist or "liberal" developments, such as the critical textual analysis of the Bible and the Freudian psychological theory of religious motivation. One of the mistaken themes in fundamentalism is that biblical authority is linked to literal biblical interpretation, whereas historic Christianity has always recognized that the different types of literature contained in the Bible and received as sacred revelation must still be engaged and interpreted on their own terms (Wright 2014).

IDT, which can be viewed as a more recent evolutionary outgrowth of creationism, employs a different strategy, essentially arguing that we find in the living world significant organic complexity that cannot be produced by natural causes. As evidence, proponents of IDT have selectively cited their preferred biological structures and have also cited even the most minimal of life forms, the cell, as displaying signs of design (e.g., Meyer 2009; Venema 2010). The "design inference," as William Dembski calls it, is a line of reasoning to an unnamed nonnatural intelligent agent—and is a strategy meant to give new impetus to the old design argument (Dembski 1999). Unfortunately, to gain plausibility for the activity of God in creation, all of these approaches still assume competition between mainstream science and religion, construct their case in terms of alleged gaps or incompletions in current scientific research, and confuse methodological naturalism in science with metaphysical naturalism as an atheistic worldview (Numbers 2006; Peterson 2010).

Posing a "what if" scenario to religious opponents of abiogenesis research proves instructive: what if science eventually finds all biochemical and environmental factors that are necessary for life and has some impressive experimental successes in putting them together? Experiments show, for example, that naked RNA molecules (given the apparatus to self-replicate) can mutate and compete against each other, thereby setting up a selective situation, leading to evolution in an adaptive direction (Eckland et al. 1995). Discovery of all natural process for bringing about life would damage claims for special supernatural action conceived in mechanical terms. Yet there are no sound theological grounds for calling a thorough biochemical description of life's origin, should we ever get one, antithetical to belief in the activity of God. There are important theological grounds for affirming that God works very much through natural processes rather than looking for gaps in those processes for God to fill. Borrowing cosmological language, are these gaps all new "singularities"? Religious perspectives that are obsessed with beginnings—specifically with the mechanics of origins—will remain at odds with science on such issues.

Theistic and Christian Belief

The key issue is how the science of life's origins relates to the worldview debate running through this book. Return to the supposition that abiogenesis research could eventually discover all natural factors accounting for the beginning of life. The absolutely crucial philosophical question would still remain unanswered:

> Does theism or naturalism make better sense of a universe in which the organic can arise from the inorganic?

Where did the matter come from that forms the universe? Our previous discussion of the cosmological argument has already shown the superiority of theism over naturalism on this question. Why does the matter that exists have the power to enter into prebiotic chemical combinations that can lead from nonlife to life? My previous point about fine-tuning is relevant here. Alister McGrath observes that the molecular basis of evolution crucially depends on certain core elements, which, in turn, depend on the apparent fine-tuning of the constants of nature (McGrath 2011a, 196).

Regardless of the amount of detail that science is able to supply about the chain of causes, no matter what steps are discovered in the biochemical narrative, life is more likely to arise in the universe if the fundamental reality is a living supreme being than if it is inherently nonliving physical stuff. Where L is the occurrence of life, T is theism, and N is naturalism,

$$P(L/T) > P(L/N).$$

Put another way, it is much less epistemically surprising that life would arise in the universe on the assumption that theism is true than on the belief that naturalism is true.

Although the explanatory advantage of theism on this point is clear, there is still room for healthy discussion of a range of metaphysical theories regarding the precise nature of divine activity in the occurrence of life. Concepts of divine energy, divine agency via secondary causes, and divine impartation of a supervening quality are possible ways of thinking about how an infinite living conscious being is the source and sustainer of finite living beings. Fuller discussion of the nature of divine activity that avoids dichotomous thinking awaits the next chapter. In any event, for theism not to produce a neat formula for divine activity is hardly a reason to think that mechanical causes must form the total explanation of life. It is simply not within the purview of science to detect divine creative involvement, but theism's assertion of divine involvement provides a metaphysical framework that certainly makes better philosophical sense of the living world that science investigates. In Darwin's own words, "There is grandeur in this view of life."

Orthodox Christian understanding augments a basic theistic perspective by supplying richer information about God's ways and God's world. Christianity answers ultimate questions about the origin of life, its source and its meaning, but not empirical questions about temporal sequence and mechanics. There is no formula for how God works with the world. The important themes of the Genesis creation story establish God as the transcendent source of all creation and all of life but do not address the age of the earth, the sequence of species, and the like. Indeed, these themes in Genesis effectively ground a polemic against ancient polytheism and its purely prudential ethic toward the divine. Theologically, these ideas give shape to the *doctrine of creation* as the central conceptual commitment in play here. The theological content correlates exactly with our best philosophical reasoning about origins. Reflecting philosophically, we previously saw that finite contingent being depends on a metaphysically necessary being, God. Likewise, finite contingent life ultimately depends on a Self-Living Life, God. The Anglican *Book of Common Prayer*, not surprisingly, employs "God, the giver of life" multiple times as a term of address.

Furthermore, Christianity affirms that God's essence is self-giving love, which implies that God's activity in bringing about finite life is a gift of love.

In Genesis, God pronounces the physical creation and the diversity of life it sustains "good." Human beings—who are made "from the dust" and yet bear "the image of God"—are pronounced "very good." There is indeed a strangeness to the Christian view that personal rational life is intimately related to physical life, which is common, frail, and perishable. But this view is not nearly so strange as the naturalist position that life comes ultimately from a fundamental reality that is essentially nonliving itself and therefore has no life to give.

According to Christian theology, God desires to enter into a relationship with creation. The doctrines of creation and eschatology are therefore inseparably linked by the overarching purposes of God: a good creation will be completed and fulfilled. Playing off the difference in meaning between two classical Greek words for "life," we might say that *bios*—fragile, temporal biological life in which there are many finite goods—is meant to be caught up into and completed in *zoe*—the higher kind of life of perfect joy and love intrinsic only to God. In a sense, then, I agree with the naturalist that there is indeed an original, nonbiological source of life. It is the Self-Living, Self-Giving Life at the heart of reality.

5

Darwin and Design

A Wider Teleology

Michael Peterson

Evolutionary science—so goes the familiar line—obviates any viable natural theology. Historically, this perception springs specifically from the fact that Charles Darwin's work on natural selection demolished William Paley's argument from design. Although Michael Ruse takes this line, I argue that Darwin's contribution to biology damages only the type of natural theology characteristic of nineteenth-century English thought, not a more classical approach. In the end, I consider the relationship of Darwinian evolution to the worldview debate between naturalism and theism, arguing that theism makes better sense of an evolutionary world than Ruse's naturalism does.

Darwin's Discovery

The idea of biological evolution—that there is a process of change and diversification of living things over time—did not originate with Darwin. By the mid-nineteenth century, natural scientists embraced dynamic and rejected static concepts of organic life. Darwin considered his major achievement the theory of natural selection, which asserts that useful variants multiply more effectively over the generations than less useful (or harmful) variants. A leopard that runs faster than other leopards will catch more prey and therefore live longer and leave more offspring than slower leopards. Of course, as environments change, over time, natural selection will change the makeup and function of organisms, thereby causing the multiplication of species.

For our purposes, the mainstream scientific theory of evolution may be understood to involve three basic assertions: (1) that organisms are related by common descent; (2) that evolutionary history details the splits in lineages and changes within each lineage; and (3) that the mechanism of evolutionary change is natural selection operating on random variation. "Darwinism" was the traditional term for this third scientific thesis, which was one of the greatest achievements in intellectual history. Readers must be aware, however, that the term "Darwinism" is now typically used to refer to a naturalist philosophical perspective that incorporates evolutionary biology. The target of my criticism throughout the book is not Darwinian science but the naturalist worldview.

Evolutionary theory today has been augmented by other developments—such as Mendelian genetics in the early twentieth century, population genetics in the mid-twentieth century, and more recent molecular genetics related to RNA and DNA. We now speak of the "new evolutionary synthesis" or the "modern synthesis" instead of using Darwin's name. Nevertheless, it was natural selection that supplied the key to understanding the evolutionary process. Remarkably, Alfred Russel Wallace discovered natural selection independently of Darwin, but it is the theory itself that concerns us here.

Interestingly, biologists now grasp the crucial step—unknown to Darwin and his contemporaries—that is prior to the process of natural selection: the stable biological transmission of favorable variations. Gregor Mendel pioneered the modern theory of genetics, which now tells us that biological inheritance occurs through particulate factors known as "genes." Evolutionary genetics attempts to account for evolution in terms of changes in gene and genotype frequencies within populations as well as the processes that convert variation within populations into relatively permanent variation between species. Over long periods of time, microevolutionary changes account for macroevolutionary patterns that characterize the taxonomic groups.

Darwin discovered natural selection by attempting to answer the same question that Paley addressed: how can we explain the adaptive configuration of organisms and their parts—which seem "designed"—to fulfill certain functions? Daniel Dennett calls natural selection "Darwin's dangerous idea" because it challenges teleological explanation and faces us with the realization that design might not need a conscious, purposive designer (Dennett 1995, 23). As far as biology is concerned, natural selection is a blind process—indeed, purely de facto, the fittest survive and pass on their characteristics, generation after generation. Mutations occur by chance (although we can calculate mutation rates) and selection simply operates on them. Thus, biological structures and functions can be scientifically explained without reference to an intelligent agent forming them according to a preconceived design. We know this much based on science.

Dennett, however, elevates Darwinian findings in science to the status of worldview, claiming that it brings together "the realm of life, meaning, and purpose with the realm of space and time, cause and effect, mechanism and physical law" (Dennett 1995, 21). What we get is atheistic naturalism—which posits a world devoid of God and purpose—shaped and flavored by Darwinian science. Is Darwinism a "universal acid," as Dennett calls it, that erodes all outmoded metaphysical ideas of God, value, and meaning? Ambiguity in the use of the term Darwinism—as either science or worldview—hinders rather than helps in answering this question. Neither is the widespread perception of inherent conflict between science and religion helpful because it pits natural selection against God as an explanation of biological complexity.

Natural Selection and Design

In his *Natural Theology*, William Paley constructed a theistic argument from design in the natural world:

> In crossing a heath, suppose I pitched my foot against a *stone*, and were asked how the stone came to be there, I might possibly answer, that for any thing I knew to the contrary it had lain there for ever; nor would it, perhaps, be very easy to show the absurdity of this answer. But suppose I had found a *watch* upon the ground, and it should be inquired how the watch happened to be in that place, I should hardly think of the answer which I had before given, that for any thing I knew the watch might have always been there. Yet why should not this answer serve for the watch as well as for the stone; why is it not admissible in the second case as in the first? For this reason, and for no other, namely, that when we come to inspect the watch, we perceive—what we could not discover in the stone—that its several parts are framed and put together for a purpose, *e.g.* that they are so formed and adjusted as to produce motion, and that motion so regulated as to point out the hour of the day; that if the different parts had been differently shaped from what they are, or placed after any other manner or in any other order than that in which they are placed, either no motion at all would have been carried on in the machine, or none which would have answered the use that is now served by it. (Paley [1802] 1809, 1)

The analogy of the watch frames the strategy directed toward this conclusion: "The inference we think is inevitable, that the watch must have had a maker" (Paley [1802] 1809, 3). This maker formed the watch for a "purpose" and "designed" its use. Paley's work proceeded to develop the argument by citing the complex organization of living things that further support the conclusion of an intelligent designer.

Unfortunately, for all its popular appeal, Paley's reasoning is weak for a number of reasons. First, like all arguments from analogy, it is subject to disanalogies. Second, the design argument also involves the erroneous assumption that the inference to an intelligent agent excludes chance because the outcomes of chance do not display organized complexity. Third, the biological structures cited in the developed line of argument are seen as mechanisms made for a purpose. The eye, a favorite example, is thus like a telescope—"made for vision"—in terms of being purposefully assembled of specific parts for the refraction of light rays.

The argument is clearly teleological—pertaining to purpose—but it involves a particularly narrow notion of teleology. Return to Paley's assumption—shared in many religious sectors today—that divine action is direct causality that excludes chance. Although Paley nominally acknowledges the possibility of "secondary causes" in nature, he insists that their existence and coordination are unfailingly ordained in God's purposes (Paley [1802] 1809, 419–420). Such a strong view of divine control implies a static and perfect creation, with the observable world, its various species, and their defining characteristics existing largely in their originally created forms. Alister McGrath explains that this particular type of teleological argument must be seen in the intellectual and cultural context of the distinctively English tradition in natural theology that sought to bolster social consensus on God without reference to biblical texts. In the late seventeenth century, Walter Charleton's *A Physico-Theological Treatise* was one of many works taking up the project. Throughout the eighteenth century, the enterprise of "physicotheology" offered rational arguments based on empirical facts to a deity governing the regularity of nature that was increasingly described in detail by mechanistic science (McGrath 2011a, chap. 3).

In the eighteenth century, the great skeptic David Hume famously criticized the design argument with parodies of its core analogy. Multiple designers are as likely as one: "a great number of men join in building a house or a ship . . . ; why may not several deities combine in contriving and framing a world?" (Hume [1779] 1947, para. 167). Furthermore, the original designer may not even remain in existence although his artifact continues to exist. Last, the "faulty and imperfect" aspects of the world could argue, as Hume says, for an infant deity or a senile deity, incompetent in either case (Hume [1779] 1947, para. 168). Christian thinkers had also critiqued the clear weaknesses in Paley's argument as well as the assumptions of the physicotheological tradition overall. Still, the argument enjoyed positive cultural acceptance in Victorian England even while the seeds of its certain destruction were being sown. In the meantime, teleological explanation persisted in biological science since there was no alternative scientific explanation of complex organic structures except to say that God made them with specific purposes in mind.

The work of Darwin completed the destruction of Paley's argument as a viable piece of natural theology. Natural selection brought biology in line with the mechanistic paradigm that had become common in the other sciences. Darwin's words in his autobiography are to the point:

> The old argument from design in nature, as given by Paley, which formerly seemed to me so conclusive, fails, now that the law of natural selection has been discovered. We can no longer argue that, for instance, the beautiful hinge of a bivalve shell must have been made by an intelligent being, like the hinge of a door by a man. There seems to be no more design in the variability of organic beings, and in the action of natural selection, than in the course which the wind blows. Everything in nature is the result of fixed laws. But I have discussed this subject at the end of my book on the *Variation of Domesticated Animals and Plants*; and the argument there given has never, as far as I can see, been answered. (Darwin 1958, 87–88)

As long as a dichotomy is presumed between natural process and divine action, natural selection operating on random mutations preempts the inference to a purposeful designer.

Understanding Evolution

Resistance to evolutionary theory as science—particularly as shaped by the core Darwinian principles of variation, inheritance, and selection—continues among various religious groups. Yet Dennett and Dawkins employ the term Darwinism to denote a worldview that combines metaphysical naturalism and evolutionary science to form a grand narrative in which nature is ultimate, physical laws displace purposive divine activity, and special status for humans is eliminated.

Darwinism or evolutionism as a worldview is inconsistent with a theistic worldview. Michael Ruse's Darwinian naturalism also involves the position that theism is explanatorily irrelevant on most points and demonstrably incorrect on others. Actually, Darwinism as a philosophical view fulfills an important function of religion—providing answers for life's great questions that are then accepted as a creed or ideology. Sensitive to misunderstandings of Darwin's contribution, Thomas Henry Huxley, one hardly sympathetic toward religion, argued that in strictly scientific terms "the doctrine of Evolution is neither Anti-theistic nor Theistic" (Darwin 1887, 312). Huxley rightly observed that science "commits suicide when it adopts a creed" (Huxley 1893, 252).

In the nineteenth century, Darwinism (a term coined by Huxley) became used to label various progressive social and economic theories. Spencer's "social Darwinism" was one of several views assuming an upward trend in human evolution because "survival of the fittest" allows the strong to advance. Darwin distanced himself from Spencer's speculative ideas, saying that they were of no scientific use and that "his conclusions never convince me" (Darwin 1958, 109). Historically, pernicious doctrines of "superior individuals" and even a "superior race" resulted from some forms of social Darwinism and provided ideological fuel for Nazism and its program of eugenics. Unfortunately, certain religious groups—such as creation science and intelligent design—foster the mistaken perception that Darwinian evolutionary biology leads to political policies that undervalue weak, minority, disadvantaged individuals.

It is of the utmost importance to distinguish the science of evolution to which Darwin significantly contributed from various philosophies that incorporate Darwin's ideas and perhaps even use his name. Religious groups that suggest that atheism and secularism are a necessary entailment of Darwinian evolutionary biology are engaging in propaganda. In part, the creationist argument for special creation and fixity of species is aimed at countering evolution and thereby undermining a mainstay of secularism. Intelligent design advocates, who argue for organic complexity that cannot occur by chance, are in their own way combating evolutionary science and thereby the unacceptable cultural results they associate with it.

As a theory in science, evolution is as well confirmed as any empirical theory could possibly be, providing the most reasonable interpretation of a myriad of facts in a wide variety of disciplines, such as paleontology, comparative anatomy, biogeography, biochemistry, embryology, and ecology. Francisco Ayala, a world-renowned biologist and former Dominican priest, has stated, "Gaps of knowledge in the evolutionary history of living organisms no longer exist" (Ayala 2007, 79). The universal tree of life—showing the pattern of continuity of all living organisms from a common ancestor to the present—is confirmed by hundreds of scientific studies published every year. We now know that all life is based on the same hereditary molecule, DNA, and that its "language" involves the same four nucleotides and the same twenty amino acids, making common origin of the diversity of living things overwhelmingly probable. The degree of correspondence between the sequences of nucleotides in the DNA supports common origin and, in fact, allows us to reconstruct the phylogenetic tree of life, with less closely related species exhibiting less similarity in their DNA than more closely related species because more time has elapsed since their last common ancestor.

In a book asking the question of how science—and particularly evolutionary science—factors into the debate between atheism and theism, we must stay clearly focused on the philosophical issues surrounding the science. Michael Ruse and I are both stipulating the validity of the science of evolutionary biology and its findings. How could we not? Theodosius Dobzhansky, a famous Russian biologist and Orthodox Christian, published an article entitled "Nothing in biology makes sense except in the light of evolution" (Dobzhansky 1973, 125). The defensive ploy stating that "evolution is a *theory*, not a *fact*" badly misunderstands that well-confirmed theories in science are considered facts.

My argument is not against evolutionary science but against its interpretation and deployment by philosophical naturalists. Dawkins and others herald the completion of an atheistic and naturalist worldview by Darwinian science, making it difficult to discern the difference between genuine scientific claims and philosophical claims made in the name of evolution. We are seeing here how Ruse combines evolution with his brand of naturalism. On the other side, some religious voices fail to recognize evolution as reliable science and have thereby forfeited the opportunity to explore a reasonable theistic and Christian interpretation. My aim throughout is to identify ways in which naturalists inflate their claims that evolutionary science contributes to the reasonableness of atheism and damages the credibility of theism. I argue that all truth—including evolutionary truth in science—finds its most fitting philosophical context in a theistic and Christian worldview.

Darwin's Gift

Michael Ruse thinks that evolution by natural selection delivers a fatal blow to the design argument and therefore puts enormous pressure on a theological perspective. Perhaps I could defend the argument from design simply because I'm a theist and think that doing so seems obligatory to protect theology. However, theists should want to support only sound arguments for the existence of God, not just any old argument made in the name of theism. Since the truth of natural selection is highly confirmed, it is much wiser—and much more faithful to a classical theological perspective—to provide a positive philosophical interpretation for it.

Evolution by natural selection—Darwin's signature finding and one of the greatest achievements in intellectual history—is a significant benefit to both science and theology. Science obviously benefits from Darwin's work by acquiring the mechanism of evolutionary change. Biology now explains complexity and adaptation in terms of natural selection winnowing random variation rather than in terms of purposive divine agency. With Darwin, efficient causation replaced final causation in the organic world, and biology took its place among all the other sciences shaped by the Newtonian revolution.

Yet we may ask, how exactly can evolution by natural selection be of benefit to theism and Christianity? Remember from the Introduction that Anglican theologian Aubrey Moore, in the mid-nineteenth century, feared that science was pushing the God of deism out of nature—a deity consistent with Paley's divine designer. The deistic Supreme Being had designed the world, its forms and functions, and then allowed it to operate without his further involvement. Then "Darwinism appeared," says Moore, "and, under the guise of a foe, did the work of a friend"—by demolishing the design argument for this kind of God (Moore 1890, 73–74).

The Catholic theologian John Haught has written of "Darwin's gift to theology" (Haught 2000, 45). Evolutionary science has changed our understanding of the natural world so dramatically that it catalyzes the rethinking and refinement of our vision of God. After all, if theology is to be relevant and meaningful, it must freshly articulate enduring truths in light of emerging knowledge in every generation. Truth in science, as in any other area, can hardly be a foe of a theistic and Christian perspective, which embraces all truth as God's.

Several aspects of God's ways and God's world are understood more clearly in interaction with evolutionary truth. First, we are reminded—as we were in the Galileo affair—that neither theology nor scripture contains detailed scientific information. Unnecessary conflict with science is invited when religion gets in the business of making pronouncements about the empirical mechanisms at work in God's world. Theology should concern itself with expressing broad principles regarding God's love and plan for humans while affirming ongoing scientific inquiry into the created world. Second, Darwin's gift encourages deeper reflection on the classical Christian doctrine of creation. Understanding the contingency of creation and its workings creates appropriate receptivity to the discoveries of science as an avenue of knowledge about God's world.

A third aspect of Darwin's gift is that it forces critical reconsideration of the Paleyite argument from design and the whole tradition of English natural theology that it represented. By discovering the natural cause of organic complexity, Darwin's discovery blocked the once-confident inference to a transcendent designer. Victorian physicotheology, which assumed static and perfectionistic ideas of nature, was to become obsolete as the dynamic and developmental processes of nature were discovered. Natural theology became freed from the strategy of arguing for God based on selectively chosen patterns in the physical world and freed to recover an approach that is at once more ancient and yet more forward looking. This more classical approach recognizes the divine bestowal of real causal powers on nature so that nature could unfold in rich and interesting ways in the economy of God.

Fourth, Darwin's gift provides the occasion for religious believers to reconsider the roles and levels of chance in created reality. Paley-type arguments from design are based on a false dichotomy between chance and intelligent divine activity. Since natural selection produces adaptive fitness by sifting through random variations, direct divine designing activity would seem to be ruled out. When religious hopes are pinned on the rejection of chance, the mistaken presumption will always be that chance in the world as studied by science gives atheism a foothold. Science, of course, identifies various kinds of chance—from radioactive decay to the strike of an asteroid. But the claim that chance—conceived as nondetermined contingency—exists within the world is not inconsistent with standard theism. Furthermore, classical Christian ideas imply that contingency is essential in a relational universe in which creatures may freely choose to love God. What is inconsistent with theism and Christianity is the naturalist claim that chance is ultimate, that the natural world as a whole exists by chance and without divine purpose. Chance *within* a possible world must not be equated with chance *among* possible worlds.

Teleology and Natural Theology

In a historical context, Darwin's discovery of natural selection as the mechanism that produces adaptive complexity undermined Paley's essential but faulty premise: that such complexity could not occur by chance. Actually, the general approach to natural theology reflected in Paley's analogical argument from design was already receiving scathing critique from some Anglican theologians who perceived in traditional Christian theology more profound concepts of God and nature. Frankly, by the publication of the *Origin*, Victorian culture was already shifting toward more comfortable acceptance of evolutionary ideas and toward disaffection with the excessive rationalism in physicotheology that attempted to infer God from aspects of the natural world. The way was opened then—and remains open now—for deeper analysis of the idea of teleology as well as recovery of a more profound understanding of the project of natural theology. I personally do not use the language of design: it is freighted with misleading philosophical and theological associations.

Static notions of design in the natural world, based on a strong interpretation of divine control, must be surrendered more to a dynamic concept of nature in which God's role is generally supportive and interactive but not always determinative. The traditional way of expressing this idea is that God works through secondary causes, but the precise conception of secondary cause at play here is vitally important. For Paley in his setting, secondary causes may be involved in the mechanisms by means of which God creates and orders the world, but God is the ultimate power regulating everything, which means that God is still the ultimate cause of their behavior (Paley [1802] 1809, 418–20). In Paley's estimation, and probably that of his reading audience, any meaningful autonomy for secondary causes would imply a "chance" element that is inimical to providential design and would, therefore, pave the way to atheism.

Aquinas's more robust theory of secondary causality far surpasses Paley's as a metaphysical description of God's providence in relation to creaturely realities. God donates to creatures their various powers and capabilities—and then allows them the dignity of their own responses—leaving open a range of contingent outcomes (Aquinas 1975, *SCG* III.i, chaps. 72–77) For Aquinas, the working of divine purposes is not incompatible with chance (*accidens*) or luck (*fortuna*). This idea is consistent with standard theism, generally acknowledged in process theism, but not accepted by versions of theism that embrace meticulous divine control. Classical orthodox Christianity speaks of *kenosis*, which refers to the humility of Christ in becoming a finite human. The notion of divine self-emptying can be applied in the present context to suggest that God empowers creatures with a "functional integrity" and gives them space to act without determining all outcomes. This is not the unorthodox idea that Ruse cites as wearing the *kenosis* label but which asserts that God lacks power to work effectively as an agent in the world and so must merely work alongside creatures. My basic point is that providence must be understood generally as God's interaction with the unfolding outcomes in the creaturely world rather than complete top-down management.

Interestingly, Charles Kingsley, a nineteenth-century Anglican minister and professor, envisioned evolution as a process in which creatures with God-given powers and potentialities could dynamically develop in relation to environmental changes. Kingsley perceptively remarked,

> We knew of old that God was so wise that He could make all things: but behold, He is so much wiser than even that, that He can make all things make themselves. (Kingsley 1874, xxvii)

There are, then, theological grounds for the idea that biological organization—the outcome of variation, inheritance, and selection—could emerge over time under the providence of God. This is an ancient theme in Christian theology. For example, Augustine wrote,

> All the normal course of nature is subject to its own natural laws. According to these all living creatures have their determinate inclinations . . . and also the elements of non-living material things have their determinate qualities and forces, in virtue of which they function as they do and develop as they do. . . . From these primordial principles everything that comes about emerges in its own time and in the due course of events. (Augustine 1982, vol. I, chap. 9, para. 17)

Michael Ruse maintains that natural selection does the work of teleology, but it actually displaces only Paley's restricted form of teleology. Interestingly, T. H. Huxley agrees that evolution devastates teleology "as commonly understood" (Huxley 1870, 301) but asserts that evolution reflects a "wider teleology" (cited in Darwin 1887, 201). Huxley writes that "the whole world, living and not living, is the result of the mutual interaction, according to definite laws, of the forces possessed by the molecules of which the primitive nebulosity of the universe was composed" (cited in Darwin 1887, 201). The point is that Darwinian evolutionary science does not prevent a sophisticated teleological argument. Richard Swinburne reasons that the best explanation of physical laws, which embody a deeper order and structure in the universe, is that they originate in the mind of

God, who is a rational and purposeful agent (Swinburne 1977, 140–41). Evolutionary laws, therefore, do not damage teleology as classically conceived but are rather one way of reflecting it.

Natural theology need not style itself as inferring God directly from empirical observations, much less conflate teleology with design. It should, however, deliberately work at presenting theism as a more reasonable philosophical framework than other worldview alternatives for making sense of all knowledge and human experience. Neither should natural theology be bonded to the science of previous eras; it should instead engage in deep and sustained interaction with the best scientific information, including information from evolutionary biology.

In this light, I ask, in what kind of world do Darwinian evolutionary processes, reflecting the interplay of chance and law and enhancing the fitness and functionality of living organisms relative to changing environments, make better sense—a world described by theism or by naturalism? A theism that embodies a proper teleology clearly makes better sense of the Darwinian processes that were previously thought devastating to a theological interpretation of nature. Put formally, where D denotes a living world characterized by Darwinian processes, T denotes theism, and N denotes naturalism,

$$P(D/T) > P(D/N).$$

After all, the adaptations of organisms are teleological in that they contribute to their reproductive success. Natural selection is a goal-oriented process of increasing reproductive efficiency and cannot be reduced to purely mechanical explanation. As Huxley observed, there is indeed still a wider—and, as theism holds, a deeper and more profound—teleology in the universe. It is a teleology explained by the existence of God.

Darwin Destroys Design

Michael Ruse

In a way, this is the key chapter in our debate. We are going to be raising fundamental questions about the nature of organisms. Note, however, that neither Michael Peterson nor Michael Ruse is a biologist. Although we both take the science seriously, and we lay ourselves right open to criticism if we get the science wrong, we don't even pretend to be biologists. One nice thing about our engagement is that, as I explained earlier, we are not arguing about the science. Without being too overwhelmingly condescending, I suspect that both Peterson and I feel rather smugly satisfied that unlike some of our good friends—those more in the center of things, like the Unitarians—we don't feel the need to argue about which parts of science are right and which are wrong. That, for us, is not our job and not really our prime interest—and certainly not our prime need. We are looking at things from a theological and philosophical perspective, and we don't feel the need to slip in solutions through selective acceptance of the scientific claims. Given the basic science, we want to look at the broader implications. Keep this in mind here and in the following chapters.

To set the context, we will continue presenting a lot of science as a prolegomenon to what we want to talk about. In his response, Peterson seeks to salvage a teleological understanding of the world in connection to evolution apart from the design argument's insurmountable difficulties at the hands of Darwin. In this chapter, I explain natural selection's devastating impact on design and contend that any notion of final causality is now explanatorily irrelevant. In fact, I venture here some reasons why even the faithful might want to abandon not only the design argument but also the whole project of natural theology. My fundamental point is that Darwinism removes major philosophical reasons for theistic and Christian belief and opens the way to atheism.

The Darwinian Theory of Evolution

Let's turn now to the actual processes and course of evolution itself. Charles Darwin's theory of evolution through natural selection is not that complex. First, he argued to a struggle for existence. Organisms have a natural tendency to reproduce at an explosive rate—following Malthus, Darwin thought that this rate would be geometric (1, 2, 4, 8, . . .). But there is only limited food and space. Again following Malthus, at most, resources can only increase at an arithmetic rate (1, 2, 3, 4, . . .). Hence, not all can survive or, what is even more important in the biological world, not all can reproduce. There is going to be a struggle, although as Darwin stressed, this struggle need not be actually physically violent:

> I should premise that I use the term Struggle for Existence in a large and metaphorical sense, including dependence of one being on another, and including (which is more important) not only the life of the individual, but success in leaving progeny. Two canine animals in a time of dearth, may be truly said to struggle with each other which shall get food and live. But a plant on the edge of a desert is said to struggle for life against the drought, though more properly it should be said to be dependent on the moisture. A plant which annually produces a thousand seeds, of which on an average only one comes to maturity, may be more truly said to struggle with the plants of the same and other kinds which already clothe the ground. (Darwin 1859, 62–63)

From this, we go on to natural selection. The success of organisms in the struggle will, on average, be a function of their different features. Over time, this will lead to change:

> Let it be borne in mind how infinitely complex and close-fitting are the mutual relations of all organic beings to each other and to their physical conditions of life. Can it, then, be thought improbable, seeing that variations useful to man have undoubtedly occurred, that other variations useful in some way to each being in the great and complex battle of life, should sometimes occur in the course of thousands of generations? If such do occur, can we doubt (remembering that many more individuals are born than can possibly survive) that individuals having any advantage, however slight, over others, would have the best chance of surviving and of procreating their kind? On the other hand, we may feel sure that any variation in the least degree injurious would be rigidly destroyed. This preservation of favourable variations and the rejection of injurious variations, I call Natural Selection. (Darwin 1859, 80–81)

In one major respect, Darwin's theory was incomplete. For evolutionary change to occur, one needs a steady supply of new variations. His knowledge of animals and plants in domestication, combined with an eight-year systematic study of barnacles, had convinced Darwin that such variation does occur. He was also totally convinced that such variation does not occur to speak to the needs of organisms but in this sense is "random." But Darwin had little idea about why and where such variation occurs and, as important, little idea about how (without being swamped out by already-existing forms) variation can gain a foothold and persist in a population. Supplying this part of the story had to wait until the twentieth century when work by Darwin's contemporary, the Moravian monk Gregor Mendel, was uncovered and biologists were rapidly able to put together a full and adequate theory of heredity. It was in the context of this theory, generalized to populations, that the Darwinian mechanism of selection came into its own and in the 1930s the amalgamated "synthetic theory of evolution" or "neo-Darwinism" was formulated. To use a somewhat hackneyed term, evolutionary studies now had its "paradigm," and this has held sway for the past seven or eight decades. Of course there have been advances and changes, many linked to the coming of molecular studies, but it is the neo-Darwinian approach that guides today's researches.

The Problem of Final Causes

The machine metaphor has triumphed. In the felicitous language of Richard Dawkins, "We are survival machines, but 'we' does not mean just people. It embraces all animals, plants, bacteria, and viruses." Continuing,

> We are all survival machines for the same kind of replicator—molecules called DNA—but there are many different ways of making a living in the world, and the replicators have built a vast range of machines to exploit them. A monkey is a machine which preserves genes up trees, a fish is a machine which preserves genes in the water; there is even a small worm which preserves genes in German beer mats. DNA works in mysterious ways. (Dawkins 1976, 22)

The story is a bit more interesting than this. (This is one of the reasons why I love working on evolutionary theory. It is always a bit more interesting.) Aristotle didn't think in terms of little men in the future reaching back to the present and altering things. But he did think it made sense to talk in terms of the future for present understanding. That is what the organic metaphor is all about. Of the newborn boy, you can ask about the function of the penis. One part of the answer will obviously refer to reproduction—something very much in the future and possibly even something that will never happen. He might become a Catholic priest! But it makes sense to say that the boy has a penis because he will need it for reproduction. He has it to reproduce or for the purpose of reproduction. As we saw in Chapter 2, in the physical world after the Scientific Revolution, this kind of thinking—"final cause" thinking—was dropped. You just focus on the machine as something going around and around according to unbroken law. You don't ask about the function, the purpose of the moon. Or if you do, you are making a joke: "It is to light the way home for drunken philosophers." But everyone agreed that in the biological world this dropping simply isn't possible. The eye obviously does exist to see and the hand to grasp—now and in the future (Ruse 2003).

The point about Darwin's natural selection is that he spoke to this issue of final cause, realizing that if the machine metaphor were to triumph in the biological world—ultimately it is all just blind law cycling endlessly—he had to deal with final causes. One way might have been to ignore them or deny that they are really that significant. Robert Chambers ignored them, and Darwin's great supporter Thomas Henry Huxley always downplayed their significance. This was not Darwin's way. He believed in final causes. Natural selection does not just bring about change. It brings about change in the direction of adaptive complexity. Organisms that have well-functioning hands and eyes do better in the struggle than organisms that do not have such characteristics. Of course, this is not always the case. A falling rock might wipe out the better organism—what evolutionists call the "fitter" organism—but, on average, quality will tell. So we have a natural explanation of final causes.

Note, and this is important, that all of the final cause work is done by natural selection. The variations that selection works on are random, although not in the sense of being uncaused. Darwin always thought that there were causes, and today (especially with the coming of molecular biology) we know a lot about them. Rather, as Darwin stated without equivocation, variations are random in the sense of not occurring according to need. A new predator arrives, and the prey needs a new adaptation. Unless the prey already has something in its tool kit, it is probably going to be out of luck. New variations, what today we call "mutations," rarely do anything to help their possessors with respect to their immediate needs. You might think that this in itself is something of a refutation of natural selection. If the right variations are so rare, how can an organism survive, let alone improve? To use an analogy, think of a class assignment where you are asked to write an essay on dictators, discussing one example in detail. The way most people think of the availability of usable variation is as if your only source material were provided by the Book of the Month Club, that is to say a book every thirty days chosen by others without regard to your immediate needs. No doubt within, let us say, ten years the club would choose some book on Hitler or Stalin or Castro or some like person, but by the time it arrived on your doorstep, the course would be long over, and you would have failed! Likewise in the biological world. By the time the right variation comes along, you are extinct.

Worries like this are surely part of the reason why many people have trouble with natural selection, and even those entirely committed to naturalism at every level argue that other causes must have been involved. In Darwin's time, the inheritance of acquired characteristics (so-called "Lamarckism") was a favorite. Darwin himself always embraced it as a secondary mechanism. However, we now know that Lamarckism—incidentally not original with Lamarck and only a side cause for him—simply isn't true. Every now and then you see claims that it has been revived, but they always turn out to be some fairly trivial, short-term effect, if that. Another mechanism (if you can so call it) that is popular in some circles today is that the unaided laws of physics and chemistry can produce complex functioning—life, we are told, is "self-organizing" (Kauffman 1993). A popular example of such a phenomenon—cutely characterized as "order for free"—is "phyllotaxis," meaning the organization of petals on plants and other fruits and seeds, including, famously, the pine cone. Non-Darwinians argue that it is simply a function of the mathematics of producing flowers and seeds (Goodwin 2001). The parts are produced in a sequential fashion and by the laws of nature they must follow a fixed pattern, a pattern, incidentally, that is governed by the so called "Fibonacci series," made famous by the thriller *The Da Vinci Code*.

Expectedly, Darwinians don't buy into alternatives to natural selection. With respect to self-organization, it is argued that at most it could cover only a fraction of the known adaptations of organisms and that investigation invariably shows that selection has been at work. No one denies that there will be constraints put on the operation of selection by the laws of physics and chemistry—you cannot make a cat the size of an elephant because whereas the legs increase linearly, the weight increases as a function of the cube—but this does not mean that selection is not at work. In the case of plants, it will be orienting petals in one way rather than another and so forth. It is not the laws of physics and chemistry *or* natural selection but the laws of physics and chemistry *and* natural selection.

This all said, there is still a worry here about the power of natural selection, and although he never broke faith either with selection or with the nondirected nature of new variations, I am not sure that Darwin himself ever got on top of this problem. Fortunately, today's evolutionists have a ready answer, suggesting that concerns of this kind are misplaced. Most new variations don't just appear on the scene, as it were. Thanks to the Mendelian system of heredity, where two units (genes) work to produce characteristics (thanks to the paired system of chromosomes), even if new variations are deleterious, if they are generally masked by their mates (in geneticists' language, if they are recessive), they can be carried on and on in populations. This means that if they meet up with an identical mate (allele), they express their physical (phenotypic) characteristic. In other words, all of the time in a reasonably large population, features stored in the genotype are reappearing in the population and can be used if they are of worth or needed (Lewontin 1974). In fact, the situation is even better than this. Apart from the fact that most mutations tend to be recessive and hence not wiped out immediately (for the simple reason that most mutations stop some biochemical processes, and the mate is there to pick up the slack), selection often works to keep variations in populations. One common reason is that an organism with just one variant may do better than either of the two possible other organisms, those with no or two variants, and so selection works to keep the variants in the population. (This is known as "balanced heterozygote fitness.")

To return to our analogy, if you were dependent solely on the offerings of the Book of the Month Club, you would indeed be in trouble. Suppose, however, you have a library at your disposal. If there were nothing on Hitler or Stalin or Castro on the shelves, and there probably would be, then surely there would be something on someone else or perhaps on someone that could be used for the purpose. Perhaps there would be something on Churchill and, although no one would say he was a dictator, one could write on his wartime powers and how they were dictatorial in one sense but not in another. You might even get an A for ingenuity! And the same is true in evolution. You might think that, with a new predator, a simple change of color to provide more effective camouflage would be best. But perhaps there is no variation speaking to color, but there is one that makes a move to a different ecological niche possible (let us say digestion of a hitherto-inedible foodstuff), and with this move the prey does even better than it did before. It gets an A for ingenuity! Just as in class there is no one predetermined best answer, so in nature there is no one predetermined best answer. Life is graded on a curve. It is not how well you do absolutely, but how well you do compared to your fellows. With a large genetic tool kit at your disposal, you are at least in the game.

Does Darwinian Selection Refute Christianity?

Now turn the story the other way. Let's continue with the focus on final cause for a moment. You might want to say that as well as having the machine metaphor, Darwin brings back or retains the organic metaphor. I am happy if you want to say that, although since presumably you are no longer looking at the inorganic world as an organism, I am not sure that we should speak of "metaphor" here since now everything seems literal. For myself, I would rather work entirely in terms of the machine metaphor. After all, machines do have ends— the automobile is for transport—it is just that in the inorganic world we drop that aspect of the metaphor as misleading or unhelpful. If I say my love is a rose, I am probably not going to spend a great deal of time talking about her root system. I would say, therefore, that when it comes to organisms, we find it helpful to use the machine metaphor more broadly when trying to understand their parts—I can ask not only how the heart works but also what it is for—but then obviously when it comes to organisms as a whole, we have the truncated metaphor. What is the ultimate purpose of organisms? In the scientific world, they have no more purpose than the rivers of the world. Organisms, of course, do things and change the environment. But so also do rivers. It is just that neither is in place to do what it does—except in special cases that rather prove the general points, as when an ant uses an aphid to provide food for its young. Overall, however, it is just blind law in action.

So where now does this leave Christianity? Something important is being said here, because second only to the cosmological argument for the existence of God—if indeed second—is the argument from design. The organic world is as if designed, and the reason why it is as if designed is because it is designed—by God! Eyes are like telescopes. Telescopes have telescope designers and makers. Therefore, the eye has a designer and maker—the Great Optician in the Sky. After the Scientific Revolution, this type of argument became somewhat of a staple in English theological circles, as Peterson notes—partly because it fit in with the scientific temperament and partly for political reasons, as the Anglican Church trod a *via media* between the authority of Catholicism and the *sola scriptura* of the Calvinists. Probably the most famous expositor was Archdeacon Paley ([1802] 1809) at the beginning of the nineteenth century, and a major reason why Darwin took final cause so seriously is because he was soused in Paley as an undergraduate at Cambridge. But the argument in some form goes back to Plato in the *Phaedo*, if not before.

Although there is debate about the different formulations of the argument, whichever way, the Darwinian story has implications for it. Some think the argument is a straight analogy. The eye is like a telescope and so forth. If this is the case, then although you don't really need Darwinism to point this out for you—Paley himself takes note of it—a weakness in the argument comes if you can show that the organic world really doesn't seem all that well designed. Those of us growing old, says this writer with feeling, know only too well the troubles of aging eyesight. God might have spared a thought for weary, elderly readers. I think it fair to say that Darwinism picks up on this point and runs with it—and this, picking up from the point left dangling at the end of the previous chapter, is a big reason why I am not inclined to give Michael Peterson even the deist God. Since everything is done by blind law, and since it is of the essence of Darwinism that you cannot go back to the beginning and start anew but must work with what you have, you are going to get an awful lot of what the English call Heath Robinson machines and what Americans call Rube Goldberg machines—ludicrous contraptions that do the simplest things in the most complex of ways. The late George Williams (1966) used to make much of the male reproductive system, where nothing seems to go from A to B in the quickest, most efficient manner, but is rather meandering and looped in almost bizarre ways. How could something like this be the production of a good God who is also all-powerful and all-knowing? Even a trainee human physiologist could have done better.

Some think the argument from design is what is known as an "argument to the best explanation"—an approach Peterson favors. The general rational order of the world—a world in which biological life occurs—cannot be by chance. Remember Sherlock Holmes speaking to Dr. Watson: "You will not apply my precept," he said, shaking his head. "How often have I said to you that when you have eliminated the impossible, whatever remains, *however improbable, must be the truth?*" You are starting with the fact that organisms are highly intricate machines, exhibiting organized complexity. Despite the optimism of the order-for-free crew, you know that normally such complexity just doesn't happen. The world is ruled by Murphy's law—if something can go wrong, it will. Nicely functioning machines don't come through chance. They never get started and, if they do, they break down. So there must be some reason for the hand and the eye, and all else eliminated, it has to be God.

Although Hume was at most a deist and not a theist, general opinion is that he was not entirely indifferent to Paley's design argument. At the end of his *Dialogues Concerning Natural Religion* ([1779] 1947), having done the world's greatest hatchet job on any system at any time, somewhat sheepishly Hume admits that there might be something—or Something. Now, however, Darwinism steps forward, and you no longer need God. The design argument collapses. Assuming that the designlike nature of organisms is the one thing holding you from falling into nonbelief, that barrier has now been removed and you are on your way. In the words of Richard Dawkins, "Although atheism might have been logically tenable before Charles Darwin, Darwin made it possible to be an intellectually fulfilled atheist" (Dawkins 1986, 6).

So, What's the Answer?

Take note of where we are now. We have not disproven the existence of the Christian God. Even given the inadequacy of male plumbing, you can still speak of God as a Creator. It is just that, assuming you want to stay with Him as loving and don't think He spends His days laughing at poor old men with urinary problems, you have to agree that speaking of God as omnipotent—able to do anything—has to be circumscribed. Of course, you knew that already. God cannot make $2 + 2 = 5$, although I think Descartes thought that might be a possibility. Now you have to recognize that there are a lot more things that God cannot do. We will come back to this point in Chapter 9. In the same spirit, it may now be that you cannot force belief in God on people, but you can still speak of God as existing and even of God as a designer. We saw that at the time of the *Origin*, Darwin wanted to do this. Admittedly, by then Darwin was probably a deist and not a theist, but there are those who were undoubtedly theists who felt the same way. The great Catholic convert John Henry Newman wrote to a correspondent, "I believe in design because I believe in God; not in a God because I see design." This wasn't just a matter of being backed into a corner. He continued, "Design teaches me power, skill and goodness—not sanctity, not mercy, not a future judgement, which three are of the essence of religion" (Newman 1973, 97).

My main point is that Darwinism does have major implications for natural theology but that they are in a sense muted. If you are a creationist, thinking that God created everything miraculously, then Darwinism is an immediate threat. I'll leave it to others to fret about whether you ought to interpret the initial breath of life as in some sense referring to a miraculous intervention but simultaneously accept the subsequent creation of animals and plants as a natural phenomenon. Personally, although I see no contradiction in such a stance, it strikes me as a little odd. I will mention the interesting point that today's creationists seem prepared to accept this in some wise, because they think that God created "types" and that after these left the Ark they evolved rapidly (thanks to natural selection) into the forms we have today. (If you don't believe me, go and see the excellent discussion of natural selection in the creationist museum in Northern Kentucky.)

At this point, the theist may be hugging him or herself—although I will leave it to others to decide whether with joy or with relief. Going back to the disjunction expressed by Aubrey Moore at the beginning of this book, you might say that Darwinism was indeed a friend because now Christianity is freed from the tyranny of natural theology. Peterson will differ from me and object to the use of the word "tyranny" or to a blanket statement about all natural theology. Here, he and I will have to differ. Or rather, he and I plus many of the major Christian theologians will have to differ. I suspect that someone like Aquinas might be able to live with the collapse of natural theology as the basis for God belief as much as Kierkegaard and Barth. Aquinas was a naturalist—his inspiration, Aristotle, I suspect would have loved Darwin—and we have seen that Aquinas ever had a nuanced view of the proofs of reason. He and the saintly Newman would have found much common ground. Design is not being denied, it is just being reframed. However, do note the other side to Moore's disjunction. Dawkins is right. A nasty roadblock has been cleared from the route to atheism.

6

Evolutionary Directionality

No Direction to Evolution

Michael Ruse

The discussion is going to take a bit more of a theological turn. I am not a theologian and don't pretend to be. Nonetheless—and this is good advice to anyone, however dignified and important he or she may be—I am happy to turn to the textbooks for information, and this is what I have done now. As you will see as the discussion proceeds, the tremendously important ideas being discussed in this chapter quickly take us out and beyond the theological to the scientific and the philosophical. So, in a sense, all of us are going to be under-qualified in one way or another. This is nothing to be ashamed of and in fact is what makes this whole topic so incredibly interesting and exciting.

In this chapter, I combat the whole idea that the universe displays a direc-tionality intended and orchestrated by God. In particular, I argue from evolu-tionary science that the biological realm was not somehow preparation for the intended appearance of *Homo sapiens* as special beings. Michael Peterson, my partner in dialogue, is committed to the opposite view. Our engagement will be the interplay of our philosophical perspectives in reference to the science.

Bottom-Line Demands

Rather than starting straight off with science, let me turn things around for a moment and start with Christianity. Acknowledge one basic fact. In the Chris-tian scenario, human beings are not a contingent add-on—I take it that this is true of any theistic religion. One presumes that God did not have to create at all, and one presumes that, having decided to create, God did not have to create humans or humanlike beings. But God did, and in the Christian (theistic) pic-ture, we have a starring role. God made humans "in his own image" to love and to have us love and worship Him in return. When we fell into sin, He went on loving us so much that He was prepared to die in agony on the cross to pave the way for our eternal salvation, whatever that might be. It isn't that God doesn't care about other organisms—He knows when every sparrow falls—but we have a special place. We have an obligation to care for other organisms, but one has a strong sense that they are there for our benefit. Jesus told us to care about the sick and the needy, even those in prison, but I don't remember any sermons on the virtues of being a vegan.

What does it mean to say that we are made "in the image of God"? A lot of theological ink has been spilled on this one. Generally—and I will go with this here—"image" focuses in on our rationality. Michael Peterson accepts this element of the image and expands on it in the next chapter. At any rate, we humans are able to think and reason, to be self-aware, to have memories that we can articulate, and so forth. This is also an essential part of God's nature, and inasmuch as we are made in God's image, it speaks of these sorts of things. Where does morality fit into all of this? The obvious answer is that it is all part and parcel of the image, as Peterson contends in Chapter 8. Recognizing that there is a huge amount of theology that needs unpacking here about the will of God and the binding nature of moral rules, we can surely say that in some sense God is a moral being and so also are we humans. This is only in a sense, of course, because there is at least one influential strand of theological thinking that claims that God is beyond or above morality—He could never be subject to external norms. This thinking comes through in places like the Book of Job, where God tells man that He, God, makes the rules: "Shall he that contendeth with the Almighty instruct him?" (Job 40:2). But whether making or following, God is good. The tricky part is that God is a supremely good being—God would never do wrong—whereas it is an essential part of Christian theology that because of the fall we are anything but supremely good beings. We know what we should do, but we don't always do it. One way around this (because of Irenaeus of Lyons) is to distinguish being made in God's likeness from being made in his image, with the former referring to our original unfallen state when we did and thought only good. I think it enough for us here to say that the important thing is that humans have a moral sense—in some wise, unlike, say, lions and tigers—and that this reflects God in important respects.

These bottom-line demands shape this and the next three chapters. Start with getting human beings in the first place, then move to mind and rationality, and then on to morality and sin and evil and those sorts of things.

Does Evolution Go Anywhere?

We must produce humans. Rather less cryptically, because obviously humans have been produced, we must show that the arrival of humans was no chance. This will be Peterson's burden. It is not enough to pull some fancy Thomistic shoe shuffle about primary and secondary causation, saying that theologically we need humans. We know that an all-powerful deity as primary cause can do this—and scientifically this is not His problem. This is secondary causation, and it is up to nature to find a solution. We must ask: "What solution?" We cannot have God left empty-handed by the evolutionary process. But is this possible? I have mentioned the history of life, and let me flesh this out a bit because it does seem promising.

First, life is approximately or, rather, more than 3.5 billion years old. It was primitive, and more complex cells had to wait until about 2 billion years ago. Coming down, less than a billion years ago, things started to pick up. The so-called Cambrian explosion didn't occur until more than half a billion years ago, and it was then that we started to get the forms that were the ancestors of organisms living today. Increasingly, however, the pre-Cambrian is being uncovered and, increasingly, it is clear that the organisms then were of a kind that one would expect would explode into being in the Cambrian. To quote J. B. S. Haldane, a precursor of what I said earlier, "No fossil rabbits in the pre-Cambrian." On the other hand, there are prevertebrates. After that, it all seems rather plain sailing. In the animal world—there is a similar story for the plant world—we have fish, amphibians, reptiles, dinosaurs (actually fancy reptiles), birds, mammals, monkeys, apes, humans.

Today, thanks both to paleontology and to molecular biology, the human lineage is well known (Ruse 2012). Living in Africa, we got up on our hind legs about 5 million years ago or less, left the jungles to live on the plains, and increasingly turned to activities that required bigger and better brains. At some points in the past half million years or so, gangs of humans left Africa and started to spread around the world. For a while, it was thought—a bit like the soldier and the tinderbox who kept emptying his pockets every time he came across better booty—that each new outward migration spelled doom for those who had gone before. But now, thanks to fabulous DNA studies, we know that there was some interbreeding. Don't run down those Neanderthals. Grandma and grandpa sometimes had wandering eyes in that direction, and it wasn't just the eyes that wandered.

All of this sounds like a smooth and predetermined progression up to *Homo sapiens.* Early evolutionists thought so. Charles Darwin's grandfather, Erasmus Darwin, was given to expressing his thoughts in (rather bad) verse, and he had no doubts that humans were the necessary end point, monad to man, as they used to say:

> Imperious man, who rules the bestial crowd,
> Of language, reason, and reflection proud,
> With brow erect who scorns this earthy sod,
> And styles himself the image of his God;
> Arose from rudiments of form and sense,

An embryon point, or microscopic ens!
(Darwin 1803, 1, 11, 295–314)

Although he was no Christian, Erasmus Darwin was a committed deist, think-ing that God started everything off and then let it unfurl through unbroken law. As noted, this was probably the position of his grandson Charles through most of his life, and although in his last decade or so he moved toward agnosticism, he remained committed to the progress of the evolutionary process from the first primitive forms of life to the apotheosis of history, *Homo sapiens*—actually, more precisely, upper-middle-class *Homo sapiens* from a small island off the coast of Europe. Remember the final words of the *Origin*:

> Thus, from the war of nature, from famine and death, the most exalted object which we are capable of conceiving, namely, the production of the higher animals, directly follows. There is grandeur in this view of life, with its several powers, having been originally breathed into a few forms or into one; and that, whilst this planet has gone cycling on according to the fixed law of gravity, from so simple a beginning endless forms most beautiful and most wonderful have been, and are being, evolved. (Darwin 1859, 490)

But here's the rub! The Darwinian process seems to knock the stuffing out of the inevitable climb to humankind. There is no necessary highpoint to the process, and indeed Darwin warned himself about such thinking. In the margin of his copy of an early evolutionary tract by the Scottish publisher Robert Chambers (*Vestiges of the Natural History of Creation* 1844), Darwin scribbled, "Never use the word higher & lower—use more complicated."

Why is this? There are two reasons. First, although natural selection is no tautology—those that survive are those that survive—it is relativistic. What succeeds in one case may well not succeed in another. There is simply no good reason to think that large brains and intelligence are always better than any alternatives. In the immortal words of the late Jack Sepkoski (one of the lead-ing paleontologists of his day), "I see intelligence as just one of a variety of adaptations among tetrapods for survival. Running fast in a herd while being as dumb as shit, I think, is a very good adaptation for survival" (Ruse 1996, 486). Second, as we saw in the previous chapter, the raw building blocks of evolu-tion, the variations on which selection works, are random, not in the sense of being uncaused, but in the sense of not appearing according to need. They are certainly not directed toward the production of human beings. Evolution through selection is opportunistic, not directed. And if further confirmation is needed, there is the case of the "hobbit," *Homo floresiensis*, discovered in 2003 on one of the islands of Indonesia. About three and a half feet tall with a brain the size of chimpanzees' (about 400 cc), it nevertheless showed advanced tool-making behaviors. It went extinct only about 12,000 years ago, and so it might plausibly have survived to the present. What price inevitable progress, were it around, or had it alone survived?

Causes

Expectedly, in the light of this challenge, there has been a century and a half of effort trying to show that progress to humankind can in fact be expected given evolution through selection. Darwin was always stone-cold certain that selection applies to humans and not just to us physically. Indeed, in 1838, in his private notebooks, humans are the focus of the first unambiguous articulation of natural selection: "An habitual action must some way affect the brain in a manner which can be transmitted.—this is analogous to a blacksmith having children with strong arms.—The other principle of those children. which *chance?* produced with strong arms, outliving the weaker one, may be applicable to the formation of instincts, independently of habits.—?" (Darwin Notebook N, 42, Barrett et al. 1987, 574). But will we win? Darwin started one of the major optimistic strategies, suggesting that the best will win out and that we are the best:

> If we look at the differentiation and specialisation of the several organs of each being when adult (and this will include the advancement of the brain for intellectual purposes) as the best standard of highness of organisation, natural selection clearly leads towards highness; for all physiologists admit that the specialisation of organs, inasmuch as they perform in this state their functions better, is an advantage to each being; and hence the accumulation of variations tending towards specialisation is within the scope of natural selection. (Darwin 1861, 134)

This kind of thinking has found supporters, right down to the present day. Julian Huxley (1912), the grandson of Thomas Henry Huxley (and the older brother of the novelist Aldous Huxley), put the idea in military garb, suggesting that there are biological "arms races," with lines of evolving organisms competing against each other. Just as with battleships—Huxley was writing just before World War I, when Britain and Germany were competing by building ever-larger naval behemoths—where every increase in gun power is matched by an increase in armor, so we find that every adaptation of one line (great speed, thicker shell) is matched by an adaptation of the other line (even greater speed, stronger boring power). Richard Dawkins is a great enthusiast for evolutionary progress: "Directionalist common sense surely wins on the very long time scale: once there was only blue–green slime and now there are sharp-eyed metazoa" (Dawkins and Krebs 1979, 508). In support of his intuition, he has whole-heartedly embraced arms-race-type thinking, arguing that in military races we have seen a move to ever greater reliance on electronic equipment and that this has implications for the world of organisms (Dawkins 1986). Those beings with the biggest on-board computers are at the top. The fact that we are twenty-three times brighter than your average hippopotamus may not tell you everything, but it does tell you "something."

I don't know whether you regard this line of thinking as flawed or merely wishful, but either way I don't see humans guaranteed. Big brains really are expensive to maintain. You need ongoing supplies of protein, meaning the bodies of other animals, and one can think of a hundred and one reasons why these might not be readily available. Again and again, the winner in battles goes with something simple, cheap, and reliable. In World War II, German tanks at their best were terrific; but the Nazi regime never really twigged on to mass manufacture, using just a few models with interchangeable parts. It made all the difference on the Allied side. Perhaps humans are likely, but Christians need more than this. Faced with this failure, other Darwinians have tried an approach that makes much of ecological niches. This was a favorite of the late Stephen Jay Gould (1985) and has been taken up with gusto by Simon Conway Morris (2003), justly famed for groundbreaking work on the fossils of the Burgess Shale. Conway Morris notes that there are many instances of evolutionary convergence, meaning that organisms that are unrelated sometimes take similar paths. There are, for instance, unrelated species of saber-tooth tiger, indeed, some being placental mammals and others being marsupial. This suggests that there is, independent of organisms themselves, a niche for predators with the kinds of shearing teeth that the saber-tooth possesses. It is just a question of an evolving line finding that niche and moving in. Perhaps, then, there is a niche for intelligence, and it was wanting to be found, as predictably happened:

> If brains can get big independently and provide a neural machine capable of handling a highly complex environment, then perhaps there are other parallels, other convergences that drive some groups towards complexity. Could the story of sensory perception be one clue that, given time, evolution will inevitably lead not only to the emergence of such properties as intelligence, but also to other complexities, such as, say, agriculture and culture, that we tend to regard as the prerogative of the human? We may be unique, but paradoxically those properties that define our uniqueness can still be inherent in the evolutionary process. In other words, if we humans had not evolved then something more-or-less identical would have emerged sooner or later. (Conway Morris 2003, 196)

This is a nice idea, but again, probably more hopeful than established. Many ecologists and evolutionists question the basic assumption that niches just wait there objectively to be found. They argue, rather, that niches are created as much as anything. There was, for instance, no niche for high-flying insects until trees evolved. Now the niche is filled and busy, but it hardly existed at all at one point. The same with culture. It is agreed that such a niche now exists, but it was not necessary that it existed at all before we came along. Contradicting himself on these matters, it is Gould who stresses the contingency of things. Making a joking reference to the asteroid that hit the earth 65 million years ago and wiped out the dinosaurs, making possible the age of mammals, Gould wrote, "Since dinosaurs were not moving toward markedly larger brains, and since such a prospect may lie outside the capabilities of reptilian design . . . , we must assume that consciousness would not have evolved on our planet if a cosmic catastrophe had not claimed the dinosaurs as victims. In an entirely literal sense, we owe our existence, as large and reasoning mammals, to our lucky stars" (Gould 1989, 318).

If natural selection seems to be a major barrier to progress, then perhaps we can sidestep it. Almost paradoxically, Darwin himself suggested that complexity might just increase naturally, and presumably, with complexity comes ever-higher life forms:

> The enormous *number* of animals in the world depends of their varied structure & complexity.—hence as the forms became complicated, they opened fresh means of adding to their complexity.—but yet there is no **necessary** tendency in the simple animals to become complicated although all perhaps will have done so from the new relations caused by the advancing complexity of others.—It may be said, why should there not be at any time as many species tending to dis-development (some probably always have done so, as the simplest fish), my answer is because, if we begin with the simplest forms & suppose them to have changed, their very changes ton tend to give rise to others. (Barrett et al. 1987, E95–97)

To be fair, I am not sure that Darwin saw this as an alternative to change through selection but more as one that augments change through selection. And this surely is that point. Starting with Darwin's contemporary Herbert Spencer, there have always been those who embrace this kind of thinking. Gould (1996) in his later years was one, arguing that evolution is a bit like a drunkard walking along a sidewalk, bounded on the one side by a brick wall and on the other side by the gutter. Eventually the drunkard will end in the gutter, simply because he cannot go through the brick wall. There is a boundary to the simplicity of life but no boundary to the complexity, so eventually it will happen. The same sort of thinking has been forwarded recently by the paleontologist Daniel McShea and philosopher Robert Brandon (2010). They see a kind of non-Darwinian upward momentum to life's history. Introducing what they call the "zero-force evolutionary law," they write, "In any evolutionary system in which there is variation and heredity, in the absence of natural selection, other forces, and constraints acting on diversity or complexity, diversity and complexity will increase on average" (3). Perhaps this is so, although I am not quite sure why complexity has to happen. But even if it does occur, it is not obvious why such complexity should be in any sense adaptive, especially not intelligence-based adaptive. A pile of chalk scattered on the ground is in some respects more complex than the pile organized to spell out simple words, but it is the latter that seems more like adaptation than the former.

Christian Escapes?

There is a major problem here for Christians. Apparently, there really is no ironclad reason why humans should have evolved—and that is simply not acceptable from a theological perspective, certainly not from Peterson's. Some religious believers take a way out by simply removing the problem from the realm of science. Since the days of Asa Gray—Darwin's American Christian supporter—this has been a favored move by theists. It is argued that God gives variations (mutations), or at least certain key variations, a shove in the right direction. Plantinga has made various remarks about this possibility. Today, it is the main plank of the intelligent design theorists, but there are others, including those who would deny absolutely that they should be categorized with the intelligent design crew. The physicist-theologian Robert J. Russell (2008) argues that God could direct variations down at the quantum level, and hence, although they could occur, we could never detect them directly: "The noninterventionist aspects of God's special action occur directly at the level of, and are mediated by, those genetic variations in which quantum processes play a significant role in biological evolution" (Russell 2008, 196).

Well, perhaps—although "noninterventionist" is not exactly the language I would use because any form of divine involvement is a problem. Scientifically, one has now simply given up the game. As Darwin noted somewhat sniffily, even if this kind of thinking does not contradict science, it certainly goes against the spirit of science. There is no evidence of directed mutations, and simply making them in principle unobservable seems close to cheating. It is not that they are unobservable because one has no choice; it is rather that they are unobservable simply to make them unverifiable. I suspect that Michael Peterson will object at this point to the use of emotive words like "cheating." He will want to draw the kind of distinction (referred to previously) that is common in Christian theology, between God's overall plan—in Creation He knew that humans would emerge—and the proximate causes—God made things so that natural selection would function but did not then keep messing around with the process. The devil of course is in the details, and one would like to know how God got His end results without messing around. In any case, theologically, the problems are horrendous. If God is willing to get involved occasionally, why not on every occasion? Every day children are dying in horrendous pain because of random mutations. Why does God not prevent these? Whether or not one thinks that God should have prevented them anyway, one can at least understand why he doesn't prevent them in individual cases if he has a general policy of not intervening or at the least only intervening when salvation matters are at stake. Better to stay out of the directed variation business entirely.

Let me offer another suggestion. The Darwinian agrees that, however improbable, natural selection could produce humans because it has in fact produced humans. I take it that what this means is that no matter how unlikely, so long as you are prepared to roll the dice billions and billions of times, you are going to come up eventually with human beings or, to help the odds a little, with beings that are rational and with a sense of morality. I don't think the Christian story cares too much if we all have green skin and are bald. Suppose the multiverse really is a possibility, billions and billions of other universes with no correlation to our own time and space. At some point you are going to get humans, and the Christian story can get underway. It is true that God is now lumbered with billions and billions—less one—worthless universes, but remember that traditionally He is outside time and space, so it is not as if He is sitting around in heaven waiting anxiously for humans to appear. In His eyes, a thousand years are as a day, and a day is as a thousand years.

Note that this is a theological solution, not really a scientific solution, which makes me feel more comfortable because (as in the case of Big Bang theory) if the science changes, you are not really caught. You have to think of something else, but you don't have to backtrack. One thing is that you are agreeing that there might be a huge number of empty universes just circling until they collapse and die. You may think that this is not really compatible with God, although as William Whewell ([1853] 2001) pointed out in the mid-nineteenth century, you basically have this problem already. Even if there are other intelligent beings elsewhere in this universe, most of the universe is empty and apparently pointless. Whewell preferred a completely empty universe other than earth because he thought that, if Jesus has to reappear again and again, and perhaps suffer again and again, this rather cheapens our relationship with God. This Friday, every Friday, somewhere in the universe, Jesus is on the Cross.

Is God Too Complex?

Richard Dawkins (2006) complains that the more complex you make the universe, the more complex you make God because He has to keep up with His creation. And the more complex you make Him, the more improbable you make Him. I am not sure that this is entirely so. The whole point of science and mathematics is that you start with the very simple—like Euclid's axioms—and quickly get a lot more complex and counterintuitive—like Pythagoras's theorem. This said, however, it does start to seem that God has fewer and fewer dimensions of freedom. Perhaps He did not have to create through law, although if He did not, one wonders what kind of world one would have. Would humans have all of the marks of evolution, even if they were not evolved? This starts to sound like the world of the pre-Darwinian naturalist Philip Gosse (1857), who suggested that God might have put the marks of the past on the world, although thereby He was deceiving us. Not surprisingly, people were not happy with that suggestion. But if He did create by law, then it does seem that God was forced to be, shall we say, a little bit exuberant to achieve His ends. A Being who had to create billions and billions of universes to get His goal strikes me as a Being not entirely in control of things.

Moreover, even if God can ride so many universes at the same time, Dawkins does have a point in suggesting that a God such as this is getting more and more distant to a God conceivable by us. God seems like He is running Walmart or Delta Airlines—and by and large the chief executive officers of large businesses don't have too much time for or knowledge of those of us down at the checkout counter or serving drinks to tired passengers. Aquinas tells us that we can know God by analogy, but He doesn't seem tremendously fatherlike anymore. You might perhaps argue that God is ineffable. The Jewish philosopher Maimonides (1135–1204) argued this way, going so far as to say that negation was positively better than alternatives: "I do not merely declare that he who affirms attributes of God has not sufficient knowledge concerning the Creator, . . . but I say that he unconsciously loses his belief in God" (Maimonides 1936, 87). By and large, however, although some like Barth have toyed with the approach, this strategy finds little favor with Christians, especially Protestants. If they are going to worship God, they want some idea of what they worship: "If, therefore, our concepts do not apply to God, then our concepts of being loving, almighty, wise, creator and Redeemer do not apply to him, in which case he is not loving, almighty, wise, a creator or a Redeemer. He won't have any of the properties Christians ascribe to him" (Plantinga 1980, 22).

I am not concluding that Darwinian theory makes impossible Christian claims about life's direction and the appearance of humans, but I am saying that there are bigger difficulties than many realize.

The Trajectory of Evolution

Michael Peterson

The sweep of evolution—from the Big Bang to *Homo sapiens*—is nothing short of breathtaking. Yet, is there a discernible direction to evolution, either cosmological or biological? Is there a trend toward increasing complexity? Is greater complexity better? Was the whole universe aimed at eventually producing humans? Michael Ruse, along with most naturalists, denies any direction, arguing that any perceived trajectory is a projection onto the facts and that there is surely no God directing the path of evolution.

Once again, we find ourselves at a major point of contact between science and religion, where both empirical facts and metaphysical interpretations come into play. In contrast to Ruse, I argue in this chapter that a realistic and total assessment of the scientific facts supports directionality at least as much as, and probably more than, it supports no directionality. I further argue on philosophical and theological grounds that the directionality is guided by God for his purposes. Part of the significance of this chapter in the overall debate is that I explain God's guidance of evolution in a way that both affirms science and preserves the essential theological vision.

How Did We Get Here from There?

A brief sketch of the major developmental stages of physical reality, as science has revealed them, is instructive. From the singularity, the Big Bang, which is considered the start of cosmic evolution, we get hydrogen, helium, and lithium aggregating into dense, giant stars. These stellar cookeries formed carbon, oxygen, nitrogen, and other heavier elements that were scattered everywhere as the giant stars exploded in death, causing the chemical complexification of the universe. Cosmic structure further developed as comets and asteroids formed. Stars and their planetary systems collected into galaxies. Although all materials are still inorganic, nonliving, directionality is apparent. The earth's environment developed life-supporting conditions, allowing increasingly complex molecules to develop, to utilize some kind of energy source, and to result in the first self-replicating molecule. From single-celled life, multicellular life eventually emerged. Over enormous spans of time, rich varieties of life forms appeared, becoming more complex and more taxonomically diverse. Sentient organisms arose and, eventually, only about 200,000 years ago, self-conscious intelligent life appeared.

The very broad stages in the history of physical reality may be said to be evolutionary in character. My rough sketch below starts with the Big Bang, skipping technical mention of its internal conditions, and helps us visualize what has happened as a basis for our conversation:

The Big Bang
[the universe studied by science begins]

Formation of Giant Stars and Chemical Complexification
[the material building blocks of the universe are developed]

Formation of Planets and Galaxies
[the large-scale structure of the universe is established]

Life on Earth
[the organic arises from the inorganic]

Sentient Life
[organisms that sense and respond to their environment appear]

Self-Conscious, Rational Life
[beings that have self-awareness and a variety of
intellectual capacities appear]

Each item on my chart abbreviates an enormous amount of information, but the chart paints an impressive picture that begs for philosophical interpretation.

We cannot talk of the sequential stages in the development of physical reality—cosmic, stellar, chemical, planetary, galactic—without realizing how puzzling it is that each stage should yield the next. Each stage represents a significant transition in the history of the universe, a major threshold that has been crossed. Science continues to advance our understanding about the processes involved at all levels. Stellar nucleosynthesis is now well understood, whereas other processes, such as abiogenesis, require further research. The point is that science is answering a lot of questions regarding the unfolding history of the universe—and, in doing so, is filling in the factual narrative of "how" we got here from there, so to speak. Ruse and other philosophical naturalists disagree with theists on "why" we got here from there, bringing worldview differences into sharp focus.

Scientific and Metascientific Questions

The universe is much more physically complex than when it began almost 14 billion years ago. Life is far more complex today than when it first appeared on the earth almost 4 billion years ago. Does increasing complexity indicate a trend or direction? Although there are technical debates surrounding the definition of complexity—as to whether it pertains to number of individual parts or functions, to isolated organisms, or to their interrelations in ecosystems, etc.—science essentially tells the story of increasing complexity. Granted, the second law of thermodynamics will eventually ensure that the overall simplicity of the universe will be realized as total entropy is ultimately maximized, but I address this point in the final chapter. In the present chapter, I focus on the trend toward increasing biological complexity and the question of whether it indicates directionality in the unfolding universe.

On the question of directionality, scientific opinions are divided. The French biologist Jacques Monod maintains that evolution proceeds by "pure chance, absolutely free but blind" (Monod 1971, 112–13). Stephen Jay Gould, a Harvard paleontologist and apologist for the supreme role of contingency, famously suggested that the Evolutionary Tree, with its upward direction, should be replaced by the "evolutionary bush," which displays great divergences and diversity, resulting from the chanciness of evolution, but no specific direction. He argues that we must

> abandon progress or complexification as a central principle and admit the strong possibility that *H. sapiens* is but a tiny, late-arising twig on life's enormously arborescent bush—a small bud that would almost surely not appear a second time if we could replant the bush from seed and let it grow again. (Gould 1994, 91)

Along with Gould, Michael Ruse rejects any idea that evolutionary sequences are like rungs of a ladder or progressive stages of improvement, particularly in regard to aiming toward the production of humans.

By contrast, Paul Davies is among the prominent scientists who discern an evolutionary trend toward greater complexity, observing that the expansion of the universe pulled the matter of the early universe out of equilibrium, allowing heat to flow and drive complex processes. Without denying the second law, many scientists now speak of a kind of temporary "sweet spot" in cosmic history in which the biosphere can develop increasing complexity. As Davies says, "The growth of complexity can occur alongside the rise of entropy" (Davies 2003, 85). As Davies explains,

> The history of the universe, then, is one of entropy rising but chasing a moving target, because the expanding universe is raising the maximum possible entropy at the same time. (Davies 2003, 82)

Freeman Dyson has even postulated a principle of maximum diversity according to which the universe in some sense operates to maximize its variety, richness, and potential as a physical system (Dyson 1979, 250). These scientific considerations support ideas of directionality toward increasing complexity.

Science can chart the path of "how" the universe developed from the Big Bang to *Homo sapiens*. But answering the question of whether the universe exhibits a trajectory or direction takes us to the borderline between scientific *description* and *interpretation*. We must proceed carefully because interpretation of scientific findings readily shades into worldview perspective. On the one hand, there are thinkers—Ruse and Gould, among others—who take the scientific fact of chance in the evolutionary process to imply utter nondirectedness in the universe and definitely in the modern evolutionary synthesis. Gould and Ruse categorically conclude from the elements of randomness in the evolutionary process that there is no inherent tendency in organic nature toward greater complexity and no other level at which evolution might be directed. But neither the affirmation nor the denial of this thesis is part of evolutionary science. Taking a position here crosses the line between scientific facts and their metascientific interpretation—which is fine as long as we recognize that philosophical commitments are involved.

Without discounting the role of chance in the evolutionary process—both as random genetic mutation and as environmental happenstance—many scientists argue for a direction to evolution. The Cambridge paleobiologist Simon Conway Morris argues that, amid the contingencies of existence, life tends, from different starting points, to find similar solutions to similar adaptive challenges. According to Conway Morris, "convergence" is the "recurrent tendency of biological organization to arrive at the same solution to a particular need" (Conway Morris 2003, xii). Although there are many theoretically possible pathways to evolutionary outcomes, the evolutionary process seems to focus on a relatively small number of outcomes. For instance, nature has a remarkable propensity to develop cameralike eyes in ever so many independent situations—and other solutions such as flight and intelligence have evolved independently multiple times.

The better part of wisdom is to acknowledge that science operating within its capabilities detects both chance and directionality—a point compatible with the theistic perspective I have been developing in previous chapters. However, science operating by methodological naturalism is not in a position to make a sweeping pronouncement that chance cancels directionality, much less that chance is ultimate. Neither can science establish that directionality is somehow guaranteed or that a trend toward increasing complexity is inherent in physical existence. Scientifically, plenty of room remains for greater understanding of the tendency toward complexity as well as its realization in variable and contingent details. Philosophically, we can reasonably interpret what science serves up as apparently nondirected (such as asteroid strikes and random genetic mutations) as well as what is apparently directed (such as fine-tuned physical laws and the fitness-producing outcomes of natural selection) as dual factors playing into unfolding complexity. Then we can begin to try to understand the "how" in terms of "why."

God and the World of Science

As we have seen, the standard scientific model of the development of physical reality provides a factual narrative of increasing complexification. At the cosmic, chemical, and biological levels, there is an overall trend toward complexity. Within the biological realm alone, evolution has led to organisms generally becoming larger in size, more complex in terms of number of cells and functions, more taxonomically diverse, and more energetically intensive—and natural selection accounts for all of this in scientific terms.

The empirical description of increasing complexity raises the question of interpretation both scientifically and philosophically—and Ruse and I disagree at both levels. In assessing the science, Ruse sees evolution as revealing a fundamental nondirectedness, as do Monod and Gould, and then fits this nondirectedness or aimlessness into a naturalist worldview in which no divine agent or teleology is at work. I hold the opposite opinion: that the scientific facts of increasing complexity reveal a general directionality in the cosmos and a kind of directionality in the biology on earth—a conclusion shared by scientists such as Simon Conway Morris and Francisco Ayala

(Conway Morris 2003; Ayala 1970). The famous biologist Theodosius Dobzhansky puts it this way:

> Viewing evolution of the living world as a whole, from the hypothetical primeval self-reproducing substance to higher plants, animals, and man, one cannot avoid the recognition that progress or advancement, or rise, or ennoblement, has occurred. (Dobzhansky 1973, 309, 311)

On good scientific grounds, it is reasonable to assert that there is directionality (Stoeger 1999).

The philosophical question then comes to the fore: which worldview—theism or naturalism—makes best sense of the entire history of the universe that displays the directionality described by science? Directionality is much more likely to be characteristic of a universe created by an extremely powerful, rational, purposeful being than it is of a universe described by naturalism. When we look at the precise kind of directionality we have—toward increasingly complex systems and indeed toward sentient and eventually self-conscious rational life—the likelihood of this is far greater given theism. Where D is the kind of directionality discovered by science, T is theism, and N is naturalism,

$$P(D/T) > P(D/N).$$

Alternatively, directionality is less epistemically surprising given theism than given naturalism.

Metaphysical naturalism simply does not have the intrinsic conceptual resources to make complete sense of the sketch of directionality offered earlier in this chapter. Given naturalism, there is little reason to expect the physical world to display directionality, much less the kind of directionality it actually does, which is a directionality leading to self-conscious intelligent animals. For the naturalist, nature is simply an ontological "given," which develops through the interplay of law and chance such that any discernible directionality is either purely accidental or post hoc reconstruction. Gould claims that the Chicxulub Asteroid that hit the Yucatan 65 million years ago and caused the extinction of the dinosaurs was the only reason that mammals—and eventually reasoning mammals—came along. Gould states, "We are the accidental result of an unplanned process, . . . the fragile result of an enormous concatenation of improbabilities, not the predictable product of any definite process" (Gould 1989, 290).

Theism provides much more reason to expect the directionality detected by science: God, who is ontologically distinct from nature, could have somehow guided the course of nature to achieve His purposes. My argument throughout is that theism makes better sense of all the topics debated in this book than naturalism does. An omnipotent, omniscient God accounts for the existence of the universe and its fine-tuning as well as for the appearance of life and its evolution toward humans. Christianity more specifically claims that a God who is personal and loving created the finite universe and willed that rational animals emerge in nature.

As a counter, Michael Ruse argues that Christian theists must show—but have not shown and perhaps cannot show—that on scientific grounds there is a *necessary* evolutionary directionality such that humans were inevitable. However, for Ruse to require that Christian thinkers prove scientifically that there is direction leading to humans is to set an artificially high standard that science rarely meets on any important issue. Gould argues that directionality is staggeringly improbable; Conway Morris states that directionality is highly probable. Technically, these scientific arguments are probabilistic and not about necessity.

Furthermore, it's a mistake to think that Christianity should be committed to any particular *scientific* theory about the necessity or high probability of directionality. As I stated earlier, it's scientifically reasonable to acknowledge that evolution is characterized by directionality as well as chance. However, the success or failure of any given scientific theory of directionality does not greatly affect the Christian view that God willed that beings who could bear His image would eventually arrive on the scene. The implication is that God guided evolution eventually to produce such beings. The guarantee of personal–rational–physical beings is theological, not scientific. Gould contends that, if we rewound the tape of evolution and then played it forward again, the significant contingency of the evolutionary process would make it extremely unlikely that we would get humans. Scientifically, Conway Morris disagrees, arguing that something like an intelligent mammal would still emerge, although its physiological details may differ from what we now know. There is certainly no theistic or Christian reason to insist that God predetermined a specific linear direction to evolution or that God arranged every detail of every creature or that the evolutionary unfolding of life would be exactly repeated if the whole process were replayed. Christian theism does entail the theological point that God guides the evolutionary process, with all its contingencies, to achieve His general purposes. In a replay, might some creatures much like humans have developed six digits instead of five? There is no theistic or Christian reason to deny such possibilities.

Note that Ruse's argument places the burden of proof completely on the Christian theist to show scientifically that there is necessary directionality leading inevitably to humans. For Ruse, if the Christian theist does not establish this point empirically, then presumably naturalism stands. Naturalistic atheism is afforded the intellectual luxury of being the default position, with nothing to prove. But why doesn't the naturalist have to meet the same standard of establishing scientifically that there is *no* necessary directionality leading to humans? Remember: there is no conclusive empirical case that evolution is nondirected. We are in a worldview dispute in which both worldviews bear equal burdens of arguing for their respective metaphysical interpretations of the mixed scientific facts.

Creation, Providence, and Evolution

There really are no convincing objections, scientifically or philosophically, to the claim that God guided the direction of evolution leading to humans. Virtually any theistic scenario that includes this claim makes the facts as we know them more probable than naturalism does. Nevertheless, what we need now is a careful analysis of the idea of God's activity in relation to the created order.

Control-oriented theisms adopt strong versions of divine providence that entail meticulous design and unilateral management of the world. Such views hold that neither natural processes nor human choices involve genuine contingency and, thus, that they pose no real risks for God. Creationism and intelligent design reflect this kind of thinking, as do certain versions of theistic evolution that envision evolutionary processes as completely divinely governed. These theisms are especially susceptible to the problem of pain and suffering because they posit divine control of all details—a point Ruse does not fail to note. I am interested in an understanding of theism that asserts that God generally gives to creatures a wide scope of operation but works with their responses to achieve his purposes. Conceptually, a theistic approach like this—which maintains that God is open to and not threatened by authentic creaturely action—is more readily compatible with the evolutionary facts, particularly in providing ontological space for genuine contingency. This is one part of my reply to the problem of pain and suffering in a theistic universe, which I develop in Chapter 9.

The classical Christian doctrines of creation and providence have implications for this discussion. The doctrine of creation affirms that God is the ultimate source of everything and that everything is radically dependent on God. Creation is "out of nothing" (*creatio ex nihilo*), leaving open the possibility that God could choose to initiate (*creatio originalis*) and then guide the subsequent unfolding of his creation (*creatio continua*). St. Augustine, for example, thought that God embedded certain principles within creation—"rational seeds" (*rationes seminales*)—which give direction to its development. St. Irenaeus and St. Origen also had their own developmental views of creation.

Doctrinally, the *point* of creation—to bring forth personal rational animals that could bear God's image and have relationship with him—is far more important than the *process* of creation. The *Catechism of the Catholic Church* makes this remarkable statement:

> God, infinitely perfect and blessed in himself, in a plan of sheer goodness freely created man to make him share in his own blessed life. (*Catechism* 1994, Prologue, 7)

Creation is an amazing gesture of self-giving love—God's giving the privilege of personal rational life to finite creatures and inviting them to participate in his own Infinite Life of unending joy and love. Thus, God's aims for creation are deeply relational, and he has chosen that these aims will be pursued in a complex and dynamic physical universe in which finite rationality is bonded to animality. Scientifically, rational animals did in fact appear in the course of evolution. Theologically, we know why they appeared.

The Christian doctrine of providence is based on the doctrine of creation. Providence implies that God pursues his purposes in creation through faithful activity in relation to both the natural world and human affairs. The theory of providence offered by St. Thomas Aquinas is helpful in explaining God's action in relation to created nature. For Aquinas, God is the "primary cause" of the origin and continued existence of everything else, but God gives to creaturely realities the role of acting as "secondary causes" (Aquinas 1975, *SCG* III.i, chaps. 72–77). Aquinas interprets secondary causes neither as mere puppets that simply comply with invisible but complete divine control nor as absolutely autonomous agents from whom God has entirely withdrawn. Aquinas reasons that God allows creatures to exercise their distinctive powers and capacities to produce uncoerced outcomes that are still within the ambit of providence. This understanding is affirming of science because the natural world enjoys a divinely donated integrity that allows creaturely realities to have their own operations that are often codified in scientific laws.

As Aquinas argues in the *Summa Contra Gentiles*, "Divine providence does not exclude contingency from things" (Aquinas 1975, *SCG* III.i, chap. 72). Providence, for Aquinas, means that the world is ruled by divine *reason* according to which everything is ordered in view of the *good*. The providential order of the world—a world that includes a large measure of contingency—is then guided by God's wisdom. God is immanently and actively present in all things, grounding their donated causal powers and seeking to draw them to himself. Yet God's providence resembles a governmental system of "subsidiarism" in which the secondary causes, sustained from within by the power of the "first cause," have their own sphere of operation, which includes the ability to reject God.

The integrity of created secondary causes is of utmost importance. In the human sphere, having the power of libertarian free will means that actions can be the rational creature's own responses to the relational overtures of God. For the natural realm, particularly the biological realm, having causal powers means the possibility to explore various nondetermined outcomes. In this light, John Polkinghorne, a theoretical physicist and theologian formerly of Cambridge University, writes of providence,

> The actual balance between chance and necessity, contingency and potentiality, which we perceive seems to me to be consistent with the will of a patient and subtle Creator, content to achieve his purposes through the unfolding of process and accepting thereby a measure of the vulnerability and precariousness which always characterize the gift of freedom by love. (Polkinghorne 2007, 82)

Thus, the unfolding future of the world is not a predetermined script but more like an improvisation between God and creatures.

Bishop Aubrey Moore, quoted in the introduction of this book, would have benefitted greatly from the Thomistic approach to secondary causality. Moore acknowledges that Darwin "did the work of a friend" for Christianity by discovering biological laws that could be interpreted theologically as God's providential activity (Moore 1890, 73). But then Moore proceeds to set up a false dichotomy between "God's activity" and secondary causes:

> [God] cannot delegate his power to demigods called "second causes." In nature everything must be His work, or nothing. We must frankly return to the Christian view of direct Divine agency, the immanence of Divine power from end to end, the belief in a God in Whom not only we, but all things have their being, or we must banish him altogether. (Moore 1890, 74)

Moore's rejection of secondary causes is an attempt to avoid deism, but his alternative is exactly what Aquinas denied, which is the unilateral operation of the primary cause within nature. With respect to creaturely contingencies, this is an open rather than a closed universe.

Moore's worry—echoed by Ruse—is that a God who patiently creates through natural processes over evolutionary time is a distant, perhaps deistic God who is not immediately present and available in his creation. Classical Christianity, however, balances God's transcendence and immanence. Just because God is ontologically distinct (meaning that the being of God is not to be identified with the being of creatures) does not mean that he is not present with his creation (meaning that God seeks to draw creation to himself and works for its good). And, contrary to Dawkins's flimsy argument, the complexity of the material universe, with its many parts and processes, does not imply the complexity of parts in God, but only a complexity in His wise providential plan. The types of complexity aren't comparable. God is not a material being such that the kind of complexity in the universe should be an indicator of the constitution of God's metaphysical nature. For example, the medieval doctrine of divine simplicity recognizes the unique being of God such that His essence is identical with His attributes (e.g., God is love), whereas finite humans can only have attributes (e.g., Mary is loving). Hence, God is simple in that His nature and attributes are conceptually distinguishable but not in reality separable. Christian theology adds that, in another sense, God is complex, at least in that He is a Trinity, three Persons in one Being (Oden 2009, 105–24).

Emergence

The Christian doctrine of creation encompasses the idea that creation is both *event* and *process*—that God as the initiating and sustaining cause guides the actualization of the potentialities bequeathed to creaturely realities. Creation, then, is not static or fixed but dynamic and emerging as each stage of development prepares the way for greater complexity in the next stage. The concept of *emergence* encompasses the appearance of new properties, powers, and behaviors at certain levels of complexity that were not present at less complex levels. Directionality toward increasing complexity inevitably raises the question of emergence, partly because we tend to value complexity as better or higher somehow. The appearance of *Homo sapiens* is of incomparable importance in the process—for here we have a creature endowed with rational, moral, and relational capacities far beyond what our evolutionary cousins display. We will pursue this point in the next couple of chapters.

Before exploring emergence further, we must deal with Ruse's contention that the Darwinian process blocks the idea that the emergence of humans was inevitable. His claim that "better" or "higher" in evolutionary science is purely relative to circumstances restricts valuation to pragmatic, survival-oriented considerations and elevates Darwinian science to serve a naturalistic metaphysical vision that opposes any intangible, intrinsic, or ultimate value to human beings. The non sequitur here is that, because a human person might not survive as well as a gazelle in swiftly evading a hungry lion, we cannot pronounce humans superior or more valuable. Wait until the next chapter where I examine the scientific discussions of superior human rational powers. Ruse's other point about the randomness of the evolutionary process overstates an aspect of what science knows about the world as a categorical philosophical thesis that there can be no context in which teleology operates in relation to chance. Since such an interpretation of the science is lopsided in emphasis and doesn't take into account all that science is telling us, we should welcome a more balanced perspective.

Emergence assumes that everything that exists in the space-time universe is constituted by the fundamental particles studied by physics. However, when these particles come to be arranged in certain complex configurations, genuinely novel properties occur that are not reducible to the properties of the lower-level components. Perhaps most amazingly, some high-level phenomena exercise downward causality on the underlying constituents. As a Christian theist, I am not committed to any new "law of emergence" or universal force or ubiquitous causal mechanism that produces higher levels of complexity in linear fashion over time, but I am committed to the idea that God bestowed potentialities on the creation that can be realized under suitable conditions. Scientific talk of self-organizing structures and self-replicating protocells is consistent with a theistic view because we are not actually talking about self-creation.

The prior discussion of fine-tuning has implications for directionality toward higher levels of emergence because the physical laws and values of the physical universe must permit it. Interestingly, naturalists insist on the self-organizing and self-replicating properties of matter, which are so essential to their purely natural explanation of life's origin. But this is an implicit admission of some kind of emergence. Furthermore, the emergence of elementary life from nonliving matter arranged in certain configurations would only be possible if there were some type of fine-tuning. Yet, naturalists vehemently deny both that the universe is fine-tuned for intelligent life and that the human mind represents the emergence of a unique and special reality. There is a significant irony here that exposes an incoherence in evolutionary naturalism. On the one hand, naturalists such as Michael Ruse desperately need emergence for the very start of life—life as a new property or reality emerging from matter configured in particular ways. On the other hand, Ruse and other naturalists cannot allow emergence in regard to the human mind, since this would mean that mind as the fruition of the evolutionary process is a new and distinctive reality, which possesses powers not predictable from the parts and constitution of the brain. Admitting an exceptional status for mind and the large gap between humans and other creatures would be too inviting for theistic interpretation.

Aristotle taught the Western world that the whole is greater than the sum of the parts. Contemporary science is revealing many different kinds of emergence in a wide variety of contexts. For example, conductivity as a property of copper atoms in aggregate cannot be predicted from the behavior of an isolated copper atom. Neither can the group behavior of various animal species—birds flocking, ants colonizing, and the like—be predicted from the behavior of individual members of the species. But the potentialities are there to be realized or operationalized at the right levels of complexity. Here I am only concerned with the preeminent reasonableness of affirming emergence as a broad scientific interpretation of directionality toward greater complexity, not with any specific physical theory of how emergence occurs.

All versions of emergence are opposed to illegitimate forms of *reductionism*. *Ontological reductionism* is the view that complex entities at any level of reality are constituted by the basic units of matter designated by physics, which is currently quarks. David Papineau, representing philosophical naturalism, argues for "the completeness of physics" (Papineau 1993, chap. 1). *Epistemological reductionism* is the idea that the concepts used to describe a particular complex system are reducible to or translatable into concepts applicable to the entities of which the complex is composed. Francis Crick, the co-discoverer of the structure of the DNA molecule, declared that "the ultimate aim of the modern movement in biology is in fact to explain *all* biology in terms of physics and chemistry" (Crick 1996, 10). The ontological reductionism here commits the fallacy of "nothing-buttery" in assuming that biological organisms are "nothing but"—that is, that they are reducible to—nonbiological entities arranged in certain ways. The correlative mistake of epistemological reductionism here is the idea that the concepts of biology are reducible to nonbiological concepts. This point is reminiscent of my disagreement with Michael Ruse on the origin-of-life question. Either life just is a certain configuration of matter—and can in principle be understood as such—or something higher than the basic material is occurring—which, as I argued, can only be fully understood in terms of emergence.

Of course, science appropriately operating according to *methodological naturalism* sometimes engages in quite legitimate *methodological reductionism* when it attempts to analyze complex systems into their constituent units as a step toward understanding them better. This kind of knowledge can be extremely helpful. But science per se makes no reductionistic metaphysical or epistemological claims. In fact, science is telling us that, when the underlying material constituents are configured in certain complex ways, new powers and properties emerge that are not adequately classified by the ontology of their parts. In a genuine sense, a new reality occurs that is classifiable in terms of its own unique ontological category.

The idea of emergence offers a reasonable account of the facts of directionality toward increasing complexity. Significant contingency in the evolutionary process is recognized, and an adequate conceptuality for understanding God's creative activity is also advanced. The evolutionary process as we know it may be seen as reflecting God's purposive activity, which supplies a more fundamental teleological character to physical reality than popular design concepts could ever capture. Huxley's idea of a "wider teleology" originally embedded in potentialities and unfolding over time—thus giving directionality to evolution—makes excellent sense of all that contemporary science has learned.

The position of *theistic evolution*—the conjunction of standard theism and evolution—accommodates the idea of a physical universe in which new levels of reality emerge over time under God's providential guidance. Unfortunately, the term "theistic evolution" has sometimes been used to speak of various nonstandard theisms combined with evolution—such as Teilhard's universe drawn toward an omega point or Whitehead's principle of unity leading the world into greater novelty and creativity. So, we must be clear about what exact elements I include in developing my very standard theistic position throughout this discussion. I do not settle for achieving the minimalist goal of showing that theism and science are compatible, which is simply to show the absence of incompatibility. My stronger argument is that theism actually explains science and the important features of reality better than naturalism does—and this point is continued as we go. But I also augment theistic evolution at key junctures with orthodox Christian theology to develop a conceptually richer position. This more nuanced perspective tells us that themes arising from the science of an evolutionary world—such as materiality, directionality, interdependency, relationality, and emergence—resonate deeply with Christian themes of the goodness of the physical, the purposive activity of God, and the profoundly relational universe, not to mention the goal of creation to bring forth rational creatures who could bear God's image (Peterson 2011).

7

Mind and Rationality

The Preeminence of Mind

Michael Peterson

The appearance of *Homo sapiens* in the evolutionary process raises important questions about the nature and status of the special kind of creature that we are. Science reveals the biological tie between humans and all other living organisms. Studies of the genome demonstrate our close tie to the primates as well as our distant kinship to fruit flies and bananas. Yet most religions affirm that humans are special in the universe and a focus of divine attention. The Koran affirms that Allah made humanity "after the most excellent of forms." The Book of Genesis, contained in both Jewish and Christian scriptures, declares that humankind is made "in the image of God."

The phenomenon of mind, which is widely viewed as the distinguishing feature of humans, generates a number of issues at the interface of science and religion that Michael Ruse and I navigate quite differently. I see powers of mind—such as self-consciousness and the capacity to form rational beliefs—as evidences of the unique and special kind of creature we are. Michael Ruse has already indicated that humans are not "higher" or "better" in some intrinsic sense, again signaling his fundamental naturalism blended with Darwinian evolution. From his perspective, rationality is an evolutionary adaptation that is incapable of delivering objective knowledge. I sketch here a theory of mind that is faithful to both science and theology, provides for objective knowledge of reality, and anchors human uniqueness. All that we know about the mind and its rational powers makes better sense given theism than given naturalism.

Consciousness and Self-Consciousness

Collin McGinn has remarked that evolution was able to "engineer consciousness from matter fairly early on" (McGinn 2000, 12). From its humble single-celled beginnings about 4 billion years ago, life flourished and eventually produced sentient creatures with primitive forms of sensory responsiveness. With the appearance of primates, consciousness becomes more complex, replete with impressive problem-solving and tool-making capabilities. In the hominins, emerging just over 2 million years ago, consciousness gets progressively more complex, leading to the appearance of *Homo sapiens* about 200,000 years ago. From Michael Ruse's Darwinian perspective, consciousness is nothing but an evolutionary adaptation, but how shall we think about this in terms of the worldview debate before us?

The academic literature these days speaks of different problems of consciousness. The "easy problem of consciousness" concerns how the brain generates consciousness, which results in abilities to discriminate and categorize stimuli, focus attention, integrate information, and the like. In principle, this problem is susceptible to the methods of cognitive science. David Chalmers argues, however, that the question of explaining why we have phenomenal experiences, or "qualia," persists even if the easy problem is solved. Chalmers says that this "hard problem of consciousness" reflects the profound puzzlement at the existence of subjective occurrences—such as the felt quality of emotion, mental images, and bodily sensations (Chalmers 1995, 201). As Thomas Nagel put it, "There is something it is like to be a bat" or to be any conscious organism (Nagel 1974, 438). The point is that what it is like to *be* conscious eludes scientific description in objective third-person terms.

With modern humans, consciousness has taken another step and turned on itself: we are *Homo sapiens sapiens*. Among our mental features, we have self-consciousness, an inner awareness that one is a "self," a unified subject or center that has emotions, mental images, thoughts, intentions, and other inner experiences. Rational self-awareness or self-consciousness is necessary for personhood, and personhood—that is, being a "self"—is essential for relations to other finite persons and to God. Classical Christian theology readily sees the arrival of finite personal creatures as a key aim of the evolutionary process and as a divine gift that mirrors the supreme personal being. Consider this moving prayer, often attributed to Brother Lawrence, a seventeenth-century monk: "O Lord, I love you and long to give myself to you, but I cannot unless you first give myself to me."

Evolutionary science sees the gradual emergence of rational consciousness as the outcome of natural history—the astounding result of the coevolution of brain, language, and culture. Abstract and symbolic thought accelerated around 45,000 years ago, as determined by the material evidence—such as the spectacular cave paintings in France and Spain from the Upper Paleolithic. This is a significant "cultural explosion." At that point in history, the modern human mind—with capabilities far beyond those of our nearest animal relatives—was already clearly, intensely, and impressively at work. Could we perhaps call this "the mind's big bang"?

Scientists in the various fields contributing to paleoanthropology are actually talking of "human uniqueness"—and they are well justified by the evidence in doing so (van Huyssteen 2006, 164ff). There are good scientific grounds for saying that we are "superior creatures" in an extremely important sense. As the Berkeley anthropologist Terrence Deacon states,

> Human consciousness is not merely an emergent phenomenon; it epitomizes the logic of emergence in its very form. Human minds, deeply entangled in symbolic culture, have an effective causal locus that extends across continents and millennia, growing out of the experiences of countless individuals. Consciousness emerges as an incessant creation of something from nothing, a process continually transcending itself. To be human is to know what it feels like to be evolution happening. (Deacon 2003, 306)

Although humans have an animal prehistory, we are rational-soulish creatures, a special type of being that begs for adequate worldview explanation.

In what kind of universe—described by what sort of philosophical worldview— would we expect to find creatures with the powers and capacities we have? For naturalists such as Michael Ruse, the appearance of humans is the result of a colossal accident or series of small accidents in natural history, such that humans do not possess incommensurable value. For theists, by contrast, finite consciousness and rational thought ultimately derive from an infinite conscious rational being. Classical Christianity goes on to declare that what we know biologically as *Homo sapiens* is, theologically speaking, *Homo divinus*—that is, *Homo sapiens* bearing God's image.

Neuroscience and the Metaphysics of Mind

We human beings have always known intuitively that mind is the fundamental feature distinguishing us from the rest of the living world and providing the basis for all other special human characteristics. For centuries, we have known that there is a particularly close connection between mind and brain. Although the old science of phrenology was badly mistaken, the idea that mental functions are correlated with different parts of the brain has proven scientifically fruitful. Advances in the cognitive sciences allow us to investigate the mind–brain connection in new ways and thus acquire important information to be interpreted by the worldviews debated in this book.

Positron emission tomography, functional magnetic imaging, and magneto-encephalography can pinpoint with great accuracy how various mental behaviors are accompanied by changes in brain activity. Moving my arm or simply imagining moving my arm, playing chess, even being in pain—all can be linked to respective areas of the brain and distinctive electrochemical responses. Ethical decision making, for instance, appears to activate one specific area in the temporal lobe and one in the frontal lobe of the cerebral cortex.

Deep religious meditation and prayer light up various areas of the brain in functional magnetic resonance imaging studies, including the parietal lobe, the visual cortex, and the caudate nucleus.

Going in the other direction, research shows that brain activity produces corresponding mental activity. Electrical stimulation or damage to the brain causes certain mental reactions to occur. Stimulation of relevant areas of animal brains has produced aggression, sleep, and other behaviors. In humans, brain stimulation has produced a wide range of conscious states—pleasure elicited from the septal region, rage from the amygdale region, and so forth. Wilder Penfield, a well-known neurosurgeon, has evoked complex, vivid hallucinations by stimulating the temporal lobe of clinical subjects (Penfield 1975). Interestingly, Stanley Koren and Michael Persinger developed the "God Helmet," which magnetically stimulates the temporal lobes in subjects in the study of correlations between neural and religious or spiritual states. Persinger indicates that many subjects have reported "mystical experiences and altered states," but these findings are controversial in the scientific literature (Persinger et al. 2010). I personally hold that seeking the transformation of everyday life—because of a clear commitment to the sacredness of the ordinary—is the mainstay of authentic religion and not peak psychological experiences that vary among personality types, traditions, and cultures. But this is a topic for another context.

Varieties of naturalism are everywhere in the larger discussion. Strict naturalists tend to be materialists about human persons: a human person is entirely a material object with no immaterial self or soul or subject. Identity theory is a common form of this reductionist materialism, maintaining that mental properties are identical to, and thus reducible to, internal bodily properties. Functionalism, also a popular view, takes mental properties to be identical to physical properties in interaction with the environment. Patricia Churchland, who works in neurophilosophy, endorses the more extreme theory of eliminativism, holding that the traditional understanding of inner mental states, such as beliefs and desires, is merely "folk psychology" that should be discarded in favor of neurobiological states (Churchland 1986).

Broader versions of naturalism hold versions of nonreductive and noneliminativist materialism, allowing that mental properties are distinct from, but supervene on, physical properties. Metaphysical supervenience (pertaining to all possible worlds) and nomological supervenience (relativized to the physical necessities of the actual world) have been explored. However, Jerry Fodor, David Lewis, and other materialists now doubt supervenience strategies because of important counterarguments, such as the possibility of disembodied beings and zombies that are like humans but lack subjective states. Jaegwon Kim has argued that both reductive and nonreductive forms of physicalism are untenable because they cannot accommodate the causal efficacy of mental states—that is, the ability to direct one's actions (Kim 2005).

Materialist theories of mind generally are far less impressive than they are touted to be. First, materialists exaggerate the philosophical implications of what brain science is learning and simply assume that *some* materialist view must be correct, although we don't currently know which one. This underwhelming intellectual orientation hardly creates a heavy burden of proof for antimaterialists. Second, materialist views make their living on weaknesses in substance dualist views without making a strong positive case *for* materialism, which is particularly difficult to accomplish in light of the unrelenting problems of consciousness in the philosophy of mind that were already mentioned.

Materialism is untenable. Although Michael Ruse endorses McGinn's skepticism that we can ever arrive at an adequate theory of mind (McGinn 2000), he still sticks with the machine metaphor, which means treating mind as a material thing. And Ruse is quick to point out that substance dualism is untenable because it cannot effectively solve its central problem of how mental and material entities can be causally or explanatorily related. I hold that both materialism and substance dualism are inadequate, that neither type of view accounts for all we know, but I don't think skepticism is warranted. There is a more adequate theory of mind that accounts for all the data.

The concept of mind as an emergent new level of reality promises important insights. Contemporary physics—the most fundamental science for materialists—now readily acknowledges lawful relationships among physical entities at different levels of reality. Talk of interaction in physics opens the door in psychophysics for mutual causal influence between the mental and the physical—something that neuroscience is detecting in its own way. It may well turn out, as William Hasker has suggested, that the problem of mind–body interaction "may well hold the all-time record for overrated objections to major philosophical positions" (Hasker 1999, 150).

I prefer to go in the following direction. That the subject of conscious experience cannot be a material object is increasingly clear, but the evidence shows that consciousness arises as a result of brain function. Emergent dualism encompasses both insights by affirming that there is an immaterial subject of experience and that it emerges from the brain and nervous system. Normally, what is generated by a healthy brain is a single, well-unified conscious subject with all of the subjective capabilities we commonly recognize. The mind is produced by the human brain, not added to the brain from the outside.

William Hasker and Timothy O'Connor, for example, are dualists who argue that mental properties are "emergent" in the following way: mental properties manifest themselves when the appropriate material constituents are configured in special, highly complex relationships (Hasker 1999; O'Connor 1994). These emergent properties are not observable in simpler configurations, nor are they derivable from the laws that describe the properties of matter in simpler configurations. To use a rough analogy, a magnetic field and its properties are generated when the physical constituents of a magnet are in certain relationships—a sufficient number of iron atoms aligned. But the magnetic field is a real, existing, concrete entity, with new causal powers of its own.

Emergent dualism makes good sense of scientific findings as well as our common human experience of ourselves. Emergent dualism agrees with materialism that the potentiality for conscious life resides in the nature of matter but avoids the mistake of denying what John Searle calls the "obvious facts about the mental," which are subjective states (Searle 1992, 20). Yet emergent dualism also agrees with substance dualism that the mind is a distinctly different reality from the physical brain but disagrees that the mind is a nonmaterial entity, separable from the brain, with no systemic or internal relationship to the physical.

Mind must then be viewed as the unique emergent reality that characterizes human beings. In theology and ordinary life, the term "person" designates the total psychosomatic unity that is a human being. As Arthur Peacocke, a biochemist and Anglican priest, says,

> There is therefore a strong case for designating the highest level—the whole, in that unique system that is the human-brain-in-the-human-body-in-social-relations—as that of the "person." Persons are *inter alia* causal agents with respect to their own bodies and to the surrounding world (including other persons). (Peacocke 2003, 197)

The emergence of the personal in evolutionary history proves to be the paragon of what the various sciences see in emergence: whole–part influence. Theism sees the emergence of personal agents as making perfect sense within a universe created by a supremely rational personal agent. Christian theism, which includes the doctrines of creation and Incarnation, affirms God's plan to be bringing forth holistic embodied personal agents—and that is indeed what we are.

Evolution and Human Uniqueness

Michelangelo's famous fresco *The Creation of Adam* on the ceiling of the Sistine Chapel depicts a bearded God, surrounded by an anatomically accurate drawing of the human brain, imparting through his forefinger the spark of life to the first human. The symbolism links brain to mind, which is associated with the impartation of the divine image. Brain is part of the physical world, developed by the evolutionary process we share with higher animals; mind gives us capacities and abilities far beyond what any other creature displays. The pressing question is, are human beings a special *kind* of creature of superior status and value—or do humans differ only in *degree* from animals?

Michael Ruse and most philosophical naturalists embrace the *continuity thesis*: that human beings *differ in degree* from animals and the rest of nature. Dawkins, predictably endorsing evolutionary naturalism on this issue, insists that "a great gulf between *Homo sapiens* and the rest of the animal kingdom . . . is fundamentally anti-evolutionary" (Dawkins 2014, 548). Traditional religious and philosophical perspectives embrace the *discontinuity thesis*: that humans *differ in kind* from all other things in nature. In a message to the Pontifical Academy of Sciences, Pope John Paul II stated, "The moment of transition to the spiritual cannot be the object of [scientific] observation, which nevertheless can discover at the experimental level a series of very valuable signs indicating what is specific to the human being" (John Paul II 1997, 383).

Scientific evidence can be deployed on both sides of the continuity/discontinuity issue. In my view, the case for continuity is not difficult to make. In *The Descent of Man*, Darwin argued for "no fundamental difference between man and the higher mammals in their mental facilities" and identified similarities in emotion, attention, and memory (Darwin 1871, 1, 35). Since animals possess the same faculties in lesser degrees of development, Darwin reasoned that humans differ only in degree, albeit an impressive degree. He even speaks of our "God-like intellect" but remarks that we bear the indelible mark of our animal origins (Darwin 1871, 2, 405). As we have already seen, Michael Ruse approves of Darwin's pronouncement that we should never call any creature "higher"—including humans—because evolutionary science provides no absolute scale of value to support the judgment. Scientists have identified similarities in anatomical structures, internal organs, DNA sequences, and many other features to show that humans are closely related to the rest of animate nature. Primatologists have argued that language, thought to be distinctively human, can be learned to some extent by apes and that basic tool use occurs among various primates, such as employing rocks to crack nuts. In the next chapter, we will consider morality in light of similarities in instincts and behavior between primates and humans.

The key lies in how we think philosophically about our similarities with animals and other aspects of the physical world. Francisco Diego, a senior research fellow in physics and astronomy at the University College London, has stated, "We are not so special because our own bodies, our own chemistry, our blood, our bones, our skin, are made of hydrogen, nitrogen, oxygen, sodium, and so forth. We find hydrogen, oxygen, and so forth in nebulae and stars in the universe. So we have the same chemistry. So there's nothing special about it" (Diego 1997). This logically inexcusable non sequitur triggering on chemistry closely resembles another triggering on astronomy: that there's nothing special about the size or location of earth; therefore, there's nothing special about us and our situation. In this chapter and the next, we face yet another non sequitur of the same sort: that humans exhibit similarities in degree with animals; so humans are not fundamentally different in kind. What we have in all these cases is the mediocrity principle hard at work, but I have previously exposed this idea as false science. Genuine science must, of course, assume the uniformity of nature and operate by methodological naturalism, which means that science simply lacks the capability to discern definitively any qualitatively unique trait in anything. However, science can hardly declare that there are no qualitative judgments to be made based on other avenues of knowledge about humans.

However, we can also make a scientific case in support of discontinuity—that is, for human uniqueness. Science tells us that the human brain is the most complex physical object in the entire universe. Features such as the ratio of brain mass to body mass and the more specialized differentiation make the human brain importantly different even from other primate brains—for example, the disproportionately large cerebral cortex in humans, which is associated with reasoning and abstract thought. Behavioral differences also factor into a scientific case for discontinuity, since language use and tool use in humans occur on a scale that is downright staggering when compared to that of our closest primate cousin.

Scientists typically consider capacities such as imagination, mathematical ability, moral awareness, and religious sensibility to be vastly beyond those of any animal. Many psychologists, linguists, and philosophers link anthropic specialness to the use of language and symbolic thought. Ian Tattersall of the American Museum of Natural History argues that increasingly complex language caused human thought to become much more efficient, allowing cognitive capabilities to grow exponentially, causing remarkable cultural transitions to occur (Tattersall 2004, 97). Cultural evolution took humans along paths completely inexplicable purely in terms of biological evolution. At a certain juncture in hominid evolution, something radically new was happening: an entity we would recognize as human was gradually appearing.

In the end, the empirical sciences provide mixed results on the question of human uniqueness. Granted, evidence is abundant for many differences in degree between humans and other animals. Yet evidence already cited also justifies those scientists who are speaking today about "human uniqueness." The cultural explosion (or creativity explosion, or cognitive explosion) of the Upper Paleolithic, for example, strongly supports an insuperable barrier between all humans and other animals. That's the human lot: both continuities and discontinuities with the rest of nature. Along with virtually all philosophical naturalists, Michael Ruse endorses complete continuity and underestimates important discontinuities that science is revealing. On the other side, many religious advocates spend too much energy defending human uniqueness by trying to prove scientifically that humans are importantly different from other animals in origin or structure or behavior.

As a theist, I recognize the mixed picture from science and instead choose to emphasize what it is that makes humans especially important to God. Theistic religions teach that humans are special in reflecting aspects of God's nature and having the capacity for relationship with God—and thus have a higher role in the purposes of God. The Psalmist could not help but declare, "You have made them a little lower than God, and crowned them with glory and honor" (Ps. 8:5). The question of human specialness can never be settled scientifically—and brings us once again to the philosophical clash between naturalism and theism.

Rationality and Evolution

Darwin believed that "*Reason* stands at the summit" of all human powers, although he understood it as the product of adaptive change (Darwin 1871, 1, 46). Rationality, with its panoply of cognitive powers, is what makes humans noetic beings who seek truth and knowledge. From evolutionary science, we can infer that our behavior is adaptive and that the neurophysiology producing our behavior is likewise adaptive. Regarding the evolution of the human brain, Patricia Churchland maintains that its principal function is to get the human organism to move appropriately (fleeing, fighting, etc.), thereby enhancing its chances of survival. Since survival is paramount, Churchland says, "Truth, whatever that is, definitely takes the hindmost" (Churchland 1987, 548). Since false beliefs may be just as adaptive as true beliefs, evolutionary science alone cannot provide a complete explanation of why our rational faculties are reliable for truth. Our rational capability for truth begs for metaphysical explanation and thus returns us to the worldview debate of this book.

Alvin Plantinga argues that evolutionary naturalism as a worldview is self-undercutting in that one cannot rationally accept both evolution and naturalism (Dennett and Plantinga 2011). However, some combination of naturalism and evolution is exactly what Dawkins, Dennett, Ruse, and many other atheist thinkers embrace. Where is this tension between naturalism and evolutionary theory? Let us start with Churchland's antirealist remark about truth, which seems to take naturalism for granted. Consider Plantinga's evolutionary argument against naturalism. Where R is the proposition that our cognitive faculties are reliable for truth, N the proposition that naturalism is true, and E the proposition that we have evolved through the natural selection of adaptive behavior,

1. $P(R/N \& E)$ is low.
2. One who accepts $N \& E$ and also sees that 1 is true has a defeater for R.
3. This defeater can't be defeated.
4. One who has a defeater for R has a defeater for any belief he or she takes to be produced by his or her cognitive faculties, including $N \& E$.

Therefore,

5. $N \& E$ is self-defeating and can't rationally be accepted.

A brief argument for premise 1 goes as follows. Assume there are beliefs. Then, since naturalists generally are materialists about human persons, they hold that a belief is an event or structure in the brain, presumably involving certain neurons and the like. However, if it is a *belief*, it will also have a mental property: it will have a *content*; that is, it will be the belief that p, for some proposition p. Since natural selection regards only the adaptive fitness, not the truth, of the belief, the falsehood of the belief does not interfere with the adaptivity of its neurophysiological properties. On purely evolutionary grounds, then, there is no reason to think that rationality reliably tracks truth—that is, that rationality generates a large proportion of true beliefs in comparison to false beliefs.

Naturalism, as a worldview allying itself with evolutionary science, provides no philosophical reason to think that natural selection on its own would produce rationality that would reliably track truth. So, given the conjunction of naturalism and evolution, the probability that rationality is reliable to track truth is low. Hence, anyone who realizes this and still accepts $N \& E$ has an epistemic defeater for R in his or her own case—that is, a reason for rejecting the reliability of rationality.

$N \& E$ generates a defeater for R. Here we have a defeater that cannot be defeated because any defeater of this defeater would have to take the form of an argument, which would already assume the reliability of rationality and thus be epistemically circular. Daniel Dennett completely misses this exact point in his reply to Plantinga:

> It is precisely the truth-tracking competence of belief-fixing mechanisms that explains their "adaptivity" in the same way that it is the blood-pumping competence of hearts that explains theirs. Hearts are for circulating the blood and

brains are for tracking the relevant conditions of the environment and *getting it right.* (Dennett and Plantinga 2011, 52)

Dennett mistakenly thinks that an account of how natural selection was involved in developing my capacity to recognize truth is an explanation of my ground for trusting my rationality. But rationality must first be trusted as reliable for truth—as Dennett unwittingly does—to give the account in the first place. Furthermore, Dennett glosses over importantly different ways in which our cognitive powers can be said to "get it right" and thus avoids addressing the special sense in which rationality operates with respect to truth as distinct from survival. Such are the trials and tribulations of those who embrace the epistemological antirealism inherent in evolutionary naturalism.

So, one cannot rationally accept both evolutionary science and philosophical naturalism. Since evolutionary theory is highly confirmed, naturalism must be rejected. Of course, the deep problem with naturalism can be exposed independently of its conjunction with evolution. C. S. Lewis explains the difficulty for naturalist metaphysics:

> All possible knowledge, then, depends on the validity of reasoning. . . . A theory which explained everything else in the whole universe but which made it impossible to believe that our thinking was valid, would be utterly out of court. For that theory would itself have been reached by thinking, and if thinking is not valid that theory would, of course, be itself demolished. It would have destroyed its own credentials. (Lewis 2001, 21–22)

Naturalism holds that rationality as we know it ultimately proceeds from the nonrational, that mind is ultimately reducible to the fundamental reality of matter. Yet, in common parlance, we often say that water cannot rise higher than its source—but this is exactly the error of naturalistic metaphysics in trying to explain the full reality of rational thought in terms of physical nature and its processes.

An important realist principle is that all humans prephilosophically and instinctively assume the basic trustworthiness of their cognitive powers. (Any *argument* for *R* would be epistemically circular!) Theism conceptually links the realist idea of rational knowers in a rationally knowable world to the idea of a rational Creator. We are made in his image in this respect. Hence, the confidence that there is "a way things are" in the world and that human beings have reliable powers for knowing these things makes sense given theism. No claim is made that our knowledge is pristine or divinely guaranteed. As Aquinas says, "Truth is the adequation of intellect to things" (*adequatio intellectus ad rem*) (Aquinas 1981, *ST* I, Q. 16, Art. 2). In a theistic universe, when our cognitive powers are functioning normally in an environment for which they were made, then we should expect them to generate many more truths than falsehoods. It is not surprising that many evolutionary naturalists are skeptical about our ability to know objective truth. The skepticism of Michael Ruse—which involves his own mix of Hume, Kant, and Darwin that makes the objective world an unknowable "thing in itself"—at best reduces truth to coherence among our beliefs. But a naturalist metaphysical framework should not be expected to support proper and healthy epistemic confidence.

The evolutionary argument *against* naturalism has led us to an argument *for* theism. Metaphysical naturalism cannot make good sense of why evolution would produce rational powers reliable for truth. Noam Chomsky, for example, claims that the congruence between the world and the human belief forming capacity "is just blind luck" (Chomsky 2001, 157). But the evolutionary facts are perfectly consistent with the theistic idea that a supremely rational God guided the contingencies of evolution to produce humans with rational faculties—indeed, that natural selection aimed at fitness and produced faculties capable of truth. Ironically, epistemology is better "naturalized"—that is, informed by what the natural sciences tell us about our evolutionary development—in the context of "supernaturalism" in metaphysics. Rational powers that are reliable for truth are far more likely to evolve given theism. Where R is the proposition that our rational powers are reliable, E is evolution, T is theism, and N is naturalism,

$$P(R/T \,\&\, E) > P(R/N \,\&\, E).$$

Theism is the proper worldview home of rationality.

Humans According to Evolutionary Naturalism

Michael Ruse

Over the past 5 million years, human evolution has been rapid and continues to the present day (Ruse 2012). For all of its cultural significance, skin color variation is recent. No more than 15,000 years ago, we were all the same color. That long-controversial notion of "race" continues to be something of heated discussion. The fact is that we can divide humans up genetically, in some respects minutely. However, the fact is also—probably a function of the bottleneck effect of leaving Africa in small groups—that overall there is nowhere near as much absolute variation as one might expect. Modern humans are a pretty homogenous group. So, let us make this our background assumption as we turn to our species and its nature.

Michael Peterson argues that human rationality is central to human uniqueness, reflecting our creation by a rational deity and enabling us to obtain objective knowledge of the world around us. To the contrary, I argue herein that rationality is an evolutionary adaptation that does not set us distinctly apart from other animals, particularly primates, which exhibit intelligence in various degrees. Although I am skeptical about achieving any definitive theory of mind or of the mind–body relation, my naturalism directs me to look at the science and interpret it rather than to embrace any special substance or quality in humans that cannot be detected by science.

Sentience

The most important thing about humans—certainly the most important thing about humans from the perspective of science and religion—is that we are conscious beings, that we have self-awareness, that we are what has been called "sentient." I don't think any Darwinian evolutionist today would doubt that consciousness is an adaptation brought on by natural selection. It may be brains that carry consciousness, and it is certainly brains that demand all of that protein, but brains are not ends in themselves. They are there because they lead to thinking. In the nineteenth century, Thomas Henry Huxley and William James argued this one out. As we have seen, although he was Darwin's great supporter—the naturalistic-evolutionary program was just what he wanted as an ideological substitute for Christianity—Huxley was never that keen on adaptation. So he had little trouble in arguing that thinking—conscious thinking, that is—is basically icing on the cake (Huxley 1874). This philosophy, epiphenomenalism, also called the "train whistle" theory of consciousness, sees us as conscious automata. We do what we do whatever we think. The train will keep chugging ahead no matter how often or seldom you toot the whistle. James (1880), who to his credit took both Darwinism and psychology seriously, retorted that if this all be so, then we might as well loathe the things that are biologically good for us and love the things that are biologically deleterious. How come we like food and drink and sex and don't like being beaten to a bloody pulp? Because consciousness affects our behavior.

As with all philosophical disagreements, the arguments and counterarguments fly back and forth, but general opinion is that James was right and Huxley was wrong. Apart from anything else, consciousness does not just arrive fully fledged in humans. It is something that builds its way up through other organisms until we get to humans. But this only prepares the way for the much bigger question. How are we to understand sentience? The options seem to be stark. Either we adopt some form of substance dualism, thinking that body and mind are separate, as was argued by Descartes (and before him in a fashion by Plato), or we adopt some form of monism in which mind and matter are features of one underlying substance, as was argued by philosophers like Spinoza (and perhaps before him by Aristotle). I think dualism is the common-sense position, and recently it has found philosophical defenders. But it has the major problem of linking mind and body. If you make them such completely different things, how then do they affect each other so intimately? As a Darwinian you want to say that consciousness gets involved in the physical world. But how? Also, if nonhuman organisms don't have mental substance, as Descartes argued, then why do they function as well as they do? But if they do have mental substance, they why aren't they as bright as humans?

Problems! Unfortunately, it seems that you have the option of the frying pan or the fire. If, to the contrary, you go with something like monism, then how do you explain how a computer made of meat can think? In what sense can one say that sparks in the brain are not just producing thought but are themselves thought? Some philosophers like Paul and Pat Churchland really do think that we are on the way to showing just this, but one would like some evidence that progress is being made (Churchland 1984). The origin-of-life problem is not solved, but suppose RNA rather than DNA as the first replicating molecule plugs a gap in the causal record. You may not have the answer, but you can imagine what an answer would be like. This is not so in the consciousness case. However much you learn about the workings of the brain, the gap to the mind remains. It is often said today that the brain is—in line with the metaphor above—like a computer and that it is the hardware and thinking is the software. Perhaps so, but it doesn't really speak to the problem. Without interpretation, the software program is just marks on paper or etchings on a disk or whatever. To take a word much appreciated by young Anglophones learning German, VATER. What do these marks mean? "Father" or, to the delight of the vulgar when you learn how to pronounce them, something about breaking wind? Software without humans is just part of the physical world.

Does this give any comfort to religious persons? I have allowed that they can offer their own answers, namely, being made in the image of God. Just as God is sentient, so also are we sentient. We could hardly be rational beings aware of moral demands if we were not. Peterson's argument is that our rational consciousness somehow reflects the divine image. But note that this is officially a theological answer and navigates the science in a way that I do not. Moreover, it comes with baggage of its own, which can be fairly pointed out, if only to suggest that one might want to retreat to the kind of skepticism I embrace. Granted, Peterson employs the philosophical theory of emergent dualism as a middle way between materialism and substance dualism regarding the nature of mind. But my skepticism about any definitive theory of mind still kicks in.

Ask yourself what on earth consciouness-sentience is all about? For us humans, sentience is very much an active, social phenomenon. We'll go into this more in the next chapter, but think of something like love. God is love; we are capable of love, precisely because in this respect we are God-like. In this context, it is not disrespectful to think not only of Platonic love (*agapé*) but also of sexual love (*eros*). It is an essential part of Christian theology that God Himself is not a sexual being, but many Christians tie in our being made in God's image with our sexuality: "So God created man in his *own* image, in the image of God created he him; male and female created he them" (Genesis 1: 27).

But note what a dynamic thing love truly is. I love my wife Lizzie dearly, and I love my five children, and I love my students. It is an ever-changing and evolving set of relationships, thank goodness. The love I feel for my wife now after thirty years of happy marriage is different from the initial passions when we first met. The love I have for my children is different from what it was when they were first born and totally helpless and dependent. The love of my students by its very nature has to change, from first getting to know them to seeing them off into the wider world, richer, I trust, from the experience of knowing me, as I am certainly richer from knowing them. Can God's love be anything like this, even analogically? Before Christians start congratulating themselves on the fact that they have a solution to the body–mind problem, they must do some spade work to show that, taken on their own terms, they have an adequate solution. I am just not sure that they do. Go back to that Christian conception of God, an uneasy amalgam of Greek philosophy and Jewish religion. Perhaps if Christians just stay with the Jewish notion of God, God's sentience and human sentience are at least in the same ballpark. God's love is unconditional, but He gets cross with us at times, and so forth. In other words, God's love is dynamic like ours. Surely the feelings that God had for and about Abraham were changed by the faith Abraham showed when tested over Isaac. But this notion of God—a god with humanlike sentience—is but one part of the claims made by traditional Christianity. It is not the God of Augustine and Anselm and Aquinas, in whose praise infant lungs used to below out at Whitehall Primary School, in Walsall, Staffordshire, in the 1940s:

> Immortal, invisible, God only wise,
> In light inaccessible hid from our eyes,
> Most blessèd, most glorious, the Ancient of Days,
> Almighty, victorious, thy great Name we praise.

This is a god who is totally unchanging, outside time and space. This is not a god who plans a special dinner for his wife on her birthday. This is not a god who picks up and comforts a small child who is crying. This is not a god who spends half of Sunday going over a doctoral dissertation that should have been handed in months ago. We are simply not made in the image of a god who has about as much emotion as a three-four-five right-angled triangle. I am sorry, but when I am confronted with the notion of a god such as this, I start to think that the critics are right that it is all a con game by a crowd of old men in skirts to control us through fear of the unknown.

Knowledge

Grant that we have consciousness. What do we do with it? One thing is we find out about the world we live in, what it is like, how it works. Although Darwinian theory may not be able to explain the very fact of consciousness, can it throw light on how it functions, more specifically how it functions as a knowledge machine? In one of his private notebooks, after he had become an evolutionist but writing just before he discovered natural selection, Darwin speculated on the nature and origins of our knowledge: "Origin of man now proved.—Metaphysic must flourish.—he who understands baboon would do more towards metaphysics than Locke" (Barrett et al. 1987, 539, M 84e, August 16, 1838, only six weeks before the discovery of selection). A few days later, he showed explicitly the line that he was following. Instinct formed by evolution gives us innate knowledge: "Plato says in *Phaedo* that our *'necessary ideas'* arise from the preexistence of the soul, are not derivable from experience.— Read monkeys for preexistence—" (Barrett et al. 1987, M 551, 128, September 4th). Most evolutionists, most scientists, would be comfortable with some kind of view akin to that being mused by Darwin in these passages (Ruse 2009). Humans are not born with their minds a blank slate—actually, even people like Locke didn't really believe that—but with certain tendencies to believe along certain lines rather than others. Those of our protoancestors who had natural tendencies to believe one sort of way rather than another and whose tendencies helped in the struggle for existence survived and reproduced, and those who did not did not. So a protohuman who saw three bears enter a cave and only two emerge was ahead of the game played against the protohuman who saw no difference between bears entering and bears leaving. Likewise, the protohuman who went down to the lake to drink and who saw trampled bushes and heard growling and who said, "Tigers!" and left quickly was ahead of the protohuman who, on seeing and hearing the same evidence, said, "Tigers! Just a theory, not a fact!"

In short, most scientists today would agree that we are born with innate dispositions toward fairly basic principles of reasoning, rudimentary mathematics, awareness of what are known as "epistemic values"—for instance, that we should try to avoid hypotheses that are too ad hoc and work from ideas already accepted, and so forth. There is a growing body of work looking in detail and empirically at these sorts of dispositions (Cosmides 1989). Expectedly, they tend to be tempered by the situations that our ancestors would have encountered, and it is relatively easy to show that we reason incorrectly if the circumstances are not natural and uncommon. Even basic rules of reasoning like *modus ponens* go awry if our heads are in a strange place. Also, of course, there is a major cultural component. The great thing about consciousness is that you don't have to have all of the necessary information transmitted through the genes—as, for instance, a bird might have a genetic predisposition to take flight and migrate at certain times of the year. You can pass on good ideas directly to others. Expectedly, however, there are going to be filters to ensure that what is good is not too idiosyncratic.

Some of the most exciting work in this direction suggests that there are two basic rules at work here. First, go with the norm:

Recall the old saw "When in Rome, do as the Romans do." This strategy makes good evolutionary sense under a broad range of conditions. A number of processes, including guided variation, content bias, and natural selection, all tend to cause the adaptive behavior to become more common than maladaptive behavior. Thus, all other things being equal, imitating the most common behavior in the population is better than imitating at random. (Richerson and Boyd 2005, 120)

Second, go with the winners. It is a good bet that the successful are using ideas or techniques that pay off, so take note and do the same:

> Mass-media celebrities notwithstanding, our attraction to the successful makes much adaptive sense. Determining *who* is a success is much easier than to determine *how* to be a success. By imitating the successful, you have a chance of acquiring the behaviors that cause success, even if you do not know anything about which characteristics of the successful are responsible for their success. (124)

Thinking about culture at a level of more immediate concern to us, I have been stressing the significance of metaphor in constructing and understanding science. It is hard to imagine that Darwin's theory of evolution formulated in the middle of the nineteenth century would have got off the ground without the socio-politico-economic changes of the eighteenth century. The struggle for existence comes straight out of Thomas Robert Malthus's worries about overpopulation, a worry shared by many at the end of the eighteenth century as people left the farm and moved to the city, where children were a bonus (because they could work in factories) rather than a burden (one more mouth to be fed off the same amount of land). Natural selection is modeled on artificial selection, a major strategy to increase foodstuffs and thus speak to the population explosion. The division of labor, a major metaphor for Darwin, is pure Adam Smith. So however important biology is, culture is vital too.

Naturalism Defeated?

How does this vision impinge on the science–religion debate? At one level, not a great deal, that is, if you have been willing already to accept human origins through evolution by natural selection. All you are doing is extending the scope of the theory in fairly obvious ways. Admittedly, there are already some interesting philosophical questions. The ethologist Konrad Lorenz (1941) embraced this kind of thinking—with reason drawing attention to its similarities to major features of Kant's epistemology (especially the way in which our thinking structures our experiences)—but believed that it is now possible to go one step beyond Kant, inasmuch as now we can claim to have true understanding of underlying reality, what Kant called the unknowable thing in itself—the *Ding an sich*. However, others, including myself, are not sure that this "realist" conclusion follows. Of course one can distinguish between the real and the apparent. It was real mice that gnawed at my cheese left uncovered on the kitchen table. It is apparent mice that I see running up the wall after a night of binge drinking. But we continue to have the same worries that post-Kantians like Fichte and Schelling had about the worth of talking of things in themselves.

Perhaps as the philosopher Hilary Putnam (1981) has suggested, we need a kind of "internal realism," where we distinguish real mice from imaginary mice but eschew talk of mice in themselves. We cannot get to this external metaphysical world, but there is no need to.

My natural inclination is to say that none of this need be particularly troublesome for Christians. However, thanks to an argument mooted by the sometime English prime minister A. J. Balfour, the Calvinist philosopher Alvin Plantinga, for one, is deeply perturbed by the implications of the ideas being expressed here and has articulated his position in the larger discussion. Peterson is appreciative of Plantinga on this point. Implicit in this line of thought, I think, is the belief that God has created this world of ours, that it exists objectively "out there," and that He would therefore have given us the ability to see and understand it truly. Our knowledge cannot be human centered because the Darwinian can provide only a relativistic epistemology and must admit that we could be fundamentally mistaken about the whole of God's creation. To get to this conclusion, Plantinga notes (correctly) that natural selection cares only about survival and reproduction and not at all about objective truth. So it has no hesitation in deceiving us if it can achieve its ends better in that way. Plantinga invites us to imagine a posh dinner at an Oxford college, where Richard Dawkins is discussing atheism with the logical positivist philosopher A. J. Ayer. Is this real? "It could be that one of these creatures [Dawkins or Ayer] believes he is at that elegant, bibulous Oxford dinner, when in fact he is slogging his way through some primeval swamp, desperately fighting off hungry crocodiles" (Plantinga 1993). The whole of life could be nothing but a sham.

This is nonsense! Philosophers love to think up these little imaginary stories to make their points. Too often, as now, the imagination outstrips the plausible. There is nothing in Darwinian theory to support Plantinga's hypothesis. You don't fight off hungry crocodiles by boozing it up with Freddie Ayer. You fight off hungry crocodiles by being quick and alert and probably scared to death. The point is that we have certain things that we know are true—crocodiles are dangerous, avoiding them is a good way to stay alive—and then if we are deceived at all by selection, ultimately we can see why the deception occurs. Take falling in love. We all know that in that first flush of emotion and passion we tend to idolize the beloved and to see him or her through rose-colored spectacles. As many of us discover in time, do we ever make false assumptions! But we can see why it happens. Nature needs to get us to hook up with strangers—inbreeding is not a good thing—and this is a good way to do it. Natural selection doesn't deceive us unless there is a good reason to do so. If every time we faced dangers like hungry crocodiles we went off into daydreams about dining with philosophers, we would not last long at all.

But still Plantinga objects. This argument depends on our having certain beliefs that we can take as given and basic, as true. Crocodiles are dangerous. Avoiding them is a good strategy. Being idealistic about a new partner is a good way to avoid inbreeding. And so forth. But couldn't it be that we are deceived about everything? Plantinga invites us into a factory where all of the widgets being manufactured are red. But are they red really, or is it all a trick of the lighting? The factory superintendent tells us that they are red, but could he be faking it or just mistaken? That's the trouble with powers developed through evolution. You can never be certain that the whole thing is not a naturalistic joke. You cannot be certain that you have any genuine knowledge in the realist sense, and of course what is even worse is that you cannot be sure that you have knowledge of God or even that He exists. Antirealism about the world and about God flourishes. If that isn't a good religious reason for disliking evolution, it is hard to know what is.

A *Sensus Divinitatis?*

At the moment, we seem to be at the stage of the argument where many religious persons should reject naturalistic science. One presumes, however, that if one is to hold to naturalistic science, one is going to reject religion, or at least Plantinga's version of it. Let's dig a little more deeply. Plantinga's argument about science—retraced by Peterson—is a direct descendent of the argument that Descartes offers in the *Meditations*. We could be mistaken about everything and are rescued only because a good God guarantees our "clear and distinct" ideas. But could we be mistaken about everything? Perhaps so, if you persist in holding to an objective external world, a *Ding an sich*. Peterson counters that God underwrites the general reliability of your rational powers. Such moves are typically tied to a correspondence theory of truth—what is true is what corresponds to that external world. But if you give up that world, not necessarily in the direction of absolute idealism (like Fichte) but more in the direction of saying that reality is always reality as experienced by us (like Schelling), then talk of "mistakes" seems less obvious. You are committed (as Putnam agrees) to some kind of coherence theory of truth, where what is true is what hangs together, but so be it. A certain pragmatism goes with being a naturalist, in the sense that we are using the term.

So we can hold to naturalistic science. What price God then? I have agreed that you can be a naturalist and have some conception of a creator, but it does seem that Plantinga's God who guarantees our knowledge is no longer needed. And this, of course, is quite apart from the difficulties of believing in such a God, difficulties that Descartes experienced before Plantinga.

Calvinists think we have a *sensus divinitatis*, something that gives us direct knowledge of God:

> There is within the human mind, and indeed by natural instinct, an awareness of divinity. This we take to beyond controversy. To prevent anyone from taking refuge in the pretense of ignorance, God himself has implanted in all men a certain understanding of his divine majesty. . . . Therefore, since from the beginning of the world there has been no region, no city, in short, no household, that could do without religion, there lies in this a tacit confession of a sense of deity inscribed in the hearts of all. (Calvin 1960, 43–46)

If faith is such a natural instinct put there by God, how then do you explain those without faith? Obviously through original sin. Their vile nature leads them to distort or ignore the avenue to God.

Apart from anything else, this kind of claim commits one to a narrowly Eurocentric view of the world that is cringe-making, even for Christians. Is one to say that the Dalai Lama is corrupted by sin in a way, say, that Pat Robertson is not? Or the dreadful Bernard Cardinal Law who let pedophilic priests move from parish to parish in the Boston area without restraint or punishment? It is true that some Christian thinkers like the English philosopher John Hick (1980) have tried to find a way of broadening faith understanding to make room for rival visions, like that of the Christian and the Buddhist. But commendable though these efforts may be—and one doubts Plantinga (2000) appreciates help offered to him on this score—the end result is clearly going to be amorphous, unkind critics might say "flabby." This said, and with an eye to the chapters to come, let us not underestimate how far we have come if we pursue the naturalistic, evolutionary strategy—even the methodological strategy. I don't think we are pitched into the absolute idealism of Fichte—we are not just brains in a vat, soothed by a surrounding chemical bath and hooked up by wires to an external picture show—but we are in a world of our own psychology where what we believe is deeply dependent on our own nature. In other words, although he was no evolutionist, we are in the world shown to us by David Hume. We shall see more of this. I think Plantinga is wrong, but if I were he, I too would be running scared. To the extent that Peterson reflects these same ideas, I completely disagree with him. Godzilla is loose.

8

Morality

An Evolutionary Perspective on Ethics

Michael Ruse

The great thing about this debate I am having with Michael Peterson is that it is not just about God. It is about human beings: who they are, what they are like, what they can know, and now, perhaps the most important issue of all, what they should do. All of us, and this applies not just to those of us living in the West, will have grown up in cultures that have particular norms of behavior. Most of the time, we don't think about them. A parent picks up the kids from school because, well, that is what parents do. But then issues do come up. I doubt that parents today would feel comfortable about five year olds walking home unaided. And yet, that is what my loving parents allowed in the 1940s, and no one thought otherwise. So we have to think about these sorts of things and what is right and proper and why it is so. What matters of fact play in decisions—is it safe, for instance? (There was, for a start, a lot less traffic when I was a kid.) And should peer pressure be a determining factor? So do note that, although this chapter is about God and morality, in the end it is about us.

In this chapter, I argue that the traditional link between morality and God can be broken by evolutionary theory. Natural selection has shaped morality in ways that cause a serious reconsideration of the ground, taking it in a subjective and relativistic direction, as well as reconsideration of some of the content of traditional Christian morality. In the course of things, I critique theistic ideas—such as Peterson's—about the objective character of morality and the universal principles that supposedly constitute its content. In place of a religious view, I advance an understanding of ethics emerging from my Darwinian naturalism.

The Moral Argument for God's Existence

The other side to being made in the image of God is that we are moral beings. We have the knowledge of right and wrong and the capacity to act on this knowledge. In this we are different from rocks that have no freedom of the will and from lions and tigers that have no sense of morality. Because morality is so central to the Christian view of humankind, it is no surprise that it is taken as the lynchpin of one of the important proofs for God's existence. Peterson is among the many who argue that the only way we can make sense of our moral nature is in terms of a deity, and that deity is the one worshiped by Christians. John Henry Newman made the definitive case: "If, as is the case, we feel responsibility, are ashamed, are frightened, at transgressing the voice of conscience, this implies that there is one to whom we are responsible, before whom we are ashamed, whose claims upon us we fear" (Newman 1870, 109). The only being who would fit this bill is God. Anything less will not do:

> These feelings in us are such as require for their exciting cause an intelligent being; we are not affectionate towards a stone; we do not feel shame before a horse or dog; we have no remorse or compunction on breaking merely human law; yet so it is, conscience excites all these painful emotions: confusion, foreboding, self-condemnation; and on the other hand it sheds upon us a deep peace, a sense of security, a resignation and a hope, which there is no sensible, no earthly, object to elicit. (Newman 1870, 110)

If conscience can produce all the moral emotions, and if the emotions can be explained as conditioned by biological factors, then the force of the moral argument is diminished. This doesn't disprove the existence of God, but it does remove one firm support of the case for believing in God.

Explaining Morality

What says the evolutionist? In light of some of the appalling revelations in recent years about the sexual behavior of clergy in the Catholic Church, combined with evangelical campaigns against gays and women and others, not to mention opposition to global warming, there is a temptation to dismiss out of hand anything Christians say about morality. Although many of today's atheists happily go this way, we must resist following them. Let us accept that, whatever the weaknesses of individual Christians, the religion itself offers an impressive attempt to articulate and justify a system of morality. For many of us, indeed, Christian morality is morality. Darwin felt this way.

A prolegomenon to the discussion between Peterson and myself is to introduce an important distinction. First, there is the question of what I should do or not do. I shouldn't kill people for kicks or for personal profit. I shouldn't say unkind things about other people just on the basis of their race or skin color. In both cases, to do so is wrong. Working out the rules of morality is known as "substantive" or "normative ethics." Second, there is the question of why I should or should not do various things. What is the force behind "Thou shalt not kill"? What is the justification for saying that the Third Reich was an immoral society because of its treatment of Jews? This question of foundations, why should you or shouldn't you do things, is a key issue in "metaethics."

I won't spend time here worrying about the content of substantive ethics. Most of us agree on the basics—caring about children, telling the truth, being loyal, and so forth. I will have some qualifications to make later, but I do note that even the worst societies like the Third Reich don't deny everyday morality. What they do is alter the realm of application, arguing that Jews and gypsies and gays are not real people. In other words, as so often, it is not a matter of substantive ethics as such but of empirical claims about realization, applicability, and so forth. For now, think about foundations, and there is a choice of ways in which you can go at this point. One way is to think of ethics (meaning substantive ethics) as "out there" in some sense, something that we apprehend in some way, and the justification (metaethics) comes from the distinct, objective nature of this (independent of us) moral code. The trouble here, without getting into either God or evolution, is quite what is meant and entailed by "out there." If you think of some kind of nonnatural domain, rather like the Platonic heaven of mathematics, it is hard to know how ethics affects and guides us, apart from how we sense it in the first place. If you think of some kind of natural domain, then you run into the kinds of problems I highlighted right at the beginning. Modern understanding of the empirical world is done in terms of machines, and machines don't, as such, have values. This is one of the basic points that David Hume made. You cannot reason from the way the world is to the way you would like the world to be—from *is* to *ought*:

> In every system of morality, which I have hitherto met with, I have always remark'd, that the author proceeds for some time in the ordinary way of reasoning, and establishes the being of a God, or makes observations concerning human affairs; when of a sudden I am surpriz'd to find, that instead of the usual copulations of propositions, is, and is not, I meet with no proposition that is not connected with an ought, or an ought not. This change is imperceptible; but is, however, of the last consequence. For as this ought, or ought not, expresses some new relation or affirmation, 'tis necessary that it shou'd be observ'd and explain'd; and at the same time that a reason should be given, for what seems altogether inconceivable, how this new relation can be a deduction from others, which are entirely different from it. (Hume [1739–1740] 1978, III, I, I)

Darwinism and Morality

What about seeing morality as subjective, a matter of emotions or sentiments in some wise? This is very much in the British empiricist tradition. Hatred of cruelty is an emotion just as is hatred of Brussels sprouts. The former is a bit more elevated than the latter, but they are essentially the same. Here, in the light of evolutionary theory, especially Darwinian evolutionary theory, a lot of people think you do run into problems. How can something that starts with the struggle for existence, that today has morphed into what Richard Dawkins (1976) memorably has called "selfish-gene" theory, account for sentiments of right and wrong, for "altruistic" feelings toward others? Surely Darwin suggests *bellum omnium contra omnes,* a Hobbesian state of existence where there is "war of all against all"? The only reason that this is not so is because, whether or not following the prescriptions of Thomas Hobbes, in some wise we have transcended our biology. Our culture has taken over.

Biologists from Darwin on feel that this is to give far less than full credence to selection theory. Remember, when we introduced the struggle, the point was made strongly that often it is metaphorical and does not at all involve bloody gladiatorial clashes. Darwin and those in his tradition are fully aware of altruism, take it seriously, and, far from explaining it away, offer selection-based explanations. Darwin himself suggested that an important factor leading to a biologically grounded substantive ethics might have been what is today known as "reciprocal altruism"—you scratch my back and I'll scratch yours (Trivers 1971):

> In the first place, as the reasoning powers and foresight of the members became improved, each man would soon learn that if he aided his fellow-men, he would commonly receive aid in return. From this low motive he might acquire the habit of aiding his fellows; and the habit of performing benevolent actions certainly strengthens the feeling of sympathy which gives the first impulse to benevolent actions. Habits, moreover, followed during many generations probably tend to be inherited. (Darwin 1871, 1, 163–64)

Then Darwin added,

> But there is another and much more powerful stimulus to the development of the social virtues, namely, the praise and the blame of our fellow-men. The love of approbation and the dread of infamy, as well as the bestowal of praise or blame, are primarily due, as we have seen in the third chapter, to the instinct of sympathy; and this instinct no doubt was originally acquired, like all the other social instincts, through natural selection. (1871, 1, 164)

He elaborated, "To do good unto others—to do unto others as ye would they should do unto you,—is the foundation-stone of morality. It is, therefore, hardly possible to exaggerate the importance during rude times of the love of praise and the dread of blame" (1871, 1, 165). He added,

> A man who was not impelled by any deep, instinctive feeling, to sacrifice his life for the good of others, yet was roused to such actions by a sense of glory, would

by his example excite the same wish for glory in other men, and would strengthen by exercise the noble feeling of admiration. He might thus do far more good to his tribe than by begetting offspring with a tendency to inherit his own high character. (Darwin 1871, 1, 165)

I should say that in recent years there has been considerable discussion about the full meaning of these just-quoted passages and their implications for our own thinking about the evolution of morality (Richards and Ruse 2015). Does selection always work for, and only for, the individual, in which case we must show that help given to others rebounds in the form of help given to us (or possibly our relatives)? Or can selection work for the group, in which case help within the group exists because overall the group benefits and thus indirectly the individual does too? We need not go into this controversy here (West and Gardner 2013). It's enough that, to a person, Darwinians today think one can explain morality in terms of natural selection working on the units of heredity, the genes, although as with empirical knowledge there is realization that culture also has its role to play. Americans, thanks to the First Amendment, let bigots get up and spout hatred toward groups. Canadian law bans such public hate speech. Both societies have the same underlying morality and want to balance individual freedom against group harmony. It is just that culturally they have different ways of trying to achieve the same ends.

Suppose we accept all of this. What now about foundations, what about the metaethical questions? We have a naturalistic position that embraces evolution, but we cannot now appeal to naturalism. Hume's is/ought barrier stands in the way. Peterson tries to anchor ethics in the intrinsic value of persons who are created by God. I think the is/ought barrier still holds. But all of this raises the question of why we should appeal to anything at all. Why not simply say that substantive ethics has no justification? Substantive ethics is just a matter of what we think, no more and no less. This position, often known as "ethical skepticism" (note that the skepticism is about foundations), seems to have one major problem, making it entirely implausible. If substantive ethics is no more than feelings, emotions, why don't people cheat? I think I should help you, and you think you should help me, but then I realize that it is all an illusion of the genes, so I might as well not help you, or pretend to help you, and nothing more. Now, to make the case complete, we have to argue that nature not only made us cooperators by filling us with moral sentiments but also made part of these moral sentiments be that we think them more than just such sentiments! We must "objectify" ethics, to use an ugly word (Mackie 1977; Ruse 1986). Part of what nature has done is fill us with the feeling that morality is not a matter of choice but something laid on us from without. So when we feel inclined to cheat, we feel that we are going against something outside us, something objective. In that way, the genes keep the whole ethical system functioning. All of this has major negative implications for theistic objective ethics, such as Peterson's.

Implications for the Science–Religion Interface

Exactly what implications does this naturalistic explanation (of substantive ethics) have for our inquiry into the science and religion relationship? Let me make the negative case as strongly as I can and then pull back and moderate. I will raise three points where I think the explanation has negative consequences for the theistic and Christian position. First, there is no longer need to appeal to a God for support of the foundations of morality. In other words, the metaethical urge to God is gone. This does not disprove God, but it does take Him out of the picture. You might well think that if God has nothing to do with morality, then this somewhat diminishes His status. He is not quite the all-important being that theists generally and Christians in particular suppose Him to be.

Second, given the nondirectedness of Darwinian evolution, my suspicion is that the naturalistic account makes substantive ethics a lot more relativistic than believers like Peterson find altogether comfortable. Let me explain this. In one way, no one is going to deny that ethics is relative in some respects, as one goes from culture to culture. I just mentioned hate speech in the American and Canadian contexts. I realize that even this kind of relativism is going to trouble some believers, especially when we get on to tricky questions like gay rights. Canada has allowed gay marriage for some time, whereas America only recently came to this position—and for all the talk about separation of church and state, it is clear that religious factors were at play here. However, this is less an issue to do with evolution and more a matter of theological disagreement among believers. In another way, evolution does argue for relativism in a way that strikes more deeply at the thinking of all Christian believers. I don't see why *Homo sapiens* should have evolved to have the underlying biologically based moral beliefs that it has. Our species might have evolved what I like to call the John Foster Dulles system of morality, so named after President Eisenhower's secretary of state in the Cold War years of the 1950s. He hated the Russians, and the Russians hated him—this really was a matter of obligation—but both sides realized that the other side felt the same way about them, so they worked together to make sure that nuclear weapons were not used against each other. There was a kind of cooperation, but based on a different kind of morality from that which we have now. This just doesn't match up with the general theistic tendency to a universal ethic.

Darwin suggests that we can go even further than this:

It may be well first to premise that I do not wish to maintain that any strictly social animal, if its intellectual faculties were to become as active and as highly developed as in man, would acquire exactly the same moral sense as ours. In the same manner as various animals have some sense of beauty, though they admire widely different objects, so they might have a sense of right and wrong, though led by it to follow widely different lines of conduct. If, for instance, to take an extreme case, men were reared under precisely the same conditions as hive-bees, there can hardly be a doubt that our unmarried females would, like the worker-bees, think it a sacred duty to kill their brothers, and mothers would strive to kill their fertile daughters; and no one would think of interfering. Nevertheless the bee, or any other social animal, would in our supposed case gain, as it appears to me, some feeling of right and wrong, or a conscience. For each individual would have an inward sense of possessing certain stronger or more enduring instincts, and other less strong or enduring; so that there would often be a struggle which impulse should be followed; and satisfaction or dissatisfaction would be felt, as past impressions were compared during their incessant passage through the mind. In this case an inward monitor would tell the animal that it would have been better to have followed the one impulse rather than the other. The one course ought to have been followed: the one would have been right and the other wrong; but to these terms I shall have to recur. (Darwin 1871, 1, 73–74)

The third point I want to make is about our own system of substantive morality that evolution challenges. Who is our neighbor? The parable of the Good Samaritan suggests strongly that everyone is our neighbor, that we have equal obligations to all humankind. Yet, a Darwinian perspective on morality could never accept this. There would always have to be a differential sense of morality, with greater obligations felt toward one's own children than to anyone else, and from there out to cousins and more distant relatives. Although no evolutionist, David Hume spotted this: "A man naturally loves his children better than his nephews, his nephews better than his cousins, his cousins better than strangers, where everything else is equal. Hence arise our common measures of duty, in preferring the one to the other. Our sense of duty always follows the common and natural course of our passions" (Hume [1739–1740] 1978, III, 2, i). Charity begins at home, and Darwinian evolutionary theory explains why we think this is so. So here, too, it seems that science leads you away from Christianity.

Of course, you might say that it does so but that it does so falsely. In fact, we really think we have universal obligations to equal treatment. But do we really have such obligations? If you heard me praise someone for his goodness—he gives 90% of his salary to Oxfam—you might well ask about his spouse and children. If you learned that the spouse and children are dressed only in cast-offs from Goodwill and that the family regularly sups at the local soup kitchen, then I suspect you would no longer think that person a candidate for sainthood. As always, Charles Dickens is good on these sorts of things. In his great novel *Bleak House*, he criticizes savagely "philanthropists" like Mrs. Jellyby who spend their time on the Africa natives in Borrioboola-Gha and yet at the same time ignore the wants of their own children and the poor, like Jo, the crossing sweeper in their own society.

Christianity on Morality: Beyond Rescue?

Christians will have counterresponses, starting with the observation that in my whole discussion I am contradicting myself because I have argued that science must remain silent when it comes to morality, and yet here I am talking about it at length. Actually, this is an easy one to counter. There is no real contradiction. My point before, still kept here, is that science cannot justify morality. Science can certainly talk about morality just as much as it can talk about the mind and the brain, even if it cannot solve the body–mind problem. I don't think anything I have said here denies Christians the right to explain morality—foundations, that is—in terms of God. It is simply that it is not necessary. The explanation via evolutionary naturalism serves well.

But doesn't the argument about the nondirectedness of the evolutionary process deny the Christian God? If God wants us to do one set of things but evolution could well have us thinking that we ought to do another set of things, this is surely not a tenable position for the Christian. God cannot be irrelevant in quite that sort of way. To be fair, things are more complex than this, although whether this lets God off the hook in the end is another matter. By and large, Christians—certainly Peterson and others like him in the Thomist natural law tradition, deeply indebted to the naturalism of Aristotle—don't think of morality as a set of statements that God has thought up and that He then applies to the world. Rather, the creation of morality and the creation of the world go hand in hand (Ruse 1988b). God makes the world in a certain way, and then certain duties and obligations emerge from this creation, not deductively—that would be to go through Hume's is/ought barrier—but from the creation and how God wants it used. Take, for instance, male and female. We have different physical natures and different passions. God made us to have sex to have children. It is "natural" to have sexual intercourse. And inasmuch as it is natural, it is good. There are all sorts of qualifications one must put around this, for instance, about sex outside marriage and gay sex, but let us put these on one side. The point is that God created in a certain way; from this creation some practices fit in and some don't—some are natural and some unnatural—and God wants us to do the natural. That is doing good. Hating your fellow humans for no good reason—the Nazis and the Jews—is unnatural and therefore bad.

Given this kind of thinking, then, it seems that Peterson and other Christian ethical theorists can get around the particular problem of nondirectedness.

In the alternative scenarios, be they the world of John Foster Dulles's morality or that world of hymenopteran morality, certain practices would fit in and be natural, and hence good, and certain practices would not, and hence be bad. At a certain level, one holds constant the claim that God created, that certain things are going to be natural and others will be nonnatural, and this determines good and bad, right and wrong. Fair enough, but there is a cost, and I am not sure that Christians want to pay it. Constants notwithstanding, natural law thinking now builds a relativism about morality right into the system, but I am not sure that this is the impression one gets from reading the Bible. There things do seem to be absolute: "Honour thy father and thy mother: that thy days may be long upon the land which the Lord thy God giveth thee" (Exod. 20:12). Now things are a bit different. Honor your mother and your father, except if he is a drone, in which case your mother probably fixed your father long before you were born. And if you yourself are a drone, then there is no father to be honored anyway. Suppose, as seems plausible, that drones are intelligent beings, at least as much as their hard-working sisters. Indeed, in a kind of Greek way, they would have had the leisure to sit around and philosophize while their sisters really had been drudges, gathering food, looking after mother and the infants, protecting the group, and so forth. No time for reading. Then, apparently, morality dictates that the drudges kill the philosophers. Is this really what the Christian God desires? I certainly hope not!

Finally, what about the worry that evolutionary morality as we have it now goes against Christian prescriptions? What about the Christian imperative to care about everyone? There are responses that Christians can make, starting with the fact that some biblical passages seem to suggest we have special obligations to relatives: "But if any provide not for his own, and especially for those of his own house, he hath denied the faith, and is worse than an infidel" (1 Tim. 5:8). And, "Behold, the third time I am ready to come to you; and I will not be burdensome to you: for I seek not yours but you: for the children ought not to lay up for the parents, but the parents for the children" (2 Cor. 12:14). The trouble with this sort of game is that there are all sorts of quotes you can give going the other way. How about, "If any man come to Me and hate not his father and mother, and wife and children, and brethren and sisters, yea, and his own life also, he cannot be My disciple" (Luke 14:26)? Everything just dissolves into a conflicting mess.

In the final analysis, theistic and Christian ethical thinking conflicts with evolutionary ethics. In addition, the total set of biblical ethical prescriptions seems to involve internal contradictions. Here we start to veer from issues evolutionary to more general theological problems about Christian ethics. Let's just leave it that even if evolution does not give a knockout blow against Christian thinking on morality, it challenges it in deeper ways than many Christians, including proscience Christians, realize.

Morality and Personhood

Michael Peterson

Charles Darwin identified morality as "the best and highest distinction between man and the lower animals" (Darwin 1871, 1, 106). Nevertheless, Darwin suggested that this noteworthy capacity is rooted in evolutionary history and therefore could, in principle, accrue to any animal. Voices in contemporary sociobiology, inspired by Darwin's observations, assert that human morality is explained by reference to its evolutionary development rather than to God. However, this unnecessary dichotomy is overcome by locating scientific information about the evolution of morality within a more adequate philosophical worldview that provides context and interpretation. I argue that a theistic position makes better philosophical sense of the scientific facts as well as the presumptive ethical realism endemic to the human community. In contrast, naturalist interpretations of the evolutionary facts about the morality of *Homo sapiens* are hopelessly reductionistic and therefore systematically misunderstand this important aspect of our humanity. Michael Ruse's naturalist position involves a thoroughgoing metaethical antirealism that I critique according to my theistic metaethical realism. For the most part, the debate here pertains to the nature and status of ethics, but some clarifications about the content of ethics will also be necessary.

A Darwinian Genealogy of Morals

The standard Darwinian account of the origins of morality involves the idea that, in the contingencies of the evolutionary landscape, certain behaviors are adaptive. Propensities for such behaviors will also be adaptive; insofar as these propensities are genetic, they are heritable. Darwin held that "social instincts" passed on from our animal ancestors form the emotional basis of our moral behavior:

> In however complex a manner this feeling may have originated, as it is one of high importance to all those animals which aid and defend one another, it will have been increased through natural selection; for those communities which included the greatest number of the most sympathetic members, would flourish best, and rear the greatest number of offspring. (Darwin 1871, 1, 82)

Both *kin altruism* (directed at family members) and *reciprocal altruism* (shown to nonfamily members and even to strangers) play critical roles in survival and reproductive success. Relevant behaviors and propensities would be naturally selected.

Conscience, according to Darwin, arises when a certain degree of rationality develops and overlays the social instincts, interpreting and orchestrating them:

> The following proposition seems to me in a high degree probable—namely, that any animal whatever, endowed with well-marked social instincts, the parental and filial affections being here included, would inevitably acquire a moral sense or conscience, as soon as its intellectual powers had become as well, or nearly as well developed, as in man. (Darwin 1871, 1, 71–72)

In the human species, tendencies toward certain behaviors—care for children, returning kindness, and the like—have been labeled moral duties because they are adaptive given the circumstances of our evolutionary path. Natural selection has shaped our evaluative attitudes so that we consider good that which promotes the survival and flourishing of our species.

E. O. Wilson of Harvard University, the founder of sociobiology as an independent discipline, has declared that "the time has come for ethics to be removed temporarily from the hands of the philosophers and biologicized" (Wilson 1975, 562). When morality is returned to the philosophers, ideas of objective moral values or universal norms will have been replaced by factual descriptions of the biological role of human behavior within groups. Altruistic and cooperative behavior, when biologicized, turn out to be forms of egoism, choosing actions that are in the interest of our survival. Wilson even analyzes the ostensibly noble actions of Mother Teresa as subtle expressions of egoism, since "it should not be forgotten that she is secure in the service of Christ and the knowledge of her Church's immortality" (Wilson 1978, 165).

The Selfish Gene by Richard Dawkins explains human values and moral practices by reference to the gene—the basic unit of biological inheritance—which seeks only its own replication. Dawkins represents genes as active agents in control of their own destiny and thus in control of their own hosts:

> [Genes] swarm in huge colonies, safe inside gigantic lumbering robots, sealed off from the outside world, communicating with it by tortuous indirect routes, manipulating it by remote control. They are in you and me; they created us, body and mind; and their preservation is the ultimate rationale for our existence. (Dawkins 1976, 18–19)

Here we have overt science—that we all carry genes—entangled with covert metaphysics—that genes completely manipulate the behavior of biological entities, even at the moral level. This is the attempt to commandeer science to deny what we recognized in Chapter 7 as the emergent top-down causality in human persons. Why not say that helpless little genes have been captured by big rational agents who have powers to act that are not available at any lower level?

Ruse distances himself somewhat from Dawkins in explaining biologically how selfish genes lead to altruistic behavior. Yet Ruse's well-known evolutionary explanation still debunks and replaces traditional understandings of morality. Interestingly, Darwin excuses himself from doing metaphysics or moral theory, let alone theology, and should not be accused of advocating for a decidedly naturalist philosophical position. He clearly states that he wants to approach moral conscience scientifically, "exclusively from the side of natural history" (Darwin 1871, 1, 71). To navigate the issues correctly, we must differentiate the scientific *facts* about animal social behavior from naturalist *interpretations* of those facts. The primatologist Frans de Waal at Emory University uses his work with higher primates to make an empirical case for human morality being a product of our evolutionary past rather than coming from God (de Waal 2006, 1–80). Michael Ruse takes evolutionary theory as supporting the same conclusion. Whether emphasizing the empirical or theoretical side of evolutionary science in this area, naturalist philosophical assumptions ensure an ethical antirealist explanation that has the ring of science. Ruse and I agree that science *qua* science—operating by methodological naturalism—cannot justify ethics. Yet Ruse relies on his combination of evolutionary science and naturalism to dismiss or discredit ideas of a universal human nature or ultimate divine source as factors in the religious explanation of morality.

A Moral Argument against Evolutionary Naturalism

A philosophically adequate worldview must meet two criteria in interpreting morality: (1) it must make sense of the scientific facts about the evolutionary development of moral instincts and behaviors, and (2) it must make sense of the facts of our common experience as moral beings, which include our having moral beliefs about what is right and wrong, good and bad. Consider how E. O. Wilson and Michael Ruse articulate their understanding of morality:

> What Darwinian evolutionary theory shows is that this sense of "right" and the corresponding sense of "wrong," feelings we take to be above individual desire and in some fashion outside biology, are in fact brought about by ultimate biological processes. (Ruse and Wilson 1986, 179)

Ruse asserts that the objectivity of ethics "is a corporate illusion that has been fobbed off on us by our genes to get us to cooperate" (Ruse 1988c, 236). Since our moral beliefs were formed by evolution, we cannot trust them to reflect objective truth.

Selection pressures strongly influenced human psychology, including the formation of epigenetic rules, developed through the interaction of human genetics and culture, giving us strong propensities to believe and behave in certain ways. Ruse states, "Epigenetic rules giving us a sense of obligation have been put in place by selection, because of their adaptive value" (Ruse 1998, 223). Ruse further explains,

> The Darwinian argues that morality simply does not work (from a biological perspective), unless we believe that it is objective. Darwinian theory shows that, in fact, morality is a function of (subjective) feelings; but it shows also that we have (and must have) the illusion of objectivity. (Ruse 1998, 253)

Here claims that human moral beliefs are illusory and serve only reproductive fitness join the factual claim that morality is subjective rather than objective in nature. This is the morality reconceived—biologicized and naturalized—that Wilson would return to the philosophers.

Evolutionary naturalists typically engage in "debunking" traditional understandings of ethics. This metaethical debunking can be taken in epistemological or ontological directions. The epistemological argument is that the shaping of our moral beliefs by evolutionary forces means that they are not rationally warranted. Even if there are moral facts, biological processes did not form our moral capacities to provide insight into an objective moral order. Regarding the ontology of morals, the claim is that there simply are no moral facts because the natural world, which is all there is, does not include them. "Error theory" is the ontological view that the traditional realist assumption that there are objective moral facts is mistaken. Michael Ruse's work embodies both epistemological and ontological antirealist metaethical positions. Interestingly, some naturalists have endorsed various versions of metaethical realism, although I would argue that even metaethical realism without theism is philosophically unsustainable (Peterson 2017).

What's wrong with the epistemological debunking of ethics? Mark Linville observes that, for evolutionary naturalists, "the best explanation of having the moral beliefs we do makes no essential reference to their being true" (Linville 2009, 179). We would have those moral beliefs whether or not they are really true—because these beliefs are *fitness aimed* rather than *truth aimed*. Darwinian evolution is thought to entail a genesis of morality that becomes an undercutting defeater for our moral beliefs. Richard Joyce suggests that it was "useful for our ancestors to form beliefs concerning *rightness* and *wrongness* independently of the existence of rightness and wrongness" (Joyce 2006, 183). Unfortunately, the disconnect between our moral beliefs and any would-be truth makers for those beliefs inevitably results in moral skepticism. In what follows, I will show that this moral skepticism results when whatever Darwinian facts there are about morality are combined with naturalism. Thus, evolution per se is not a defeater for a realist understanding of morality.

Historically, the human community has been gripped by the profound conviction that we have *true* moral beliefs—and many people today basically understand that assorted factors contribute to these beliefs, ranging from biological propensities to mother's instruction. *Conscience* (from the Latin *cum* and *scientia*) means "common knowledge"—a grasp of the common fund of deeply held beliefs about what is right and wrong. The metaethical epistemological antirealism of evolutionary naturalism, then, clearly conflicts with a traditional realist metaethical understanding of morality, which takes our shared moral beliefs as knowledge.

The mistakes evolutionary naturalism makes about morality can be turned into an argument against it. Where N is the proposition that naturalism is true and E is the proposition that we have evolved through the natural selection of adaptive behavior,

1. If N & E is true, then human morality is completely the result of natural selection.
2. If human morality is completely the result of natural selection, then there is no objective moral knowledge.
3. But there is objective moral knowledge.
4. Therefore, N & E is false.

Let's talk through why this is so damaging to naturalism.

The conjunction of N and E in Premise 1 generates a defeater for our moral sense and any beliefs it produces. The resulting moral antirealism in Premise 2 entails that there is epistemic impropriety in taking our moral beliefs as really true. But Premise 3 is supported by the deep human conviction that our most basic moral beliefs are objectively true—a belief too strong epistemically to be overturned by skeptical arguments, Humean or otherwise. The skeptical doubts about or alternative proposals to Premise 3 always have less epistemic standing than our trust in our moral capacity to form reliably true beliefs. All of this means that evolutionary naturalism is completely unacceptable. N and E cannot both be accepted as true if we are to make full sense of our moral beliefs. Since evolutionary theory (E) is well confirmed as science and cannot be easily dismissed, philosophical naturalism (*N*) must be rejected.

The reason why there cannot be an *argument* or line of reasoning for why our moral capacity is valid is similar to why there cannot be an argument for the validity of rationality. Although we might initially grant the legitimacy of reason in justifying our moral capacity, there are no nonmoral starting points for reason that could ever result in a moral end point. At the most basic level, then, our moral capacity simply must be accepted as delivering to us fundamental moral insights or principles that are not derived from prior premises of any sort. They are self-evident moral truths. Hence, Hume is mistaken, argued his contemporary Thomas Reid, in thinking that, since moral conclusions cannot be derived from statements of fact, morality lacks objective status. Just as our rational capacity must be accepted and trusted before using it, so must our moral capacity. However, this doesn't mean moral beliefs are not objective knowledge (Reid 2010, 173).

That it is wrong to murder, steal, and lie—these are simply things we can't not know. C. S. Lewis employs the Chinese term *Tao* to signify objective morality:

> In the *Tao* itself, as long as we remain within it, we find the concrete reality in which to participate is to be truly human: the real common will and common reason of humanity, alive, and growing like a tree, and branching out, as the situation varies, into ever new beauties and dignities of application. (Lewis 1947, 86)

The tradition of objective morality is the realist view that certain attitudes, actions, and aims are aligned with the universe and with the kind of thing a human being is. However, morality is not objective in the sense that it is out there, independent of us and imposed on us; moral reality is objective in the sense that it is not subject to our desires or agendas. The idea of a natural law, or law of our natures, finds resonance in the book of Romans: "The work of the law is written on their hearts, while their conscience also bears witness" (2:15 English Standard Version). Rooted in universal human nature, objective moral principles are expressed somewhat differently across cultures and religions and are subject to situational application.

When Michael Ruse interprets morality purely as a Darwinian phenomenon, the facts of our common experience are dismissed and distorted. Thus Ruse's metaethical view falls short of a major criterion that I proposed for an adequate worldview interpretation of morality. All things being equal, that failure is a powerful reason to reject evolutionary naturalism. What science is telling us about the evolutionary precursors of morality in animal behavior that developed in response to the contingencies of evolutionary history is best interpreted by a realist metaethical approach, which, in turn, is best interpreted within the theistic worldview.

Theism and Personal Dignity

A moral argument for God can be reasonably based on the ability of the theistic worldview to meet both of our earlier criteria—accommodating the facts of evolutionary science and adequately explaining our common moral experience. Intellectual history has witnessed a wide variety of theistic moral arguments: that moral law requires a moral lawgiver; that moral choice is motivated by prospects of heaven and hell that must be ensured by God; and that God is the only way to make coherent rational sense of the human moral enterprise à la Kant. None of these arguments is on offer here.

Theism implies that God willed that our moral faculty be reliable in delivering true moral beliefs. In conjunction with evolution, this further implies that God somehow guided or influenced evolutionary processes so that rational moral animals would emerge and acquire a trustworthy capacity to form true moral beliefs. On evolutionary theism, moral beliefs possess reproductive fitness *because* they are true; fitness is not the only reason we have them. A mother has natural instincts to care for her children; it is also morally right that she care for them. With such thinking as part of my total set of background beliefs, the evolutionary story about morality doesn't become a defeater for my moral beliefs. Contemporary epistemology tells us that defeaters are person-relative and depend for their force on the other beliefs an individual holds—a point not noticed by naturalists who advance evolution as a rationality defeater for our moral beliefs. Evolution as an intended defeater is filtered and interpreted by my theistic perspective in ways described above. Of course, the naturalist mistakenly interprets evolution as a defeater simpliciter for theism. But, as a theist, I remain justified in having confidence that our moral faculty produces true moral beliefs.

Our moral faculty is much more likely to have evolved in ways that make it reliable for producing true moral beliefs on theism than on naturalism. Where M is the proposition that our moral faculty is reliable in delivering true moral beliefs, T is the proposition that theism is true, N is the proposition that naturalism is true, and E is the proposition that we have evolved through the natural selection of adaptive behavior, I contend that

$$P(M/T \ \& \ E) > P(M/N \ \& \ E).$$

Unlike the conjunction of naturalism and evolution, the conjunction of theism and evolution does not discredit the reliability of our moral sense in producing true beliefs. Instead, on theism, the moral epistemology works because God willed that our moral faculty be reliable. Moral truths are *mediated* through evolutionary processes but not *created* through evolutionary processes such that they cannot be completely relativized and subjectivized. Evolutionary theism accounts for both the scientific facts and the shared human moral experience. Thus, we have in our moral experience good reason to believe in God.

Having established that our moral judgments may be taken as generally reliable for truth, a further question arises: what would reality have to be like for our moral judgments actually to *be true*? Since morality deals with persons and their interactions in community, we are really asking for an ontology of persons that would provide adequate grounding for our moral beliefs about good and bad, right and wrong. It is important to recognize that a profound concept of *personal dignity* is implicated by our ordinary, pretheoretical moral beliefs—that is, the concept that human persons have intrinsic, unconditional value such that they should act and be treated in certain ways and not others. Beyond Michael Ruse's epistemological critique of morality, his "error theory" is that moral beliefs are false because there are no moral facts—that is, they have no ontological ground.

Significant overlap between naturalists and theists regarding classes of actions that are deemed right or wrong (substantive ethics) is witness to the force of our common moral intuitions. However, the disagreement between naturalists and theists over the ontology of persons (an infrequently visited area of metaethics) generates greatly different explanations of *why* certain actions are right or wrong. At a minimum, personal dignity—as entailed by our ordinary prephilosophical moral experience—requires that there *be persons*, that persons be genuine moral agents, and that they possess inherent value. Naturalism encounters serious difficulties in meeting any of these requirements and thus fails to support personal dignity. Theism, by contrast, supports personal dignity and all it entails.

Michael Ruse says we can't be sure that materialism is a correct view of mind but explicitly treats mind and persons as material things in his philosophical perspective. Most naturalists, as we have seen, are outright materialists of one stripe or another about human persons, denying that there is any such thing as a unique enduring conscious self or person. Francis Crick is doctrinaire in his reductionism of personhood to physical components:

> The Astonishing Hypothesis is that "You," your joys and your sorrows, your memories and your ambitions, your sense of identity and free will, are in fact no more than the behavior of a vast assembly of nerve cells and their associated molecules. (Crick 1994, 3)

Broader versions of naturalism, which often rely on minimal physicalist theories that appeal to supervenience, fare no better. Jaegwon Kim says that such theories seek to "declare amnesty for all of those valuable and obvious mental concepts that have lived in exile throughout much of the previous century" (Kim 2005, 15). Unfortunately, the causal closure principle, on which virtually all naturalists agree, fatally damages concepts of the supervenience of the mental on the physical. Thus, no mental event, however irreducible, can be a cause of a physical event—which means that there can be no real agency, operating by incompatibilist free will, that can be the cause of events.

Furthermore, Michael Ruse's naturalist universe exists purely by chance, which, in effect, makes it impossible to support the intrinsic value of persons. When evolutionary information about morality is elevated to the role of total explanation, moral antirealism results. In an effort to salvage some form of moral realism on behalf of a nontheistic worldview, Erik Wielenberg has ventured the hopeless naturalist thesis that "from valuelessness, value sometimes comes" (Wielenberg 2009, 40 n68). Wielenberg believes that objective values supervene on certain nonmoral states of persons, but the causal closure principle still thwarts supervenience, and a pointless naturalist universe does not support intrinsic value.

By contrast, evolutionary theism makes good sense of finite personhood such that its inherent value and contracausal free agency are part of the total picture. Personal dignity is conceptually at home within a theistic worldview framework in which finite personhood comes from the infinitely personal and morality and value derive from a supremely moral being of unsurpassable value. What a stark contrast this presents to the naturalist worldview that purports that the personal ultimately derives from the impersonal, the moral from the nonmoral, and value from the valueless.

For evolutionary theism, *Homo sapiens* represent the emergence of persons with rational and moral capacities. But theism takes the personal and the valuable as basic features of ultimate reality, not as derivative features. Personhood is the most fundamental reality and, in fact, in the order of reality, the nonpersonal derives from an infinite personal being. This personal being is the one thing that is both metaphysically and axiologically ultimate, such that personhood and value are necessarily united in that being: "At the heart of 'the natural order of things' is a divine consciousness" (Goetz and Taliaferro 2008, 84). For theists, this being is God.

A Theistic Genealogy of Morals

The conceptual power of theism is clearly displayed in a theistic genealogy of morals. God, who is an infinite personal–rational–moral being, willed that there be finite rational persons that reflect his moral nature. This means that God and human persons share an overlap of kind membership in personhood itself. Human dignity is found precisely in membership in that kind. Personhood *just is* the kind of reality that is intrinsically and unconditionally valuable. Persons have inherent worth—and we are to value them accordingly. According to the theistic worldview, human persons have been fashioned after the most ultimate and sacred feature of reality and thus participate in that sacredness. Moreover, God chose that human personhood would emerge in a sufficiently complex animal form over evolutionary time.

Our moral faculty, then, is aimed at valuing persons and making objectively true judgments about how to treat them appropriately. Obviously, if we were not biological beings, some moral considerations would not apply to us—say, regarding sexual behavior or gratuitously inflicting pain. But even our biology is nevertheless that of a certain kind of personal being—a rational moral animal—of exquisite worth. It is not simply that rationality now adjudicates among instincts, as Darwin indicated, but that our rationality uplifts and elevates human morality far above the most advanced instincts of our animal ancestors. This theistic conception of humanity—both scientifically informed and yet profoundly realist—underwrites moral life.

Christian orthodoxy adds to the theistic understanding of the human moral endeavor that God is a Trinity. The doctrine of the Trinity implies that God's own inner life is inherently social, interpersonal, and relational, characterized by unending joy, peace, and love. God's purposes in creating finite personal life are therefore relational: God invites finite persons—who are made "in his image"—into fellowship with himself and with other persons. *Human* personal dignity, although intrinsic, is derivative. This means that human beings have a distinctive destiny or *telos*—which is to participate in the very life of God. In other words, the qualities of God's own life are to take root and grow in our lives in a transformative way. No wonder Jesus promises in the Gospels that life in God is abundant and joyous. The emerging picture is of a relational God creating a relational universe in which relational beings are very much at home.

In a relational universe, morality guides our interactions with others. Jesus taught that all commandments rest on two foundational principles: that we are to love God with our whole being and love our neighbor as ourselves (Matt. 22:36–40). Morality, then, has a point and a purpose: fostering and protecting loving relations among all personal beings. Love, for example, would not defraud, damage, or destroy others: thus, we have moral prohibitions on treating persons in such ways. Although morality developed along an evolutionary path, it is not purely a product of the evolutionary process. Explaining the evolutionary development of our capacity to make moral judgments no more undercuts the objective truth of those judgments than explaining the evolutionary history of the eye preempts its ability to see a real external environment.

There are no essential conflicts between a Christian perspective and evolutionary science regarding morality. Christianity contextualizes the findings of evolutionary science within a larger framework of God's purposes for humanity. Michael Ruse argues that Christian and biblical viewpoints have problems with the nondirectedness of evolution because it leads to ethical relativism. But it is no part of science to claim that evolution is nondirected and thus supports ethical relativism; that, too, is part of the naturalist world picture. And it is clearly not against the spirit of science for theists to hold that God worked through evolutionary processes to bring about higher moral beings—and that God did this while respecting the integrity of created secondary causes and the nondetermined contingencies that occur in their operation. I discussed these matters extensively in Chapter 6. Again, it's not really the evolutionary facts—but rather the naturalist interpretation of those facts—that conflicts with theism and Christianity. Minus naturalism, the evolutionary facts about morality are able to be sensitively explained within a theistic and Christian worldview.

What about Ruse's claim that the moral teachings of the Bible seem to be absolute and thus in conflict with evolutionary relativistic ethics? First, any literature on any point must be read in terms of its historical epoch, social circumstance, and cultural forms. Second, normal literary devices and figures of speech must be recognized as well: we can thus correctly understand Jesus's hyperbole as "hate your parents *in comparison to loving me*." Fairly interpreted, the moral understanding arising from the anthology of biblical books, written by multiple authors over a long period of time, represents properly ordered moral principles as well as practical maxims and embedded explanations that constitute an enlightened moral tradition.

Defending his view that morality is cut off from any foundation, Ruse also argues the Humean line that we cannot derive moral obligations from empirical facts, including the Darwinian facts. However, Hume's alleged is/ought barrier mistakenly assumes that there are only concrete, empirical facts that are completely value neutral. By contrast, the theistic and Christian analysis above shows that metaphysical facts—particularly about human nature—are required to make full sense of morality. The metaphysical facts of what a person is and of how the unconditional dignity of finite persons is linked to the value of God as an infinite personal being ground our moral beliefs about the treatment of persons in the very structure of reality. From these fundamental metaphysical facts about the inherent value of persons, we derive our beliefs about our moral duties.

Ruse is likewise mistaken that evolutionary ethics and Christian ethics are incompatible in that kin altruism (in evolutionary ethics) and neighbor love (in biblical ethics) cannot be reconciled. Darwinian ethics, as Ruse points out, explains why we have a greater sense of obligation to one's own children than to anyone else, whereas the Christian ideal of neighbor love recognizes the equal intrinsic worth of all persons *qua* persons in God's image. But there is no essential conflict here. In a Christian moral universe, both conceptually and practically, there is indeed an ordering of the loves—*ordo amoris*, as Augustine said (Augustine 2009, Bk. XV, chap. 22). This ordering is patterned on the nature of the different relationships and roles people represent in our lives.

Aquinas correctly reasoned that, in general, the natural law morally requires one to love one's family members more than one's extrafamilial neighbors, both "in regard to inner affection and in regard to outward effect" (Aquinas 1981, *ST* II.ii, Q. 26, Art. 6–8). Our more elevated moral capacities had relatively primitive evolutionary precursors, which is why evolutionary biology has information to contribute to the more refined understanding of morality made possible by Christian moral teachings. Still, in the worldview of Christian theism, moral life is a central aspect of the temporal fulfillment as well as the ultimate destiny of our humanity. According to Aquinas, natural law morality is thus "participation in the eternal law on the part of the rational creatures" (Aquinas 1981, *ST* II.ii, Q. 94, Art. 2).

9

Evil and Suffering

Theism, Atheism, and Evil

Michael Peterson

Evil and suffering are the basis of the most serious challenge to religion generally. What is typically known as the problem of evil is most acute for theism because of its strong claims regarding the unrivaled power, wisdom, and goodness of God. Essentially, the challenge for theists is that of reconciling the negatives of this world with their high and lofty claims about God. Evolutionary science further complicates the problem because various types of pain, suffering, and evil are now known to be inherent in the very fabric of the living world. In this chapter, I engage this most difficult of issues, discuss it in light of science, and develop a theistic response.

As an evolutionary naturalist, Michael Ruse takes the position that evil and suffering are strong reasons to reject theism and embrace atheism. Our disagreement is deep and involves differing perspectives on free will and sin as well as the acceptability of different proposals for God's purposes. Even in the face of the difficult phenomena of evil and suffering, my contention, as always, will be that theism rather than atheism provides the more reasonable and plausible explanation.

The Argument from Evil and Suffering

The philosophical problem of evil is best understood as an argument that is problematic for those who find the premises credible and yet don't like the atheistic conclusion. The logical argument from evil, which prevailed throughout much of the twentieth century, was based on the contention that the claim that God exists and the claim that evil exists are inconsistent. During the 1970s, philosophers recognized that the free will defense as crafted by Alvin Plantinga was successful against the logical formulation of the argument (Peterson 1998, chaps. 2 and 3). However, the demise of the logical argument simply cleared the way for a more accurate version of the objection from evil.

The evidential argument—classically advanced by William Rowe and effectively echoed here by Michael Ruse—has long been considered the strongest formulation (Rowe 2014). A basic version goes as follows:

1. There are evils that are not necessary to a greater good.

(Factual Premise)

2. If an omnipotent, omniscient, wholly good God exists, then he would not allow evils to exist unless they are necessary to a greater good or the prevention of an evil equally bad or worse.

(Theological Premise)

Therefore,

3. God does not exist.

(Conclusion)

Premise 1 is a factual claim, a statement of the evidence; Premise 2 embodies a typical position on how God could be morally justified in permitting evil.

Now, let us use the term *gratuitous evil* to refer to an evil that is not necessary to a greater good or to the prevention of an evil equally bad or worse. The theological premise construes theistic claims about God's power, wisdom, and goodness to entail that God would not allow gratuitous or pointless evils to exist. That is, all evils allowed by God would serve a greater good. The factual premise is a placeholder for generalizations about pointless evils or for specific instances of evil that seem pointless. Since the argument is logically valid, if there are good reasons to believe 1 and 2, then there are good reasons to believe 3. Debate therefore revolves around the truth or plausibility of the premises. Interestingly, most theists and their critics accept the theological premise, making the factual premise the main focus of controversy.

Ruse, like Rowe, cites dramatic examples of evil to justify acceptance of the factual premise, arguing that, on careful reflection, we see no greater good to which these evils are necessary. Both *natural evils* (evils caused by the operations of nature) and *moral evils* (evils caused by the wrongful actions of human persons) supply ample material. Rowe's fawn suffering an agonizing death in a forest fire or Ruse's antelope caught by the cheetah seem to be unnecessary evils in a theistic universe. An Indonesian tsunami wiping out thousands and pancreatic cancer killing a young mother just begin the list of natural evils affecting humans. Many moral evils also appear pointless—a five-year-old girl raped and strangled by her mother's drunken boyfriend, cited by Rowe, and the extermination of Anne Frank, cited by Ruse. All provide rational grounds for believing Premise 1.

Skeptical theist defense rejects the factual premise on the basis that we humans cannot know that such evils are not connected to any greater goods (Wykstra 1984). Finite humans, it is said, cannot fathom God's infinite wisdom and cannot perceive all of the goods there are or all of the connections between goods and evils. Hence, it is not reasonable for critics to claim that the failure to discern any goods for the sake of which God allows some evils is an adequate reason for thinking that there are no such goods—and thus that the evils in question are gratuitous. I don't embrace this defensive strategy because of my realist presumption about the reliability of our created moral belief-forming capacities. It's appropriate simply to remind us that human moral evaluation of the pointlessness of a given evil may be mistaken but not to pronounce our judgments in these matters to be systematically mistaken. Besides, theodicy, not defense, is the traditional approach that theists have taken in response to the problem of evil.

Science and Approaches to Theodicy

A theodicy is an explanation of God's permission of evil—coming from the Greek *theos* and *dikē*, it is technically a "justification of God." Most theodicies function by connecting evil to a greater good or set of greater goods that could not otherwise be realized—goods ranging from moral development to deeper appreciation for the good. Gottfried Leibniz is famously summarized as contending that this is the "best of all possible worlds" because a perfect deity would choose the best possible world (Leibniz 2001, 67, 128). Accordingly, the actual world contains the least amount of evil commensurate with its being the best world on the whole, such that eliminating any evil would actually make the world worse on balance! Unfortunately, theodicies grounded only in basic theism may make interesting proposals about God's *possible* reasons for evil but lack the resources for making claims about God's *actual* reasons that must be drawn from a living religious tradition. In the present discussion, I'll draw from major Christian thinking on the subject of evil.

Augustinian and Irenaean theodicies loom large in Christian history (Peterson 1998, chap. 6). Themes from St. Augustine continue to dominate thinking about theodicy in the Western church: the familiar V-shape pattern of creation–fall–redemption. God created an originally "good" world in which a completely innocent, sinless couple, Adam and Eve, the parents of humanity, had the power to sin or not to sin. Although blessed in the paradisal state, Adam disobeyed God, thereby falling into sin and becoming deserving of punishment. All humans inherit "original sin" from Adam via human generation, become unable to refrain from sin, and are subject to damnation. Augustine thought that the negative consequences of sin also include pain, suffering, and death in the physical world. God's plan of redemption is aimed at restoring fallen humanity—and all of creation—through the death and resurrection of

Jesus Christ (Augustine 2009, *CG*). Although themes in Augustinian theodicy include the idea that God's redemption is unilateral and selective (monergism), the larger context of church doctrinal reflection affirms that divine grace extends to all humanity and enables authentic response to God's salvific offer (synergism) (*Catholic Catechism* 1994, 482–484).

For Augustine, the "greater good" is the overall beauty and worth of a created universe that experiences sin and the wonderful redemption it necessitates. Augustine says, "God deemed it better to bring good out of evil than to permit no evil to exist" (Augustine 1955, *Ench*, Bk. VII, sec. 27). Following this tradition, Alvin Plantinga offers the interesting argument that God's goal was to bring about an unsurpassably good world—a world containing the incomparable good of Incarnation and Atonement (Plantinga 2004). As Plantinga explains, Incarnation and Atonement are necessitated only in a world that falls into sin—what the ancient Easter liturgy calls a "fortunate crime" (*felix culpa*).

Science is relevant to various renditions of Augustinian theodicy. First, paleoanthropology, genetics, and related sciences indicate that there cannot have been a single primeval couple—a point conflicting with literal interpretations of Genesis. The rub is not so much against Augustine, who advocates properly understanding the meaning of scripture that is embedded in various literary formats (Augustine 1982), but against Augustinian-type theodicies involving verbatim readings. Second, science questions whether it is meaningful to say that early humans were "perfect," either morally or physically, since moral maturity can't be created by fiat, and physical perfection incoherently suggests biological immortality. Third, both genetics and common sense indicate that sin isn't transmitted by human procreation, which opens the way for other thoughtful explanations of the reality of transmission. For example, the cultural transmission model of Karl Rahner, which recognizes the historical situation of human beings, is insightful (Rahner 1982, 110–11). John Wesley's interpretation of historic orthodoxy on this point is that sin is a spiritual disease of preferring one's selfish interests, rather than an entity or state that is transmitted (Wesley 1988, Sermon 13). Such issues deserve detailed analysis in another venue to clarify what is theologically essential in creation–fall–redemption in a manner consistent with well-known scientific and other extrabiblical facts (e.g., see Alexander 2008; biologos.org).

St. Irenaeus, a bishop in the early Eastern Church, provides a somewhat different theological vision for theodicy. Irenaeus pictures Adam and Eve as childlike, innocent, immature, and imperfect and therefore needing to grow and learn. The sin that comes signals weakness and vulnerability as much as deliberate revolt. God-given freedom and responsibility are strongly emphasized; wrongdoing is straightforwardly blamed on the individual sinner; the universality of sin among the human race is affirmed; and the need for all persons to be redeemed through Jesus Christ is declared. The world is an environment where human beings, originally created in God's "image" (Greek: *eikón*), can be brought by a more difficult aspect of divine creative activity into God's "likeness" (Greek: *homoiósis*). The overarching good in Irenaean theodicy is, then, the development into greater moral and spiritual maturity (Irenaeus 1869, v.vi.I).

British philosopher John Hick articulated his "soul-making theodicy," inspired by Irenaeus, which was crafted around correlations between theological themes and evolutionary claims about the developmental trajectory of humanity. Hick states,

> At the very least we must acknowledge as two distinguishable stages the fashioning of *Homo sapiens* as a product of the long evolutionary process, and his sudden or gradual spiritualization as a child of God. . . . The first stage . . . was easy for omnipotence. By an exercise of creative power God caused the physical universe to exist . . . and finally to produce out of organic life personal life; and when man had thus emerged out of the evolution of the forms of organic life, a creature had been made who has the possibility of existing in conscious fellowship with God. But the second stage of the creative process is of a different kind altogether. It cannot be performed by omnipotent power as such. For personal life is essentially free and self-directing. It cannot be perfected by divine fiat, but only through the uncompelled responses and willing co-operation of human individuals in their actions and reactions in the world in which God has placed them. (Hick 2010, 255)

A person who attains goodness by mastering temptations and overcoming evil is good and virtuous in a richer sense than one created from the beginning in a state of innocence or virtue. (Logically, of course, it is impossible to create virtue by fiat because virtue entails having developed moral dispositions by habitual action over time.) The world, which includes pain, hardship, catastrophe, and suffering, thus serves as an environment for the soul-making process.

One thing is clear: that classical Christian theology contains important conceptual resources for addressing the problem of evil and suffering. The Augustinian approach is historical and causal, whereas the Irenaean approach is forward looking and eschatological. Yet neither of these great traditions is incompatible with science, and both gain by allowing well-confirmed scientific knowledge to inform and check the implications they draw for theodicy. Interestingly, both traditions, in their own ways, designate greater goods that could not be attained without evil.

Theodicy for a Scientific Age

What we need is a theodicy that is theologically orthodox and scientifically informed. Traditional theodicies address the argument from evil by proposing some good or set of goods for which evils in the world are necessary—essentially denying the critic's claim that there are gratuitous evils. Although containing interesting insights, such theodicies will always seem strained and unrealistic. The way forward for theodicy is to admit that it is still more reasonable than not to accept the factual premise. The common human judgment that there are gratuitous evils has weighty philosophical and theological support.

On philosophical grounds, there is strong presumption in favor of the general reliability of our rational and moral faculties. Therefore, when reflection on certain evils detects no goods for which they are necessary, it is reasonable to believe that the world would be better, or at least no worse, if God had prevented them. Granted, not everything is as it appears, and some apparently pointless evils may, on further consideration, be seen as having a point. But we are talking here about general trustworthiness, not exceptions, in our moral evaluations. Most thoughtful people believe there are many evils without which the world would genuinely be better. The realist in me agrees with Michael Ruse and other critics that it is entirely reasonable to believe that many apparently gratuitous evils are really gratuitous. But Ruse isn't a moral realist—and we must think about that in a moment.

Theologically speaking, the judgment that there are gratuitous evils also has strong support. God endowed finite human persons with rational and moral faculties that reflect powers God himself possesses in infinite measure. The reliability of our faculties does not mean that all beliefs we form enjoy a divine guarantee, but it does mean that the orthodox Christian cannot take a position that implies that our rational and moral judgments about evil and other basic matters are systematically mistaken. Traditional theodicies mistakenly overrule the persistent human judgment that there are gratuitous evils by specifying some good or goods that our careful evaluations supposedly don't reveal. Skeptical theist defense mistakenly exaggerates the implication of the finite–infinite gap between human and divine to mean that human moral judgment on these matters is incompetent and that only God's infinite wisdom sees how evils are connected to greater goods. One wonders how Christian theodicists, who hold either that all evils are connected to greater goods, or skeptical theists, who hold that humans are in no epistemic position to discern such connections, can marshal moral energy to try to alleviate, change, or reform bad situations.

Speaking of positions that undercut the status of our moral evaluations, what about Michael Ruse's own metaethical antirealism that was discussed in the previous chapter? If our moral beliefs aren't about objective moral truths, and if there really are no objective moral truths, then the critic's factual premise claiming the existence of gratuitous evil lacks the evaluative force it needs. Yet the premise is advanced as being objectively true and reasonable to believe— that certain negative states are not or could not be justified by any greater good. My ready response is this: the atheistic critic—just as much as the believer—is made in God's image and therefore possesses the capacity to make reasonable objective moral judgments in this area. Atheist and theist both believe at a deep level that there are evils without which this world would genuinely have been better. However, the metaethical antirealism of Ruse's atheistic naturalism can't provide adequate standing for this belief, which is needed in forming the factual premise in the atheistic argument from evil. Intriguingly, theistic metaethical realism can properly support this belief.

Since I take the factual premise as well grounded, I take the real weakness in the argument from evil to be the theological premise, which assumes that God would not allow the existence of any gratuitous evil. The premise assumes what I have called the principle of meticulous providence: the idea that God arranges the evils of this world such that they are all necessary to a greater good (Peterson 1982; Peterson et al. 2012, 189). Versions of theism that are committed to meticulous providence will never generate a satisfactory response to the argument from gratuitous evil. In fact, under the auspices of the meticulous providence principle, some Christian believers have too often spoken with sermonic certitude and in sweeping fashion about why God allowed or brought about various evils. Theodicies in this vein are themselves, as Terrence Tilley has observed, the cause of much psychological and emotional damage (Tilley 2000). For such statements about God's purposes, sincere, humble apologies to a hurting world are long overdue.

A theodicy is needed that rejects meticulous providence and develops a conception of God's general providence that accounts for existence of gratuitous evils. Since standard theism lacks sufficiently detailed information on this matter, certain implications of Christian orthodoxy will also be required. The doctrine of the Trinity implies that God is an inherently personal, relational, self-living Life whose nature is self-giving, self-sacrificing love. Creation by this Three-Personal Life graciously placed finite reality on an evolutionary trajectory that would eventually bring forth personal–rational–moral beings that are intimately related to the physical realm and can relate to God.

This mainstream construal of the doctrines of the Trinity, creation, and humanity entails that this is a deeply relational universe. Only in a truly relational reality can certain great goods—such as love, self-giving, free pursuit of the good, and interpersonal communion—be realized by finite rational–moral creatures. For the universe to be genuinely relational, it must possess two important features: free will and physical law. Yet these features involve risk or contingency in creaturely outcomes—risk that free beings will not always do what is right and risk that the operations of the physical order will not always accommodate human aims and agendas. Nevertheless, this world, with its inherent risks and dangers, is a good type of world that makes possible all sorts of great goods. To those who say it was not worth it for God to create, I ask, not worth it for whom? Surely it was worth it for humans: otherwise we would not exist and the whole moral enterprise would not be underway.

Human free will—conceived in libertarian terms—is necessary to moral and spiritual growth. Libertarian free will is incompatible with any form of determinism, physical or divine. My friend Michael Ruse endorses a compatibilist view of free will, maintaining that actions caused by the operation of scientific laws can still be called "free." Among the laws at work are Darwinian laws, which explain much about human drives, instincts, and behaviors, as we have seen. Interestingly, Augustine's theology of divine sovereignty takes human free will in a compatibilist direction as well. Irenaeus is more clearly an incompatibilist, stating, "God preserved the will of man free and under his own control" (Irenaeus 1869, Bk. IV, chap. 37, para. 5). I argue that incompatibilism is the only view that makes sense of authentic moral and spiritual life. I believe, with Michael Ruse, that physical laws are a necessary structural feature of reality, but I also see them as crucial to the emergent human self. However, the self as agent can, in turn, exercise top-down causality, which is the power to bring about new events that would not have occurred by the normal workings of laws. I made this argument in Chapters 6 and 7.

Physical laws provide a stable structure in which libertarian free will can operate and choices can have predictable consequences. C. S. Lewis makes the point that a lawlike natural world is necessary for a relational or interpersonal reality:

> As soon as we attempt to introduce the mutual knowledge of fellow-creatures we run up against the necessity of "Nature." People often talk as if nothing were easier than for two naked minds to "meet" or become aware of each other. But I see no possibility of their doing so except in a common medium which forms their "external world" or environment. . . . What we need for human society is exactly what we have—a neutral something, neither you nor I, which we can both manipulate so as to make signs to each other. . . . Society, then, implies a common field or "world" in which its members meet. (Lewis 1962, 30–31)

Indeed, there is a vulnerability to our material existence as personal beings that makes it possible for us either to help or to hurt one another. And the operations of the physical world itself can be either favorable or unfavorable to human agendas and aims.

Animal suffering is also an integral part of the way the physical world works. The same evolutionary processes that make for increasing health, function, and complexity also involve pain, predation, and death in the subhuman animal world. Science tells us that these processes have been going on for a long time, well before the appearance of humans, and yet are responsible for the biological creature we are. Obviously, theological explanations that make animal pain and suffering a result of human sin stand corrected by the known facts, but none of this detracts from the theodicy I'm articulating. Although the problem of animal pain deserves thorough treatment, I here briefly suggest that part of the answer runs along lines discussed above—that lawlike natural processes involving pain and death contribute to the survival and flourishing of species by providing warning systems and the like, and thus aiding evolutionary advance.

Our world involves the interplay of chance and law, contingency and necessity, which makes possible many goods. Particularly for our purposes, these goods include relational goods. Yet a world constituted in this way makes possible evils that are not necessary to any greater good. To eliminate the very possibility of unnecessary evils is extensionally equivalent to eliminating the possibility of important goods. The stock broker who says he has an investment for you that involves all reward and no risk is lying because upside and downside potential are commensurate. The more wonderful the goods made possible by the very makeup of the world we inhabit, the more horrendous the possible evils. The significant degree of freedom that makes possible amazing deeds of nobility and love also makes possible senseless and destructive acts of hostility, cruelty, and greed. Many terrible evils are not necessary to greater goods, but their *possibility* is necessary in a world in which higher goods may be sought (Peterson 1982, chap. 5).

God allows creaturely realities—or secondary causes—a range of operation that he does not meticulously control. Nondetermined contingency, in human action as well as in the natural world, makes this a world open to various alternative possible outcomes. In creating an environment in which great relational goods may be sought, God thereby opens himself to the outcomes of creaturely decision and the resulting challenge of drawing free creatures to himself. All of this means that the existence of gratuitous evil does not count against the existence of a God who is not conceived as ruling it out. When evils come, however, the Christian emphasis is always that God works redemptively to bring good out of them. Marilyn Adams has even argued that, for those who experience horrendous evils, which cannot be outweighed by any set of finite goods, the redemption of their situations may come only in the eschatological fulfillment of all things in the presence of God himself (Adams 1999).

Evil and the Clash of Worldviews

Although theism faces the difficulty of explaining evil, every worldview must explain evil based on its own conceptual resources. Convinced atheists must also provide an explanation of evil based on their worldview commitments. Just as theism finds larger context in Christian orthodoxy, so atheism finds larger context in philosophical naturalism. Then how does atheistic naturalism fare in the debate over evil?

Consider William Rowe's final assessment that the problem of evil and suffering in our day, coupled with "reason and science," makes atheism more rational to believe than theism:

> In an age of faith, before the growth of scientific knowledge that produced alternative, credible explanations of the emergence of human life, [the problem of suffering] would not lead to disbelief. But the age of faith has been replaced by an age of reason and science. And in this age of reason and science, for many human beings the idea of God no longer plays an essential, rational role in explaining the world and human existence. The idea that human suffering may be divine punishment for human sin and wickedness is no longer a credible explanation for many educated human beings. (Rowe 2006, 87–88)

Rowe commits the fallacy noted earlier that theism and science offer competitive explanations, whereas they actually offer quite different types of explanations, without being compartmentalized, as I have already argued. Rowe's calculus is that theism's inadequacy in explaining evil could not lead to atheism until a more complete explanatory alternative emerged, which we allegedly now have in science. We are already familiar with Michael Ruse's perspective combining naturalism and science.

As I have argued, theism is not under pressure from science and actually provides the most adequate worldview framework for interpreting the reality of science itself. The real conflict is between theism and naturalism at the worldview level. In this light, I have contended throughout the debate with my friend Michael Ruse that naturalism, even coupled with science, does not provide an explanation at the worldview level that explains important phenomena as well as theism coupled with science explains them. The philosopher Paul Draper also takes this matter in terms of worldview comparison but thinks that "evolution is evidence favoring naturalism over theism" (Draper 2008, 208). All else held evidentially equal, according to Draper, evolution makes naturalism much more probable than theism, at least twice as likely. Speaking directly to the problem of evil, he argues that the patterns of pain (and pleasure) in the biological world, which are closely linked to reproductive success, are more probable on evolutionary naturalism than on evolutionary theism.

However, the whole idea that selecting one piece of evidence and stipulating that all other evidence must be given equal weight in the rational scales is an artificial and misleading setup of the situation. For one thing, even if we pretend that all else is evidentially equal, the description of the evidence of evolution, including the pain involved in the biological world, seems to tip the scales toward naturalism only if a minimal, unsympathetic, and unnuanced definition of theism is in play. Yet, for one thing, the theistic deity might well have chosen evolutionary laws to characterize created nature. For another thing, all else really isn't evidentially equal. There are many other probabilities in the neighborhood that strongly favor theism. In previous chapters, I argued that the very fact of finite existence, life itself, and the appearance of rational and moral beings are all more probable on theism. Without discounting the challenge of evil for theism, naturalism certainly doesn't account for evil better—say, by contending that the evils of the exact texture and depth we have in our world are much more probable on naturalism than on theism.

Naturalism fails in explaining the depth and texture of evil that occurs within a total world context that includes natural law and personal beings with a variety of special characteristics. Naturalists assert that nature is the fundamental reality, hold a materialist view of persons, typically endorse a relativist theory of morality, and deny that the universe has any purpose or meaning. Pain and suffering, then, fit into a naturalist universe as effects of the operations of the total system; evildoing occurs perhaps as maladaptive social behavior. Given naturalism, it is difficult to see how the objection from evil against theism can assume the moral significance and high regard for persons that it does. However, critics of theism, who are made in the image of God and share our common humanity, know at a pretheoretical level that this world is not as it should be. Understandably, their reactions to evil are better than their philosophy.

Comparison of theism and naturalism on the question of evil reveals that naturalism has its own difficulties in accounting for all we know about evil and suffering. Just as theory choice in science must ultimately be based on all of the relevant evidence, so the choice between theism and naturalism should be based on how well each worldview explains a wealth of important phenomena—such as rationality, morality, and personhood. I have already made the case for the superiority of theism in explaining these other phenomena (Peterson 2013, 83–85). Now, in the theistic context already developed—where persons are intrinsically valuable, moral ideals have objective status, and the whole universe is given purpose by God—the theistic explanation of evil begins to make sense. More remains to be said to fill in this sketch. But this kind of world—including its inherent possibility for evil—is very much worth creating. No wonder that our world has the feel of a good world that is damaged, not of a world described by atheistic naturalism.

Darwinism and Evil

Michael Ruse

The problem of evil is generally taken as furnishing the strongest of all arguments against the Christian God. He is all-loving. Hence, He does not want evil to exist. He is all-powerful. Hence, He can prevent evil. And so evil should not exist. Yet it does exist! Hence, God is not all-loving, or He is not all-powerful, or both. There are various ways of blocking this argument, and I think it fair to say that today many Christian philosophers are congratulating themselves on their successes in this direction. You can point out that love does not necessarily mean no pain or strife. The parent chastises the child (these days more figuratively than literally) to bring on a greater good, namely an obedient and helpful adult. Likewise, sometimes God punishes us for our greater good. Think of David and Bathsheba and how much better he was when God took strong action against the killing of her first husband. You can also point out that power does not necessarily mean the ability to do anything whatsoever. We have seen God's limitations with respect to mathematics, and although it was dismissed as heretical, we have seen how some (process theologians) want to limit God's powers generally. Neither Michael Peterson nor I want to go too far down this path here. These are more theological issues than strictly to do with science, including evolutionary biology.

I will say in passing, however, that I do not find the defenses to be convincing, and there is a strong feeling within me that I don't want to find an escape clause for the problem of evil. I can think of no way one can excuse the death of Anne Frank in Bergen-Belsen, and if my eternal salvation demands her death, I am just not interested. I am, of course, not the only one to feel this way. Ivan Karamazov powerfully makes the point in Dostoevsky's novel *The Brothers Karamazov*:

> "Imagine that you are creating a fabric of human destiny with the object of making men happy in the end, giving them peace and rest at last, but that it was essential and inevitable to torture to death only one tiny creature—that baby beating its breast with its fist, for instance—and to found that edifice on its unavenged tears, would you consent to be the architect on those conditions? Tell me, and tell the truth."
>
> "No, I wouldn't consent," said Alyosha softly. (Dostoevsky [1880] 2007, 229)

It is hard to know what to add to that.

In this chapter, I make the case that pointless evils are telling against theistic and Christian belief and, thus, why I embrace atheism. Rather than attempt defensive ploys, Peterson engages the issue head-on with his own theistic explanation. Yet I argue that his and all other theistic and Christian explanations of evil are unsatisfactory.

Does Darwinism Intensify the Problem?

What about Darwinian evolutionary biology in particular? From Darwin on, there have been thoughts that no good can come from it, at least no good for Christians. Writing to Asa Gray in a letter, part of which was quoted earlier to show his deism, Darwin was blunt:

> With respect to the theological view of the question; this is always painful to me.—I am bewildered.—I had no intention to write atheistically. But I own that I cannot see, as plainly as others do, & as I sh^d. wish to do, evidence of design & beneficence on all sides of us. There seems to me too much misery in the world. I cannot persuade myself that a beneficent & omnipotent God would have designedly created the Ichneumonidae with the express intention of their feeding within the living bodies of caterpillars, or that a cat should play with mice. Not believing this, I see no necessity in the belief that the eye was expressly designed. (Darwin 1985–, 8, 224)

Expectedly, this problem has not escaped the eagle eye of Richard Dawkins. Using the notion of "reverse engineering," for the process of picking backward to try to work out something's purpose, and of a "utility function," for the end purpose being intended, Dawkins draws our attention to the cheetah/antelope interaction, asking, "What was God's utility function?" Cheetahs seem wonderfully designed to kill antelopes: "The teeth, claws, eyes, nose, leg muscles, backbone and brain of a cheetah are all precisely what we should expect if God's purpose in designing cheetahs was to maximize deaths among antelopes" (Dawkins 1995, 105). But, conversely, "we find equally impressive evidence of design for precisely the opposite end: the survival of antelopes and starvation among cheetahs." Do we have two gods, making the different animals and then competing? If there is only one god who made the two animals, then what on earth is going on? What kind of god is this? "Is He a sadist who enjoys spectator blood sports? Is He trying to avoid overpopulation in the mammals of Africa? Is He maneuvering to maximize David Attenborough's television ratings?" In a like vein, the philosopher Philip Kitcher, who once argued for the compatibility of science and religion, now finds the horrors of the evolutionary process too great to stomach or ignore. He fears that "the story of a wise and loving Creator, who has planned life on earth, letting it unfold over four billion years by the processes envisaged in evolutionary theory, is hard to sustain when you think about the details" (Kitcher 2007, 122–23).

Expectedly, Christians are not insensitive to these worries and do argue back. The retired British philosopher-theologian Keith Ward finds comfort in a gentler evolutionary process than the stark traditional picture of conflict. He writes, "On the newer, more holistic, picture, suffering and death are inevitable parts of a development that involves improvement through conflict and generation of the new. But suffering and death are not the predominating features of nature. They are rather necessary consequences or conditions of a process of emergent harmonisation which inevitably discards the old as it moves on to the new" (Ward 1996, 87). Here Ward stands in a tradition that goes back at least to John Muir, the Scottish transplant who founded the American environmental group the Sierra Club: "I never saw one drop of blood, one red stain on all this wilderness. Even death is in harmony here" (Muir 1966, 93).

This is all very well, but we do still get pain and suffering. Tales of "emergent harmonization" are of little comfort to the fawn facing the hungry wolf. And as I pointed out in the previous chapter, there is still considerable debate about how holistic the evolutionary process truly is. For every evolutionist who thinks that selection can work for the good of the group, there are probably at least ten who think that it can work for and only for the good of the individual. Muir was deeply influenced by the Romanticism of Wordsworth, with its nigh-pagan beliefs in world spirits and living earths, "a spirit, that impels / All thinking things, all objects of all thought, / And rolls through all things."

Original Sin

Can we dig ourselves out of this hole? Yes, but there are costs, and they may be higher than Christians are willing to pay. Start by making a traditional distinction between two kinds of evil. On the one hand, we have moral evil. This is the evil of Auschwitz brought on by human action. On the other hand, we have physical or natural evil. This is the evil of the tsunami brought on by the forces of nature. Focus for the moment on the former. Anne Frank died in Bergen-Belsen. Sophie Scholl, one of the leaders of the White Rose group opposing the Nazis, died on the guillotine in Munich. How does one explain these evil events? Through free will: "God therefore neither wills evil to be done, nor wills it not to be done, but he wills to permit evil to be done, and this is good" (Aquinas 1981, *ST* I, Q. 19, Art. 9). The freedom of Hitler and of Goebbels and the rest of the sorry Nazi crew is an absolute good and outweighs the suffering of those two young women and all others who died because of the Third Reich. God Himself is free. God is good. We are made in His image. Hence, we too are free. Our freedom, therefore, is good. We could not speak of Hitler and Goebbels as evil were they not free. The wolf is dangerous; it is not evil.

I am not now in the business of asking whether this is an adequate answer. You know my opinion. Peterson differs from me here, although I suspect that it is true to say that he has as little sympathy as I do for the softening moves of someone like Keith Ward. Not only—in line with points already made—does Peterson think the science points unambiguously to pain and suffering, but also at some theological level, he does not want to minimize this fact. He does see this as a harsh world, and for him that is what makes truly meaningful the sacrifice on the cross. But we have already seen the case that Peterson makes that a theistic world allows the possibility of real evil.

Here, I am particularly interested in whether Darwinism impinges on the relation of evil and freedom—and I can see that it does in two ways. First, ask why it is that creatures made by a good God would sin in the first place. Why wouldn't they always behave themselves? This seems logically possible. Apart from anything else, Christians believe that Jesus was sinless. The Christian answer—that is, the Augustinian Christian answer—is that Adam sinned and the rest of us are tainted by this act. We are born without sin but we have an initial predisposition toward it and so, rapidly, we fall into it:

> Therefore original sin is seen to be an hereditary depravity and corruption of our nature diffused into all parts of the soul . . . wherefore those who have defined original sin as the lack of the original righteousness with which we should have been endowed, no doubt include, by implication, the whole fact of the matter, but they have not fully expressed the positive energy of this sin. For our nature is not merely bereft of good, but is so productive of every kind of evil that it cannot be inactive. (Calvin 1960, Book II, chap. i)

We are still free agents, so we are responsible and deserving of punishment. It is because of this that Jesus died on the cross, thus taking up the burden and freeing us from our rightful (unpleasant) merits.

As always, rush past the theological questions—about whether such a dreadful punishment as being expelled from paradise was merited for the failure of a naive man bewitched by a scheming serpent, or about how we get tainted because of what Adam did, and about why Jesus's death on the cross pays off our debts. Is the Father quite such a sadist as this? Turn to the science. What about Adam and Eve? No sin up to that fateful moment when they took a bite, and then all hell let loose. Part of the reason why there was no sin is because there was no one else around—they were supposedly the first unique human couple—and part of the reason is that everything was perfect in paradise until they fell. Here, I am afraid we get just as much of a clash between science and religion as we do with Noah's flood or Jonah's whale or Joshua's stable sun (Ruse 2012). Given Darwinian evolutionary biology, it is just not true that humankind was ever reduced to one pair—at the least there were always thousands—and they had ancestors like them who fought and squabbled and made up and loved. Sin did not arrive on one afternoon when the fruit was hanging low on the bough. It just didn't. I don't know how far developed was the thinking of "Lucy," *Homo afarensis*, that little hominin that Don Johanson found back in 1974 in the Ethiopian wilds—she lived about 3 million years ago, had a brain about the size of a chimpanzee, and walked upright—but I (and any professional paleoanthropologist) would be willing to bet that sometimes she did things that were wrong and knew pretty much that what she was doing was wrong. Dogs certainly feel this way, so why not our ancestors?

Is there no way out? A number of thinkers have pointed out that Augustine's take on sin is not the only Christian option or even the first (Schneider 2010). It is the standard for Catholics, Lutherans, and Calvinists, but the Eastern Orthodox have always been more inclined to the earlier thoughts of already-mentioned Irenaeus of Lyons, who argued that original sin refers less to an actual act by one rather pathetic human and more to the whole developmental nature of the creation. God made us incomplete, and the story of salvation is God working out His long-determined purpose of making us whole. Apart from getting around the Adam and Eve problem, this viewpoint rather expects sinners before them, and hence it makes God far less of an improviser. On the Augustinian position, the Incarnation is Plan B. Things have gone wrong, and God has to rally around to put them right. On the Irenaean position, God anticipated the need of the Crucifixion from the beginning. Since Michael Peterson is a Methodist who looks to a more ancient orthodoxy (rather than a Calvinist), he is inclined toward "Arminianism," meaning that he thinks we have freedom in (what is generally known as) the incompatibilist sense to accept God's offerings or not. He is less inclined to put everything down to the harsh judgment of God and sees more freedom in human life than does a Calvinist. For him, the Augustinian doctrine of original sin does not have a stranglehold, and many of the theological themes in Irenaeus are attractive for addressing the problem of evil and suffering. Theologically, of course, there are still issues about why this kind of suffering was needed in the first place, but God is off the hook for making an inadequate human and then overreacting rather badly when things went wrong.

Free Will

Move on. Ignore the fact that faculty at Christian colleges lose their jobs for this kind of thinking. Let us assume that we at least are willing to jettison 1,500 years of Western Christian theology for the sake of staying onside with modern science and keeping the faith. What about that free will for which so much is being sacrificed? Basically, there are two philosophical strategies on offer here. First, you have "libertarianism." This is not the philosophy of Ayn Rand, so beloved of the American Tea Party, where the state is kept out of individual life. This is the incompatibilist idea that free will is genuine and not bound by the laws of nature. It does not so much break them as stand outside them. The great German philosopher Immanuel Kant is the touchstone here:

> Since the conception of causality involves that of laws, according to which, by something that we call cause, something else, namely the effect, must be produced; hence, although freedom is not a property of the will depending on physical laws, yet it is not for that reason lawless; on the contrary it must be a causality acting according to immutable laws, but of a peculiar kind; otherwise a free will would be an absurdity. (Kant 1959, sec. 3)

This certainly goes with our intuitions. The rock falls and has no choice in the matter. At the end of a long day of writing on science and religion, I turn to the drinks cabinet and decide whether to have a gin and tonic or a glass of sauvignon blanc. It is my choice. I could have done otherwise. The point is that I am beyond cause—I drink because I am thirsty—but into reasons—I anticipate the bouquet of the wine and decide to forgo the tangy tartness of the g and t.

But apart from questions about whether reasons could be causes, do I really freely decide here? I could no more end the day with a Babycham—a rather disgusting sparkling pear cider—than I could fly to the moon. You could make me of course. You could put a gun to my head. You could offer me an all-expenses-paid, business-class flight, week in Paris with Catherine Deneuve. Best of all, you could bribe me with a season's pass to the Metropolitan Opera. But then I wouldn't really be free. For an evening of Donizetti I would even drink Diet Coke. This points to the second philosophical strategy tackling free will, compatibilism, which I embrace. Here you agree that everything is determined. Humans are as subject to the laws of nature as are rocks. The crucial distinction is between constraint and liberty. A person in chains, a person hypnotized, a Ruse with opera tickets dangling before his eyes, is not free. An end-of-the-day philosopher choosing gin or vino is free, although he or she is causally bound in his or her decisions. Indeed, argues the compatibilist, without law there is no freedom. If I suddenly start yelling in the middle of *The*

Marriage of Figaro and there is no reason for it, I am not free. I am crazy and no longer responsible. And don't think, as some do, that appealing to quantum mechanics is going to make any difference. It is true that an individual quantum event may not be predictable, but apart from the fact that group events are predictable, if I suddenly fly off the handle because of an unpredictable quantum event, I am even crazier than otherwise.

Obviously, you can be a libertarian and a Darwinian because this is the position of Michael Peterson. But the more Darwinism succeeds, then the less libertarianism seems an attractive option. The more the rule of law applies absolutely and completely to humankind, the more compatibilism seems the way to go. I pay exorbitant fees to put my kids through college. Part of this is the genetic drive to care about family and see that my genes keep going. Say what you like, a child who is a schoolteacher is going to be better fixed than a child who is a homeless bum. Part of this is cultural because I would not dare do less for my children than my colleagues in the department. "Oh, hi Mike, you're looking relaxed." "Yes, I just got back from a month in the south of France. Cost a fortune though. You look pale, how about you?" "Well it was a tough summer doing that extra teaching, but the fees at Harvard are so very high." Yeah! This is Diet Coke territory, at least as far as I am concerned. Not much libertarianism around the Ruse household as the kids grow up. Compatibilism starts to look like an attractive option. Humans are bound by laws like everything else, and in our case the laws involve a lot of Darwinian biology; but there is not total constraint—I am just about free to tell my kids that, after the pension meltdown of 2008, I am prepared to sock it to them for a good state college, but some fancy liberal arts college is out of the question. On the freedom front, after nigh 4 billion years of evolution, this may not seem like much of a bargain, but as any parent will tell you, you take what you can get.

Interestingly, at this point Darwinism speaks up on behalf of compatibilist free will. Forty years ago when understanding of the evolution of human social behavior (sociobiology) was being developed, there were somewhat hysterical fears expressed that we were on the road to "genetic determinism" (Ruse 1979b). Humans will have no more responsibility than ants. We really will be Dawkinsian gene machines. These fears were grotesquely overblown. Humans have taken an evolutionary strategy that points in a different direction. Ants really are genetically determined. They need no schooling to do what they do instinctively. This is a good policy because teaching takes effort from other needed activities, like food gathering. But it comes with a cost. If something goes wrong, a genetically determined insect has no recourse. It cannot change strategy. It cannot go around the new puddle caused by the rain because it doesn't know how. In the nest, this doesn't really matter because so many offspring are being produced. If an individual is killed, there are lots more to take its place. Humans have gone a different route. We produce just a few offspring, and so we cannot afford to lose them when things go wrong. We have to have built in the ability to go around the puddle because there are no ready replacements. So we have to have a dimension of flexibility—call it freedom—not possessed by ants and rocks. As Daniel Dennett (1984) has pointed out perceptively, we are like the Mars Rover that, although causally determined, thinks for itself. Ants are like rockets with no homing devices: cheap, but not that reliable.

One final point about free will: you may complain that, no matter how the compatibilist reframes free will, in the end there is no freedom anyway. An omniscient being can tell you from the beginning what is going to happen. Taking allowance for quantum effects—which, as suggested, really don't help with free will—this is true. So doesn't everything collapse in the end? Yes and no. Many Christians will find it threatening, but Calvinists will welcome it. On the one hand, we have enough freedom to be responsible for our acts, and if we sin, we can be sent to hell legitimately. On the other hand, who ever thought that God would not know even before He created what would happen? God is totally sovereign. It was His choice absolutely who would go to heaven and who to hell. Our future is "predestined." God is just as well as merciful, a judge as well as a parent. Let us never forget that. You may not like this kind of Christianity. I suspect that many Christians do not like this kind of Christianity. To be fair, Peterson doesn't like it and embraces an alternative vision in which God allows a significant range of contingent outcomes for creatures. But many, including those who do not much like it, think it true. And those like Peterson who do not think it true have problems of their own, like how much control God has over the universe and why He has to keep bailing us out when He Himself was responsible for our unfinished nature.

Natural Evil

We have a good idea now where we are going here. It's all a matter of what God can and cannot do. We start with the fact that God is constrained to create through laws and to use these laws to keep the whole system afloat. Did God have any choice on this? Who knows, but we can be certain that had He gone other routes, He would have created as many problems as He solved. Without gross deception about our origins, humans would need to be made eliminating all of the putative marks of natural ancestry. Could this even be done? I am not sure. Of course, He could have been a lot more into the miracle business, as many Christians—for instance, the supporters of IDT, not to mention theistic evolutionists who have God busy at the quantum level—think that He is. But the science apart, note that you are now starting to raise theological worries. If God was prepared to get His hands dirty in the creation of, let us say, *Australopithecus afarensis*, an early hominin, then why was He not prepared to get His hands dirty to prevent the death of Anne Frank? And if you say He is not in the business of saving children from the Nazis, then—to pick up on a point made earlier but sufficiently important to be made again and again—why does He not prevent the horrendous effects from deleterious mutations? My oldest son worked for several years at a camp supported by the March of Dimes. I cannot speak sufficiently highly of his love as year after year he and his fellow workers gave kids (and their families) a little break from the horrendous routine of daily life—a time to forget and to laugh and to enjoy childhood—or of the heartbreak as year after year children he had grown to know and love no longer came to camp. This is why simplistic design arguments always fall to the problem of evil.

Given law, I have spoken already of what I think is the solution open to Christians at this point. It is one made famous by Leibniz and, although parodied by Voltaire in *Candide* as pointing to undue optimism, makes good sense. Creating through law poses restrictions. Even God cannot make a functioning cat the size of an elephant. Weight goes up by the cube, whereas legs go up linearly. A cat the size of an elephant needs tree-stump legs like an elephant, not the elegant limbs of the felid. Yet, whatever the restraints, organisms need adaptations to function—organisms without eyes and ears and bark and leaves are not organisms. Adaptations are designlike; they exhibit organized complexity. How can this be done, given the constraints of nature? Richard Dawkins (1983) argues that the only way you are going to get this is through natural selection. Things like random macromutations on their own lead only to disaster, malfunctioning. And other putative processes like Lamarckism just don't work. So I think God is off the hook for natural suffering, at least in the immediate sense. In the long run, things may be otherwise. I have made it clear that I am not in the John Muir–Keith Ward camp about animal suffering. I am more with Darwin and Dawkins and Ivan in the Dostoevsky novel. I am just not convinced that the end is worth the means. And if you say that it is, then I think you must qualify what you mean by "loving," and I, for one, wonder about God's omnipotence and even more about His freedom. It all starts to seem to me that God, if such there be, creates out of divine necessity, that this was bound to happen, and that He does not have a great deal of control over the process. Perhaps predestination applies not only to humans.

10

Meaning and Purpose

A Stark Picture Indeed

Michael Ruse

I will switch tactics now and plunge into the sociological, but only for a short while, as you will see, because then the conversation will swing right back to the philosophical. As you will also see, if you have not yet realized, although I have my beefs with the Christians, they are nothing to the beefs I have at times with my fellow nonbelievers. Now I will sound smug and self-satisfied. For me, it is never the conclusion alone that counts. It is always how I get to that conclusion. I guess that is the result of years of undergraduate teaching and trying to get students to reason properly. I don't want to base my nonbelief on what I think are faulty premises and arguments, and I think too often that is just what happens. So the fact that I sometimes criticize those with whom you might think I should feel solidarity does not prove me to be a Doubting Thomas. Let me quote that very Christian poet T. S. Eliot in *Murder in the Cathedral*: "The last temptation is the greatest treason: To do the right deed for the wrong reason" (Eliot 1935, Act 1). I would say the same of beliefs. If we are to hold a position of importance, let it be for the right reasons.

Where Are We?

Let's sum up. I argue that science is deeply metaphorical and that the root metaphor of modern science is the machine. This means that science simply rules out certain questions as unanswerable: about the fact that there is something rather than nothing, the foundations of morality, the nature of mind, and the ultimate ends of things. I argue also that, thanks to Charles Darwin, evolutionary biology entered fully into modern science. We are survival machines. In this sense, therefore, I am an accommodationist, thinking that science and religion can coexist, because although I personally am skeptical about the answers to the unanswered questions of science, I think it perfectly legitimate for the religious person to offer answers. It is just that they cannot be scientific answers. This does not mean that I am backed into accepting religion, the Christian religion, as true. On the one hand, it is fully open to someone like me to criticize the basic claims of religion on philosophical or theological grounds.

On the other hand, the Christian religion wants to make many more claims than these basic claims, and there it opens itself up to criticism, including criticism based on science.

As you have seen, I do think that there are theological and philosophical problems with the Christian religion. I think its notion of God is an unhappy and probably, in the end, irresolvable amalgam of Greek reason and Jewish faith. I think its notion of God as a necessary being is nigh incoherent, at least very implausible. I do think that science, Darwinian evolutionary biology in particular, poses grave problems for Christian believers. We have just seen that it makes simply untenable the idea of a unique founding pair of humans, Adam and Eve—and because of this, the venerable Augustinian explanation of original sin is blown to smithereens. Earlier, we saw that the nonnecessity of the evolutionary process leads to big problems about the appearance of humankind at all, and most of the possible solutions in the literature are just not up to it. To solve this issue, it might be necessary to have God doing all sorts of things—billions of multiverses, for example—that themselves create horrendous new theological problems. Overall, Darwinism causes massive headaches for natural theology, that branch of the business devoted to proving the existence of God through evidence and reason. It is true that not all Christians want to go the route of some kind of natural theology, but many have so wanted and still do—Catholics, for instance, and this is true also of Michael Peterson. But the argument from design is an argument in tatters—a point on which Peterson agrees—and the argument from morality is in no better shape—a point on which Peterson disagrees. Moreover, I have suggested that the freedom of God is starting to look severely compromised. He is starting to seem more like an elemental life force acting through necessity than a being with personlike qualities who freely decides and acts.

Why Do We Believe?

So, this leads me to my final question. What has gone wrong? Why do humans believe in God or gods? Why are so many of my fellow Americans such deeply committed Christians? What is it about human nature that makes us so susceptible to such a pack of untruths? Understand, now, I am not talking deliberate deception. I am not with the Grand Inquisitor saying that we all know that this is a pile of bunkum, but we need it to keep the troops happy, although I am also not saying that religion has never been used this way. There is a fair amount of cynicism about religion in American politics. I am interested in why people believe and what this means for our discussion. One thing is certain, namely, that someone like me needs a natural explanation of religion; otherwise, I am open to the objection—one Peterson endorses in his own way—that people believe because it is true. Some even say that, if it is true, no further explanation is needed. I have to have an explanation.

For the past 150 years, anthropologists and sociologists have been providing such explanations. Emile Durkheim sets the pace: "A religion is a unified system of beliefs and practices relative to sacred things, i.e., things set apart and forbidden—beliefs and practices which unite in one single moral community called a Church, all those who adhere to them" (Durkheim 1912, Bk. 1, chap. 1). Note here how the emphasis is on the group experience rather than the isolated individual. Religion gives people a sense of belonging, of community. Perhaps understandably, over the years the biological sciences and the social sciences have not always been the best of friends. To a great extent, this has been a matter of territory, about who has authority to speak in what realm. This is still true, but it is also true that, with more or less sensitivity, evolutionists have been moving into the area of cultural explanation and that religion and its underpinnings have been a big focus of attention.

Traditionally, evolutionists' thinking on the subject goes back through Darwin to David Hume. Although no evolutionist, Hume was very much a naturalist. It is all a matter of mistaken perceptions: "We find human faces in the moon, armies in the clouds; and by a natural propensity, if not corrected by experience and reflection, ascribe malice or good-will to everything, that hurts or pleases us" (Hume [1757] 1963, 78). From such simple beginnings, we build up the elaborate edifices of medieval Catholicism and more. Darwin (who read Hume on this subject with some care) took up the refrain. He thought his dog—"a full-grown and very sensible animal"—a good guide to the reason why there is "tendency in savages to imagine that natural objects and agencies are animated by spiritual or living essences." The dog was disturbed by a parasol blowing in the wind: "Every time that the parasol slightly moved, the dog growled fiercely and barked. He must, I think, have reasoned to himself in a rapid and unconscious manner, that movement without any apparent cause indicated the presence of some strange living agent, and that no stranger had a right to be on his territory" (Darwin 1871, 1, 67). Thus, from moving umbrellas to Jesus Christ walking on water in one or two easy steps.

Of course, even if we accept that because religion is not about the real world and that there must have been some mistaken perceptions in its genesis, if it does persist, it must have some function that selection picks up and improves. There is nothing odd about this. The Darwinian thinks that this sort of thing often happens in the physiological world. Picking up on themes from Durkheim, Edward O. Wilson tries his hand: "In the midst of the chaotic and potentially disorienting experiences each person undergoes daily, religion classifies him, provides him with unquestioned membership in a group claiming great powers, and by this means gives him a driving purpose in life compatible with his self interest" (Wilson 1978, 188). Culture is involved, but biology is the foundation: "Because religious practices are remote from the genes during the development of individual human beings, they may vary widely during cultural development. It is even possible for groups, such as the Shakers, to adopt conventions that reduce genetic fitness for as long as one or a few generations. But over many generations, the underlying genes will pay for their permissiveness by declining in the population as a whole" (178). Culture can play the variations, but the underlying themes are biological.

If only for the sake of argument, let us give their case to Wilson and his fellow Darwinians. Remember how Stephen Jay Gould used to complain that many such explanations of this ilk are akin to what the English novelist Rudyard Kipling called "just-so" stories (Gould and Lewontin 1979). I am sure there is truth in this complaint of Gould. If anyone, say, tried to put down a belief in transubstantiation to a peculiar gene, one would rear back. Did a convert to Catholicism like John Henry Newman have a biological disposition that was not possessed by his fellow members of the Oxford Movement who did not convert? I doubt it. The truth, however, is that so much to do with religion does seem so biological or molded to fit with biology. Food taboos are an obvious example, but there are other things. I am always fascinated, given the supposed sanctity of marriage, how it is that, when a spouse dies, there are no major theological objections to taking up with a new mate. Why are the priests not losing sleep over the possibility that, when we get to heaven, we are all like the unfortunate husband in Noel Coward's farce *Blyth Spirit*, where he has two wives—eventually both dead—nagging him and making life impossible? Perhaps this is so, although for personal reasons I very much hope not. But the real reason surely is that people need mates—to live, to have love and friendship, to raise children, and all of those sorts of things. Successful religions keep in biological line or, like the Shakers, they end up on the garbage dump of history.

Evolutionary Debunking?

Agree, then, that it is not a matter of being true or false but whether religion plays a useful biological function, and let us agree that it does. In this respect, it is not much different from morality. We are better off with it than without it, although I do think we have an empirical question here. I cannot imagine a society without morality. I can imagine a society without religion. Indeed, some societies in Europe seem already to be on that way, and the same can, in respects, be said of some of the members of the British Commonwealth—New Zealand, Australia, Canada (Ruse 2015). There is still a lot of religion if you look, but it is less and still declining. In the Province of Quebec, for instance, in the past half century the drop has been dizzying. I suspect that much has to do with what comes in replacement. A good state social net may be both a necessary and a sufficient condition. But let us leave this and related questions. Instead, let us agree that the skeptic like myself can find in evolutionary biology, fleshed out by the findings of the social scientists, reason enough to explain the existence and persistence of religion, true or false.

The question that must be raised now is whether giving a natural explanation automatically implies that religion is false. Wilson seems to think that the very act of giving such an explanation is enough. He thinks that because of our biology, not only are we religious, but also we must have a religion. We must therefore turn to new alternatives: "But make no mistake about the power of scientific materialism. It presents the human mind with an alternative mythology that until now has always, point for point in zones of conflict, defeated traditional religion." We must now have a kind of secular religion, based on evolution: "Its narrative form is the epic: the evolution of the universe from the Big Bang of fourteen billion years ago through the origin of the elements and celestial bodies to the beginnings of life on earth." He concludes, "Theology is not likely to survive as an independent intellectual discipline" (Wilson 1978, 192).

All of this is fine and dandy but in itself doesn't show religion is false, any more than an evolutionary explanation of how I see and hear the locomotive heading down on me means that the locomotive is not really heading down on me. After all, if religion be true, it would be odd if it did not give group cohesion and support. The New Atheists do try to plug the gap that Wilson leaves open. Dawkins, for instance, sees all sorts of good biological reasons why we might believe the sorts of things our elders tell us. Adopting a version of the theory of cultural transmission we saw earlier, he writes,

> When a child is young, for good Darwinian reasons, it would be valuable if the child believed everything it's told. A child needs to learn a language, it needs to learn the social customs of its people, it needs to learn all sorts of rules—like don't put your finger in the fire, and don't pick up snakes, and don't eat red berries. There are lots of things that for good survival reasons a child needs to learn. (Dawkins 1997)

All of this is supported by natural selection: "Be fantastically gullible; believe everything you're told by your elders and betters." In the case of religion, we have a virus of a particularly pathological kind. Before you know where you are, you are in deep trouble:

> "You must believe in the great juju in the sky," or "You must kneel down and face east and pray five times a day." These codes are then passed down through

generations. And there's no obvious reason why it should stop. Even worse is the fact that those viruses that are really good at their job are precisely those with the most awful and dangerous messages. So, if the virus says, "If you don't believe in this you will go to hell when you die," that's a pretty potent threat, especially to a child. (Dawkins 1997)

All of this may be true, but I am not sure that it shows that, simply because it has a natural explanation, religion is false. I am not even sure that it shows that religion is bad. At least part of the trouble here is that Dawkins is priming us with emotive language like "gullible" and "virus." These are not part of the argument proper, and there are indeed some viruses that have good effects. The same verbal trickery can be found in Daniel Dennett's explanation of the spread and hold of religion. He works more at a cultural level than a biological level, and rather than a virus, he uses the metaphor of a parasite:

> You watch an ant in a meadow, laboriously climbing up a blade of grass, higher and higher until it falls, then climbs again, and again, like Sisyphus rolling his rock, always striving to reach the top. Why does this happen? The ant gets nothing out of all of this activity. Its brain has been commandeered by a tiny parasite, a lancet fluke (*Dicrocelium dendriticum*), that needs to get itself into the stomach of a sheep or cattle in order to complete its reproductive cycle. This little brain worm is driving the ant into position to benefit *its* progeny, not the ant's. (Dennett 2006, 3–4)

Religion apparently is playing the same trick. It makes you believe because, if you believe, then you are more likely to spread the message. In other words, those religions that are really good parasites do better than those that are not.

Again, however, if you look through the emotive example, one is not sure why religion is necessarily false. Why not simply say that a true religion will play better than a false one? I am not saying that debunking arguments never work. Mrs. Ellen G. White, one of the founders of that distinctively American, nineteenth-century religion Seventh-day Adventism, claimed to have all sorts of visions that convinced her that the creation of the world took but six literal days and that God expects us to rest on the seventh day—the Sabbath—and so forth. Then, a hundred years later, a young historian, brought up in the faith, discovered that Mrs. White had cribbed her visions from the printed writings of earlier nineteenth-century visionaries (Numbers 1992). I would say, as did he from then on, that this is good reason to give Seventh-day Adventism a wide berth.

What about a more general debunking argument against religion, Christianity in particular? My inclination is to go back to ethics and why Darwinian evolution debunks the claims that it makes. (I say debunks in the sense of showing them without objective referent, not in the sense of exhorting you to ignore morality.) The trouble with claiming objectivity in ethics—in claiming that substantive ethical claims refer to real matters of fact—is that the nondirectedness of Darwinian evolution makes for the possibility of different end points, and it really doesn't seem that all of them can be true. If we should love our neighbor, then we should not find ourselves in a position where our evolution convinces us that we should hate our neighbor—but treat him carefully because you know that he hates you. If you should care about your family members, then evolution should not convince you that you should put some of them out in the cold when winter comes. It really shouldn't.

We have an analogous situation in religion. It seems that, by and large, from a Darwinian evolutionary perspective, Christianity is a good religion. But so also is Islam! And for all of their troubles, Jews seem to have good staying power. And what about Hindus? Don't forget the Buddhists and the Jains. And so the story goes. We know how John Hick (1980), much to his moral credit, tried to find common ground between the faiths. But it isn't easy—in major part because most people don't want to find common ground—and what is left to be shared is pretty thin. Forget God—the Buddhists don't want Him. Out with Jesus as the son of God—Jews and Muslims agree on this. Love your neighbor. Well, yes, but within the constraints of the caste system. Priests? Not for Quakers, thank you. And so it goes. In the end, I am inclined to think that the right response is, "A plague on all your houses." A Calvinist like Plantinga (2000) would argue that it could just be that one and only one of the religions is right, and this religion is a form of Protestant Christianity. This is possibly true. As in ethics, an evolutionary explanation does not show that there is no objective reality, just that it is unlikely that there is, and it also floats the wonder that God would open the possibility—actuality in the case of religion—that so many people would be deceived. Leave it at this, and remember that this is only one part of the overall picture.

Evolutionism as Religion Substitute

So, finally, where do we finish? There are those, as we have just seen (Edward O. Wilson is one in this generation, and that grandson of Thomas Henry Huxley, Julian Huxley, was one in a previous generation), who think that evolution can offer a kind of religion substitute—*Religion without Revelation* (1927), to use the title of one of Huxley's books. Usually (inevitably), this starts with the belief that evolution is progressive and leads up to humans. This gives us a background history, substituting for the history of the Bible and, like

Christianity, puts humans front and foremost. It also gives ethical directives. We must do that which will keep evolution going and humans at the top. For Huxley, writing in the 1930s, this meant major state-run projects. He was much impressed by the Tennessee Valley Authority that brought power to the South and wrote a book about it (Huxley 1943). For Wilson (2002), writing in the new century, it is the environment that is all important. Above all, he would have us promote biodiversity. A world without a myriad of animals and plants is a world doomed to failure and death.

Unfortunately, this philosophy or religion substitute—it often goes by the name "humanism"—is no better in the end than Christianity. Life is not progressive in the needed way; humans are top only by courtesy of our interests; and, although it may explain morality, evolution as a mechanism provides no guide to moral conduct. Julian's grandfather knew the score on this. Why have we succeeded as well as we have? "For his successful progress, throughout the savage state, man has been largely indebted to those qualities which he shares with the ape and the tiger; his exceptional physical organization; his cunning, his sociability, his curiosity, and his imitativeness; his ruthless and ferocious destructiveness when his anger is roused by opposition" (Huxley 2009, 52). Alas, "in proportion as men have passed from anarchy to social organization, and in proportion as civilization has grown in worth, these deeply ingrained serviceable qualities have become defects" (Huxley 2009, 52).

Christianity will not do and neither will Christianity substitutes. I don't want to underestimate or conceal the radical picture to which I think we are being pointed. If there is no God or afterlife or hope or objective ethics, then what is there? You are left with one of those bleak landscapes—fog or ice or water—painted by the early-nineteenth-century German artist Casper Friedrich David. There is nothing, or if there is something, you cannot know it and should not hope for it. All we have is existence today. In the nineteenth century, John Stuart Mill faced this problem and had no doubt as to the right course of action and belief: "It is better to be a human being dissatisfied than a pig satisfied; better to be Socrates dissatisfied than a fool satisfied. And if the fool, or the pig, are of a different opinion, it is because they only know their own side of the question" (Mill 1863). David Hume knew the story. All we have left is our psychology:

> Most fortunately it happens, that since reason is incapable of dispelling these clouds, nature herself suffices to that purpose, and cures me of this philosophical melancholy and delirium, either by relaxing this bent of mind, or by some avocation, and lively impression of my senses, which obliterate all these chimeras. I dine, I play a game of backgammon, I converse, and am merry with my friends; and when after three or four hours' amusement, I would return to these

speculations, they appear so cold, and strained, and ridiculous, that I cannot find
in my heart to enter into them any farther. (Hume [1739–1740] 1978, 175)

But isn't this in the end something akin to religion? After all, as was pointed
out in an earlier chapter, aren't we just as dependent on faith as the religious
person? We are assuming without evidence that it will all hold together and
keep functioning. And don't we have a world picture as much as the religious
person? Well, of course, both of these points are well taken. The question is
whether they make us religious. I have tried to suggest that believing that
things do work is a reasonable strategy given that in the past they did work and
that there is no reason to quit now. Moreover, this is a strategy open to everyone. Revealingly, it is a strategy adopted by the religious as much as by the
nonreligious. There is no converse. If religion worked in this way, if faith delivered the goods, then it might have a dog in this fight. But it doesn't. Time
and again, people pray for deliverance and it doesn't come. Time and again, a
person from one culture has one insight—Jesus loves me—and time and again,
a person from another culture has another insight—Mohammed is the greatest
prophet of them all. Of course, the evolutionist—especially the evolutionist
like me who is a philosopher—is trying to offer an overall picture, as best he
or she can. But it isn't a picture with hope or meaning or value. It is just a
picture.

Saint Paul said, "For now we see through a glass, darkly; but then face to
face: now I know in part; but then shall I know even as also I am known" (I Cor
13: 12). I don't know if we shall ever see face to face. But I do think that, thanks
to Darwinism, we have been able to scrub a little dirt from the glass. As grown-
ups, it is our moral obligation to look through it. Fear of the unknown is not an
excuse.

The Deep Structure
of the Universe

Michael Peterson

Socrates in the *Theatetus* says, "I had a dream, and I heard in my dream that the primeval letters or elements out of which you and I and all other things are compounded, have no reason or explanation" (Plato 1892, 201e). For normal persons, this dream is a nightmare because we have a deep longing to make sense of life and the world. The Spanish philosopher Miguel de Unamuno objected that the world without meaning is completely unbearable. Yet we humans are instinctively on a search for meaning, pondering and debating whether the universe and our lives within it have significance and purpose. Meaning and purpose have always been tied to religion—and now science has been brought into the discussion. The key is how all of this is philosophically construed.

Michael Ruse recognizes that science can't answer questions of purpose but predictably takes a negative position on purpose based on his combination of science, evolutionary theory, and philosophical naturalism. His antirealist commitments entail that there is no objective meaning and that we could not know it if there were. To the contrary, I affirm that there is a sacred reality that is good and purposive and that we can have knowledge about these purposes. My recurring theme is that we must make a comparative judgment about the plausibility of theistic and atheistic visions of the world. In previous chapters, I showed that theism explains the existence and nature of all the relevant phenomena better than atheistic naturalism does, which already establishes the basis for a much more accurate understanding of their meaning. My total theistic case includes identifying fatal flaws in naturalism, including Ruse's version, and displaying the capacity of theism to answer pertinent objections.

Science, Evolution, and the Search for Meaning

The human search for meaning is inextricably bound to answers to life's big questions: Where did it all come from? Why is the universe intelligible? What is the basis of morality? What is a human person? Every worldview provides a set of answers to such questions and, in so doing, projects its distinctive understanding of meaning. Popular and academic cultures perpetuate the impression that science shows religious accounts of answers to these questions to be false, implausible, or unnecessary—and thus that science discredits religious accounts of meaning as well. But such stereotypes actually emanate from a naturalist worldview that enlists science in its service. Michael Ruse finds himself somewhere in this camp.

The name "Darwinism" is often associated with the rejection of a religious interpretation of the world—including religious ideas of meaning and purpose—but this requires clarification. Darwin was a scientist of the first rank, second to none, who believed in rigorous scientific investigation. He recognized that his findings had a destructive impact on a badly conceived form of natural theology and its peculiar form of teleology, but he was not an advocate for atheism. The science of Darwinian evolution is not inimical to more classical theistic ideas of meaning and purpose. However, as we have seen, the term "Darwinism" today typically refers to an atheistic perspective, philosophical naturalism interlaced with Darwinian categories, which is of course antithetical to theism at every point.

As Peter Medawar, a Nobel Prize winner in medicine, has stated, ultimate questions are questions that "science cannot answer, and that no conceivable advance of science would empower it to answer" (Medawar 1985, 66). If science can't answer ultimate questions, then evolutionary science certainly can't answer them. However, when naturalists seek to incorporate science and evolution into their worldview and their criticism of theism, the boundary between science and philosophy is blurred in confusing ways. Hard-liners Dawkins and Dennett use science and evolution to deny religious answers to meaning out of the gate; Ruse ends up rejecting religious answers as lacking rational credibility to one who is committed to science. But naturalism is the dominant thought in any case. As a theist, I refuse to surrender science or any well-confirmed findings about God's creation, even the facts of evolution, to the naturalists as if they fit much more obviously with their perspective. Love of God's world plays out in honest investigation of the scientific facts. Without a reliable factual picture of the physical and biological facts, any answers to ultimate questions are doomed to irrelevance anyway.

The intellectual strength of any worldview is based on its ability to offer a coherent, credible interpretation of all the relevant data, not on airtight chains of evidence. To use a metaphor, a worldview is an "interpretive lens" through which we look at—that is, philosophically explain—important features of reality. Natural theology in our day must seek worldview engagement: the comparison of explanatory frameworks that philosophically address the same common set of data known by common sense and science. Theism, and indeed

Christian theism, will be well served by an informed, balanced, and interactive approach. Naturalism can't just market its criticisms of theism as its best feature, since it too must bring its conceptual resources to the table and try to parlay them into credible explanations of the same data.

I have argued, subject by subject, that theism makes better sense than naturalism—of the existence and intelligibility of the universe, the appearance of life, consciousness, rationality, morality, personhood, and so on. Theism allows us to see these phenomena for what they really are, in their full dimension, not reduced or distorted. In this vein, the quest for meaning—that is, the search for a framework that makes consistent, credible sense of reality in all its key aspects—assumes the fundamental explicability of the world. Albert Einstein once remarked, "The eternal mystery of the world is its comprehensibility" (Einstein 1950, 60). On the face of it, comprehensibility intimates an underlying meaning that must be pursued. Cruel irony it would be if the best, most enlightening explanation turned out to be a philosophical account of why there is no meaning.

Naturalism and the Denial of Meaning

For naturalism, nature is the fundamental reality and has no intrinsic value or purpose. Since everything that exists is a part of the totality of nature, nothing in the universe has intrinsic value or purpose. Rationality, morality, and personhood are nothing but products of the evolutionary process and should not be assigned any ultimate significance. Michael Ruse has given voice to this view, saying that the discovery that "we are the contingent end-products of a natural process of evolution, rather than the special creation of a good God, in His own image, has to be just about one of the most profound things we humans have discovered about ourselves" (Ruse 1998, ix).

Although Ruse correctly states that science cannot address questions of meaning, his default naturalism is an interpretive framework that excludes objective meaning. Physical nature as ultimate reality is simply not sufficient to generate an explanation of positive meaning. Science then comes in to offer a mechanical explanation of everything and to diminish religious answers as being nonscientific. Scientific naturalism commits various reductionistic fallacies—reducing all key realities to the material and reducing teleological explanation to mechanical explanation. Reductionism, in turn, spawns the fallacy of false alternatives: Ruse contends that the appearance of humans is either the result of evolution or God—but not both.

Reductionism plays out in spades as Darwinian naturalism addresses the big questions regarding the origin, structure, and destiny of the universe. Why is there a universe? There is no reason—existence is purely by chance. Brute nature has no purpose, and empirical science can't discern purpose in the operations of nature. As Jacques Monod states,

> Pure chance, absolutely free but blind, [is] at the very root of the stupendous edifice of evolution. . . . It is today the sole conceivable hypothesis, the only one that squares with observed and tested fact. And nothing warrants the supposition—or the hope—that on this score our position is likely ever to be revised. (Monod 1971, 112)

Here is naturalism using science as its public face to proclaim that there are no detectable purposes in nature, no gods, no designing forces.

Exposing the reductionism of naturalism further: what is the significance of being human? There is no transcendent significance—the contingencies of our evolution shape our morality and religious aspirations. Stephen Jay Gould was fond of saying that humans would not even be here if it were not for the purely accidental event of a giant asteroid strike that caused the extinction of the dinosaurs. What is the destiny of the universe? Science tells us—scientific eschatology, we might say—that there can be no optimism about the future of the cosmos. Death is the ultimate end for the physical universe and everything in it—whether it will be a Big Crunch, a Big Rip, or Heat Death. "Human destiny," as Ernest Nagel observes, is "an episode between two oblivions" (Nagel 1954, 16). If we reductionistically look for meaning in the elemental stuff out of which everything is made—matter plus time plus chance—then no meaning can be found. The universe so constituted—and the amazing realities emergent within it—must be explained by something outside themselves, something that makes it likely they would come to be. Otherwise, Socrates's dream will indeed become a nightmare.

At this juncture, the evolutionary explanation of religion offered by atheistic naturalists proves fascinating but inadequate. Darwinian theory assigns the origin of religion to survival value, but individual naturalists play different variations on this same theme, from Dennett's overly active defense mechanism to Dawkins's self-replicating but destructive "meme" (Dennett 2006; Dawkins 1976; see also Blackmore 2000). Ruse likewise advances the theory that religion is based on underlying biological functions—mistaken perceptions, social needs, and so forth.

What exactly is the impact of evolutionary explanations in the hands of naturalists? Remember that these are a type of causal explanation, which has been around for a long time, used by naturalists as complete explanations of free will, mind, and other key features of reality. For Ruse, an evolutionary/causal explanation serves to "debunk" religious belief, just as it debunks moral beliefs.

As with ethics, debunking comes in both epistemological and ontological versions—and Ruse endorses both. The epistemological thrust is that, if natural selection is causally responsible for the human ability to form religious beliefs, then the rational warrant for those beliefs is undercut. The ontological thesis is that there is no divine referent that is the target of religious beliefs. Let's look at each line of attack.

The epistemological debunking of religion has its problems. Mistakenly thinking that identifying the origin of a belief obviates the need to engage its truth or credibility on its own merits is technically called (pardon the pun) the "genetic fallacy." But why are disciplines such as evolutionary biology and cultural anthropology—which are employed by naturalists to undercut the rational warrant of religious belief—not themselves undercut when their origin in the human psyche and social experience is empirically described (Trigg 2014)? Evolutionary naturalists cannot claim validity for their preferred discipline without allowing that it is motivated by the same search for truth that they wish to suggest in religious believers is merely a result of social or psychological adjustments and adaptations that foster survival. I am herewith debunking debunking.

As we observed in Chapter 8, there is really no such thing as an epistemic defeater *simpliciter*. Whether the evolutionary history of religion serves as a defeater for the truth of a person's religious beliefs depends on many of the other background beliefs that he or she holds. My own background belief set includes evolutionary theism, which accepts and interprets the evolutionary facts (just the facts, not philosophically driven extrapolations) as revealing something of how God made the world to work. So, the evolutionary facts of religion are not a defeater for me. Of course, the subterranean conflict here is between epistemic realism and epistemic antirealism about religion (Peterson et al. 2012, chap. 2). The epistemological realist in me holds that we can reasonably assess theological claims on their explanatory merits and that this is a distinctively philosophical rather than scientific activity.

Ruse acknowledges that "evolutionary debunking" used as an epistemic defeater doesn't really prove religion false. However, at rock bottom, he still holds that religious beliefs about a divine being are in fact false because of his naturalist ontological commitments. This other aspect of Ruse's debunking posture is his explicit error theory about religion, which is parallel to his error theory in metaethics. Ruse holds the ontological position that there are no objective religious facts that make religious beliefs true—no transcendent, no divine being. On one level, Ruse claims that an evolutionary explanation of why we form religious beliefs makes it unlikely that there is a divine reality to which those beliefs correspond. Yet the assessment of the low probability of claims about the divine is not straightforwardly objective but is instead a function of Ruse's deeply held background assumptions—chiefly, naturalism as the correct worldview picture and mechanical explanation as exclusive. My theism leads me to assess the probability differently because I see God as guiding evolution to make us religious as well as moral creatures. On another level, let us not forget that Ruse's default naturalism absolutely guarantees (not just in degrees of probability!) that no divine reality exists. This is the clear result of Ruse's ontological antirealism about religion.

A further word about Ruse's biological explanation of religion: to say that religion serves biological functions (and cultural functions as well) is nothing new to the informed theist. The theist readily expects that there are biological as well as cultural aspects to religion because God created us as biological and cultural beings. It is totally predictable, then, that religion would be intertwined at multiple levels with the complex total reality that human persons are. Of course, religion will have a concrete origin and expression within the natural world, which makes it open to several types of scientific investigation—psychological, sociological, anthropological, and so forth. Evolutionary explanations of religion, then, highlight aspects of our creatureliness but don't show that religion is *purely* a "natural phenomenon," as Dennett has proclaimed. Thus, religion is not explained away as a vehicle for truth.

Within the Judeo-Christian tradition, for instance, biological interests are clearly involved in ideals of human flourishing (the marriage bond, feeding the hungry, etc.) since both our essential physicality and the goodness of the material world are strongly affirmed. The contingencies of life, such as death of a spouse, don't cancel the ideal of faithful, loving marriage. Rather, a fuller interpretation of the ideal is required in the context of the eschatological fulfillment of all things—a state in which the physical is not discarded but is transformed and superseded such that all important relationships are continued and redeemed. If our personal identity is largely formed by our various relationships, why think that a fulfilling afterlife would level or diminish or deny them? Then no criteria of personal identity could justify saying that the earthly John Smith is the resurrected John Smith.

In addition to debunking religion generally, Michael Ruse offers specific criticisms of theism and Christianity. First, he argues that the wide diversity of religious concepts of the divine makes it unlikely that just one religion is true. However, a multiplicity of ideas on any topic, religious or otherwise, does not in itself mean that none is likely to be true. Classical Christian orthodoxy makes no claim that other religions are complete falsehoods but rather appreciates and explains the basic desire for the divine within the human heart that is expressed in various ways across cultures (Newbigin 1995). Augustine said, "You have made us for yourself, O Lord, and our hearts are restless until they find their rest in You" (Augustine 1998, Bk I, para. 1). The Christian emphasis is that fuller, more accurate knowledge of God is found in the life and ministry of Jesus Christ. In the end, a God of infinite goodness and wisdom, who seeks to draw all persons to himself, must know the trajectory of each individual life and be trusted with its ultimate disposition. A more complete Christian theology of the world's religions must await another time, but helpful sources are available for further study (Peterson et al. 2012, chap. 14; Pannenberg 1971, chap. 4; *The Documents of Vatican II* 1966, 656–77).

A second argument Ruse deploys is that adopting a scientific point of view—that is, assuming everything operates by natural laws—intellectually disposes one against religion. In Chapter 1, Ruse suggests in his own way that a scientific mind-set will not acquiesce in the wishful thinking of religion or ignore the failure of prayer. Let's consider the comment that science works but religion doesn't. Classical Christianity certainly doesn't peddle some neat formula for what prayer is or what it means for prayer to "work," let alone offer a complete explanation of prayer in the providential activity of God. No doubt, there are petitionary prayers for divine aid whose consequences appear to be the further unfolding of negative circumstances rather than their reversal. In contrast, there are innumerable reports that associate prayer with improving and transforming otherwise hopeless situations. A fuller theology of prayer—explaining various qualifications and nuances generally understood by sincere believers—lies beyond the scope of our present consideration. Yet what Christianity does clearly teach is that prayer is very much about relationship with God and its transformative effect on the believer.

The form of my argument throughout the debate is that basic theism explains key features of life and the world better than naturalism does and that Christian theology adds to the greater explanatory power of theism. To be sure, there will always be more details to probe, more questions to answer, and more objections to overturn. But this is true for any worldview framework whatsoever. The way is now open to pursue any issue in this debate in greater analytical detail. What I have done in this exchange is to make a cumulative case for theism and Christianity. To make this overall case, I argued, point by point, that the conceptual resources of theism and Christianity provide more credible explanations of important phenomena than naturalism is able to provide. Along the way, I answered objections and clarified misconceptions. All things considered, then, a theistic and Christian worldview has greater explanatory power than naturalism does. This is a strong reason to take seriously theistic and Christian ideas about meaning and purpose.

Let's look more closely at the other side of the ledger. Michael Ruse states that Darwinian naturalism proffers a bleak picture of a universe with no meaning or purpose, but he expresses a commendable resolve to make the best of the existence we have. Although Ruse says that science itself can't detect meaning, his Darwinian naturalism entails that life and the world are without meaning. Nature as brute ultimate, operating by physical and biological laws and yet involving significant contingency, supplies no meaning and has no inherent purpose. What Dennett has called the "universal acid" of Darwinism erodes all traditional knowledge and values and religious beliefs (Dennett 1995, chap. 3). Of course, in the rationality chapter, we noted the irony that Darwinism as a totalizing philosophy also erodes its own claim to being objectively rational. I believe in taking Darwin seriously in terms of the important science he inspired but oppose enlisting Darwinian concepts in the service of a naturalist worldview. Promoted beyond its pay grade to do metaphysics, epistemology, and ethics and to speak to meaning and purpose, Darwinism distorts, denies, and dismisses all the important phenomena at stake in this book.

Theism and Meaning

For theism, an infinitely rational, good, and powerful God is the ground of meaning. God is the basis for making sense of the existence and rational structure of the universe and of the existence of finite rational moral beings within it. Reality as we know it is not the result of tremendous "dumb luck" but rather is dependent on the nature and purposes of God. Within the theistic universe, we can make good sense of rationality, morality, and personhood and of how they are all connected in a unified reality—and we can do this in positive interaction with science and evolution. Whether we call this perspective theistic evolution or evolutionary theism, it provides a holistic, integrated worldview framework that entails an understanding of meaning and purpose anchored in divine activity.

Christian theology adds information about God's nature and purposes to the principles of theism. In Christian teaching, the kind of goodness behind the universe is characterized as self-giving love. And the power behind all things is seen as humbly stepping back to give contingent creaturely action a wide scope, so that finite beings may authentically choose to love God and each other. Such concepts enrich the framework for understanding the meaning of the universe and the purpose of the human venture. However, Michael Ruse and some other critics contend that the Christian God cannot anchor meaning because the very concept of this God is an incoherent mixture of Greek and Hebrew elements. How can the aloof, immutable God of classical Greek thought, they ask, be the personal–relational God described in Christian thought? There are important issues here. But let's be clear. Christian theology affirms that God is unchangeable in his essential nature while being relational to creation in ways already explained. Employing pure reason, the Greeks gained glimpses of this Supreme Reality but froze it and detached it from the world. Christian theology corrects, refines, and refocuses any glimpses of God attained through rational reflection on the world and what is behind the world—what is typically known as general revelation. By the same token, classical orthodoxy also corrects and puts in theological perspective misleading anthropomorphic ideas of God drawn from the figurative language of some biblical texts and popular religious discourse.

Central Christian doctrines are threads woven into a rich tapestry of meaning. The doctrine of creation implies that there is value and purpose to the physical universe and to human history. The doctrine of Incarnation—that God, in the Second Person of the Trinity, became bonded with a historical human being, Jesus of Nazareth—signifies how close God wants to be with humanity. The Christian understanding of sin and the fall identifies the damage to creation caused by humans organizing their lives apart from their True Source. Although essentially good, human persons do not live up to the highest and best—and somehow the world of nature reflects this incompletion and need for restoration. Eschatology affirms that God is working to redeem and transform humanity and the material creation—and that the future holds an unimaginably wonderful destiny for finite reality. Theological eschatology reframes scientific themes of contingency, finitude, and death in the larger context of hope, joy, and the ultimate ground of the worth and dignity of all things (Polkinghorne and Welker 2000; Wilkinson 2010).

Nothing in a theistic perspective or orthodox Christian worldview conflicts with science as a discipline or the facts of evolution. Owen Gingerich, Francisco Ayala, and Francis Collins are among the many noted scientists who are Christians advocating harmony between science and faith (Gingerich 2006; Ayala 2007; Collins 2006). These scientists know well the scientific story of the origin, nature, and course of the world—from the Big Bang to the future demise of the physical universe. Yet they also know that the scientific story doesn't address questions of meaning, purpose, and value. Alister McGrath puts it this way:

> Science tells us a story about the history and nature of the world which we know and inhabit. But it does not tell the full story. Christianity is consistent with the story told by science, but it takes that story further. It tells the full story, of which science is but a part. (McGrath 2011b, 44)

Even scientists, who by definition work in restricted fields, need a more complete understanding that encompasses science and also satisfies their need as total human beings for meaning and purpose.

Follow the Argument Wherever It Leads

At every juncture of this debate—the existence of the universe, the fine-tuned structure of physical reality, the nature of rationality, morality, and personhood—I have argued for the superior explanatory power of a theistic worldview over a naturalistic worldview. My general point has been that theism makes the existence of these phenomena much more probable than naturalism does. Alternatively, these phenomena are much more epistemically surprising on the assumption that naturalism is true; we would not rationally expect them. The momentum of my cumulative case now carries into our discussion of meaning.

A theistic universe intrinsically possesses meaning because it is created and guided by God, who is a purposive agent, whereas a universe described by evolutionary naturalism—which excludes personal agency at the core of reality and rejects teleological explanation as fundamental—can have no objective meaning. The theistic worldview reveals the "deep structure" of reality that contains important clues to its meaning and purpose. This deep structure involves the key features of life and the world that are illumined and explained within the more comprehensive perspective of Christian theism. Therefore, it is not surprising that the universe is invested with meaning and that persons within it have a purpose. Theism establishes the framework; Christian orthodoxy provides detail, texture, and depth.

In *The Republic*, Socrates admonishes his dialogue partners: "We must follow the argument wherever it leads" (Plato 1974, 394d). The atheist philosopher Antony Flew lived by this motto, which eventually led him to the astonishing reversal of his position. Flew became persuaded that a supremely intelligent and powerful being behind the universe was required to make sense of the intelligible and purposive dimensions of the world revealed by reflection on science. Considering that the ultimate origin of the universe lies beyond science, that the laws of nature form a rationally coherent system requiring explanation, and that the appearance of life from nonlife is incomprehensible given naturalism, Flew concluded that there must be a God. Believing that there is an essential teleology at work in the world and that this teleology must ultimately be rooted in a supremely intelligent being, Flew adopted a sort of deism during the last decade of his life (Flew 2007, chap. 4). By his own account, if he were to move further along his intellectual trajectory, he would seriously consider historical Christianity (Flew 2007, 185–87).

Following the evidence, in the current context, means discerning which worldview makes best sense of the evidence. For theism, the most fundamental reality is an intelligent personal agent who has purposes and intentions—which implies that the most fundamental kind of explanation is ultimately teleological, pertaining to the purposes and intentions of the supreme agent. Mechanical explanation, then, is derivative in the order of reality, not primary as Ruse and other naturalists would have it. Both types of explanation are legitimate in their appropriate contexts, and both together provide a fuller explanatory picture. Philosophical naturalism sees nature as ultimate, makes mechanical explanation primary, and elevates science as the paragon of knowledge. Dimensions of meaning and purpose in the universe are thereby illicitly ruled out.

Driving on a family vacation years ago with my wife, Rebecca, and my two sons, Aaron and Adam, I passed the time by asking the boys questions. "Why is that billboard standing alongside the road?" I asked. Adam, who was six years old and fascinated by building things, said, "Because trucks and high lifts came in and put it all together." Aaron, twelve years old and wiser about life, responded, "Because the owner of that business wants to market a product and make a profit." Here we have a mechanical explanation and a teleological explanation—both are correct, and both pertain to the same reality. These two kinds of explanation are neither mutually exclusive nor compartmentalized; they are complementary in providing important information about the same subject. Throughout this debate, we have observed how atheistic naturalism works from false dichotomies—either evolution or God, either mechanical explanation or teleological explanation, and so forth. It is critical that we are clear about the different kinds of questions we are asking, what disciplines properly address them, and how they are related. Scientific explanation appropriately addresses questions about how things operate—the mechanics of physical cause and effect—but theological explanation addresses questions about God's purposes for humanity and nature.

The famous biologist Francisco Ayala indicates that some idea of teleology is actually indispensable to modern biology's description of the functional roles that the parts of living organisms fulfill (Ayala 1970, 10; also Lenoir 1982, ix). What is reproductive fitness if not a goal? Ayala's observation echoes the statement by Thomas Huxley, Darwin's eloquent interpreter, that Darwin's destruction of Paley's badly formed design argument does not discredit a "wider teleology" that is evident in nature. Moreover, the operation of various levels of teleology in the natural world does not necessitate that every detail is predetermined but can allow significant nondetermined contingency in outcomes.

In the final analysis, theism simply provides a more accommodating worldview home for all the important realities we have discussed. This is not wishful thinking but a frank comparative analysis of the explanatory power of competing worldviews. An intelligible fine-tuned universe, consciousness, rationality, morality, and personhood—all fit together and take on coherent meaning in light of a God who has consciousness, rationality, and moral goodness and is himself a personal agent. Christian orthodoxy says that God's relational, self-giving nature is demonstrated in his free choice to create a finite world and will that personal beings eventually arise and have opportunity for fellowship with him. Yet humanity and all of creation have sustained damage and have become the focus of God's loving, redemptive activity. Within this framework, all important elements of the world—even the challenging facts that we have considered, such as evil, chance, and unbelief—can be reasonably explained.

Atheistic naturalists who insist on nothing but conflict between science and theism are mistaken. Also mistaken is Michael Ruse's version of atheistic naturalism that allows religion to address some questions while still rejecting the answers based on a mix of Darwinism, empiricism, and naturalism. Yet we have seen that neither science in general nor evolution in particular can be credibly construed to tip the rational scales toward naturalism and atheism. The material world, which physics, evolutionary biology, and the other sciences investigate, has theistic meaning both as a creature and as a context for finite personal life. Theologically, this is a meaningful world, a world invested with significance and developing within the ambit of divine purpose—an evolutionary world.

We began the introduction of this book with a quote from Bishop Aubrey Moore that correctly stated that Darwinian science did the work of a friend for Christianity. Although Moore was mistaken that Christians should envision God as always acting directly rather than through secondary causes, he was exactly right on the more basic point: that Christians must carefully articulate how God relates to nature in a manner faithful to classical Christian orthodoxy. Although science will always be a factor in this articulation going forward, the reasonableness of the Christian position must be displayed in worldview engagement. The interaction between my Christian theism and the atheistic naturalism of my friend Michael Ruse has created a spirited exchange that I hope was as enlightening and enjoyable for you the reader as it was for us. In our debate, I consistently argued that Christian theism embraces whatever is true about reality, as revealed by science and all other fields, philosophically framing and explaining it better than atheistic naturalism does.

As an atheist, C. S. Lewis was committed to seeking the truth among competing worldviews and found himself on an intellectual journey. Over the course of many years, he came to accept theism and then finally Christian belief. Dedicated to finding the best total explanation of reality and all we know about it, he became convinced of the explanatory power of orthodox Christianity. Christianity, Lewis found, makes good rational sense on its own terms and illuminates key features of reality better than other worldview alternatives (Lewis 1955, chap. 14). Lewis eloquently wrote, "I believe in Christianity as I believe the Sun has risen, not only because I see it, but because by it I see everything else" (Lewis 1980, 140).

GLOSSARY

abiogenesis   The origin of life from nonliving matter.

absolute idealism   The philosophy that reality is one whole (often termed the Absolute) and is of the nature of Mind or Idea.

accommodationism (accommodation)   Compromising with or adapting one's position to make room for another viewpoint.

adaptation   Any heritable characteristic of an organism that improves its ability to survive and reproduce in its environment. Typically, the process of genetic change within a population, as influenced by natural selection.

agent (agency)   A personal rational being with power of choice and the ability to perform actions.

agnosticism   The state or position of not knowing, the lack of knowledge.

altruism   The principle or practice of unselfish concern or behavior for the welfare of others.

analogy (argument from analogy)   The comparison of likeness between two things, which can be the basis for inference to further likenesses. Used to infer further similarities, although the inference is subject to logical scrutiny.

Anglicanism (Anglican)   A tradition within Christianity tied to the Church of England that positioned its theology as an ecumenical compromise between Catholicism on the one hand and Lutheranism and Calvinism on the other.

antecedent probability   An approach to probability calculating or estimating the probability that a certain event would occur assuming in advance that some hypothesis is true.

anthropic argument   One version of teleological argument claiming that the existence of God is the best explanation of the unlikely fine-tuning of the fundamental physical constants of the universe that were necessary to intelligent life.

anthropic principle   Thesis in cosmology stating that the universe must allow the observer to exist (weak version) or that the universe must possess those properties that make the existence of intelligent life inevitable (strong version).

antirealism   The position that there are defects in our belief-forming capacities that discredit any claims that the beliefs they form can constitute knowledge (epistemological version) or the position that there is no reality or kind of reality to which our beliefs can correspond (ontological version).

apologetics   The intellectual activity of giving positive reasons for religious belief as well as rebutting objections against it.

Arminianism (Arminian)   A theological view, breaking from classical Calvinism, which asserts that divine grace empowers free will to receive or refuse salvation.

Ascension (the)   The teaching in historical Christianity that Jesus was taken into heaven forty days after his resurrection.

aseity   God's property of self-existence according to medieval Christian thought.

atheism   The outright denial that there is a god (positive) or the refusal to affirm that there is a god (negative).

Big Bang   The prevailing model in cosmological science stating that the universe rapidly expanded from a high-density state known as the Singularity.

Calvinism   Body of theological doctrines taught by the Protestant reformer John Calvin dealing with absolute divine sovereignty over human destiny (opposed to Arminianism).

Cambrian explosion (Cambrian radiation)   The relatively brief evolutionary event beginning about 530 million years ago when a wide variety of animals burst into the organic world as indicated by the fossil record.

Catholicism (Roman Catholicism)   A major historic branch of Christianity of which the Pope in Rome is the worldwide leader and authority.

causality   The power or potency of natural objects to bring about effects (see also final cause, efficient cause, primary cause, and secondary causes).

Christianity   A religion based on the life and ministry of Jesus Christ understood as God incarnate, particularly the belief that his death and resurrection provides for forgiveness of sins and right relationship with God.

classical orthodox Christianity (orthodoxy)   The framework of common or ecumenical beliefs endorsed by the Seven Great Councils of the early Christian centuries.

coherence (logical)   The relation of beliefs that not only are consistent (not inconsistent) but also have natural conceptual connections.

coherence theory of truth   The theory that a proposition is true when it fits or has a conceptual connection with other already accepted propositions.

common descent   In evolutionary biology, a group of organisms that share a most recent common ancestor; ultimately, all life on earth is descended from a last universal common ancestor.

compatibilism (compatibilist)   The view that free will is compatible with some or all forms of determinism, such as divine or scientific determinism.

confirmation   The judgment, often by a community of researchers, that a scientific hypothesis is supported by a sufficient amount of evidence to be accepted as true.

consistency (consistent)   The logical relation that obtains between two or more propositions when all can be true together.

constructivism   See social construction of knowledge.

contingency   A state of affairs that is neither impossible nor necessary; often associated with chance.

contradiction   The logical relation that obtains between propositions such that if one is true the other must be false and vice versa (see also law of noncontradiction).

convergence (evolutionary)   In evolutionary biology, the thesis that relatively unrelated organisms develop along similar evolutionary paths, developing similar structures for similar adaptive functions.

Copernican principle (mediocrity principle)   The idea that the replacement of geocentrism by heliocentrism in astronomy implies that human beings are not special.

correspondence theory of truth   The theory that a proposition is true when it corresponds with some aspect of the objective world.

cosmological argument   A type of theistic argument, taking various specific forms, that essentially reasons that the universe requires God as a cause or sufficient reason beyond itself.

cosmology   The consideration of the origin and development of the universe either as a scientific endeavor or as a philosophical and reflective activity.

creation   In theology, the divine act of bringing the universe and everything in it into existence (see also doctrine of creation).

creationism (creation science, creationist)   The view generated by Protestant fundamentalism that God created the universe and all life in its present form in six literal days or relatively short time periods.

Darwinism (Darwinian)   Classically, the biological view advanced by Darwin that the evolution of species is by natural selection.

debunking argument   Generally, an epistemic argument based on an evolutionary explanation for a belief that is supposed to discredit or defeat the rational warrant for that belief.

defeater   In contemporary epistemology, a belief that, if accepted, makes it irrational to accept another belief that is in question.

defense against problem of evil   A reason or argument why the argument from evil is not effective, not credible.

deism (deist)   The view popular in the Enlightenment that God created the universe to work by laws and does not intervene.

design argument   One type of teleological argument that reasons that the order of the world requires an intelligent being to design it using the analogy that artifacts of intelligent design (e.g., a watch) require an intelligent designer (e.g., a watchmaker).

determinism   The view that every event is caused to happen, either by some causal factor or by divine will, such that there is no genuine contingency or human libertarian free will.

Ding an sich   German term for "thing-in-itself," which is the object of knowledge unaffected by human mental structuring activity.

directionality   In evolutionary discussions, the idea that the universe is developing in some direction characterizable as more complex, higher, or more valuable.

DNA   Deoxyribonucleic acid, in a double-helix structure, which carries the genetic instructions used in the development, functioning, and reproduction of all living organisms (see also RNA).

doctrine of creation The teaching in theistic religions that God alone is self-existent and brought about and continues to sustain all finite existence.

Drake equation A formula advanced by astrophysicist Frank Drake to identify the key factors—astronomical, biological, psychological, etc.—relevant to there being active, communicative extraterrestrial civilizations in the Milky Way galaxy.

dualism In philosophy of mind, the view that mind (soul) and body are distinct and separable substances.

Eastern Orthodoxy (also Orthodoxy, with capitalization) Major Christian denomination or tradition that is geographically eastern in relation to the Western Catholic Church centered in Rome.

efficient cause From Aristotle, that which brings something about, produces it, puts it in motion (see also final cause).

eliminativism (eliminative materialism) In philosophy of mind, the strong view that our common-sense understanding of mind is deeply wrong and that mental states do not exist but can be eliminated in favor of physical states.

emergence (emergentism) The process whereby larger or more complex patterns or powers occur through the interactions of smaller or simpler entities.

emergent dualism A view of the mind–body relationship which holds that mind and mental properties arise from complex physical arrangements in the brain rather than being separate nonmaterial substance or being completely reducible to the physical brain.

empiricism The epistemological view that genuine knowledge is grounded in sensory experience.

Enlightenment (the) An intellectual and cultural movement in Europe during the seventeenth and eighteenth centuries emphasizing the sufficiency of human rationality.

epigenetics In genetics, the study of heritable changes in gene expression that do not involve changes to the underlying DNA sequence but are rather caused by age, environment, lifestyle, disease, etc.

epistemology (epistemological) The branch of philosophy dealing with belief and knowledge, its ground, justification, and structure.

eschatology The area of theology pertaining to the ultimate culmination of history and fulfillment of God's plans for creation and humanity.

essence The metaphysical concept of the necessary traits or underlying substance for a given kind of being.

ethics The study of ethical conduct, rules, and reasoning (see also moral theory).

ethology (ethologist) The scientific study of animal behavior, usually in the context of natural habitat and conditions.

evidentialism A philosophical thesis regarding justified belief being a function of one's evidence.

evolution The change in heritable traits of biological populations over successive generations that gives rise to diversity in individuals and among species.

evolutionary theism See theistic evolution.

existentialism   The philosophy that the individual search for meaning is found more in a subjective personal choice, which can be religious or atheistic, about the kind of person one will be than in objective rational theories.

exnihilation (exnihilate)   Bringing and maintaining a being in existence.

faith   The religious attitude or orientation that properly relates a person to the divine.

fallacy   In logic, a mistaken type of reasoning that derives a conclusion from insufficient evidence or irrelevant points.

final cause   From Aristotle, a type of cause involving a purpose or end, that toward which something is directed (see also efficient cause).

fine-tuning (argument)   The argument that the precise balance of the fundamental physical constants of the universe could not have occurred by chance and must have been produced by a supremely intelligent and powerful being.

forms   From Plato (with roots in Parmenides), the belief that the unchanging abstract ideas are the most fundamental kind of reality as opposed to the changing material realm.

free will   The power of choosing between alternative courses of action, although views differ with regard to whether there must be no restraints whatsoever (incompatibilism, libertarianism) or simply no external restraints (compatibilism).

fundamentalism   A religious outlook based on belief in strict, literal interpretation of sacred scripture.

gene   Most basically, the molecular unit of heredity that contains an organism's inherited phenotypic traits or, more technically, the locus of DNA that encodes a functional RNA product.

general relativity (theory of)   The concept, originally proposed by Albert Einstein, that the force of gravity arises from the curvature of space-time, which is a dynamic entity that is distorted by matter and that in turn controls how the matter behaves.

genetics   The scientific field that studies genes, heredity, and genetic variation in living organisms.

genome   An organism's complete set of DNA, including all of its genes, which contain all information needed to build and maintain that organism.

genotype (genotypic)   The collection of genes specific to an individual.

God of the gaps (God-of-the-gaps argument)   Refers to the concept of a deity that causes certain phenomena in nature for which science knows no physical cause.

hominids   Often known as the Great Apes, the large taxonomic family of primates that includes orangutans, gorillas, chimpanzees, and humans.

hominins   The group consisting of all humans, modern and extinct, which are in turn a part of the larger family of primates known as hominids, which includes orangutans, gorillas, chimpanzees, and human beings.

Homo sapiens   *Homo* is the genus, followed by *sapiens* as species, to form a term that literally means "wise man" or "knowing man."

humanism   The perspective that human life, thought, activity, and achievement are valuable; occurs in both secular and religious forms.

hypothesis (theory)   An if–then statement in which the antecedent clause states the initial conditions and the consequent clause states the proposed outcome, thus allowing considerations of testability.

idealism   The philosophical view that mind or idea is more fundamental in the order of reality and that matter is either less important, less real, or unreal.

imago Dei   The theological term meaning "God's Image," which reflects the view that humans reflect or resemble God in certain important ways, usually in regard to rationality, morality, personhood, and will.

immanent   The divine attribute of being present with the whole of creation while remaining ontologically distinct.

immutable   The divine attribute of being unchanging and unchangeable.

impassible   The divine attribute of being unable to be affected by emotions or to be acted on by external beings or forces.

Incarnation   The Christian doctrine that God in the Second Person of the Trinity became one with the first-century person Jesus.

incompatibilism (incompatibilist)   The view that free will is not compatible with any form of determinism; libertarianism.

inconsistency (inconsistent)   The logical relation that obtains between two or more propositions when they cannot all be true together.

inorganic   Not consisting of or deriving from living matter.

instrumentalism   The view in philosophy of science that concepts and theories have worth as useful instruments, not in terms of being true about reality.

intelligent design argument   An argument that the low odds that certain kinds or levels of organic complexity could not have occurred by random chance support the conclusion that it is probable that there is a powerful, intelligent being (see intelligent design theory).

intelligent design theory (IDT, ID)   The theory, which claims to be a scientific theory in biology, that certain kinds or levels of organic complexity (irreducible, specified) cannot have been produced by natural selection operating on chance variations and thus are evidence of a designing intelligence (see also intelligent design argument).

kin altruism   Engaging in behavior helpful to one's biological relatives.

law of noncontradiction   Fundamental logical principle that contradictory propositions cannot both be true; if one proposition is true, the other must be false.

liberalism (liberal)   The theological view that supernaturalism in scripture reflects a prescientific mentality, that literal interpretation of scripture is unnecessary, and that social action is more important than individual salvation; often contrasted with fundamentalism.

literalism   See fundamentalism.

logic   The branch of philosophy that studies correct argument and formulates principles and rules for their evaluation.

materialism   The philosophical view that everything that exists is material or physical in nature.

mechanistic explanation   The type of explanation that cites a physical cause or causes as bringing about the phenomenon in question.

mediocrity principle   See Copernican principle.

meme   Term coined by Richard Dawkins to mean an idea or behavior that spreads from person to person, which makes it a unit of cultural transmission (by imitation, replication), just as the gene is a unit of biological transmission.

metaethics   The second-order discipline studying the grounds of ethical obligation, the structure of ethical arguments and reasons, and the meaning of ethical terms.

metaphor in science   Metaphor as such, a controlling idea in science (related to social dimension of knowledge).

metaphysical naturalism   The philosophical position that only physical nature is real and there is no supernatural (see also naturalism).

metaphysics (metaphysical)   The branch of philosophy dealing with the nature and structure of ultimate reality.

metazoa   A zoological group consisting of the multicellular animals, living or extinct, that have cells differentiated into tissues, organs, etc.

methodological naturalism (methodological)   The philosophical position that science proceeds by seeking natural causes for natural phenomena and not recognizing supernatural causes as the basis for its explanations.

miracle   Classically, a violation of a law of nature, which is an event that otherwise would not have occurred in the regular course of nature.

modus ponens   A basic rule of logic stating that if the antecedent of a conditional statement is true, then its consequent must also be true.

monism   The philosophy that reality is one neutral substance and that mind and matter are aspects or modalities of that substance.

moral argument   A type of theistic argument, taking various specific forms, that essentially reasons that human morality is ultimately caused or explained by the existence of a moral God.

moral evil   The wrongful actions of personal beings (or institutions) or character defects of personal beings.

moral law   The general principle of right conduct, often thought to imply or contain multiple duties that apply to all of humanity.

moral theory   The branch of philosophy dealing with moral conduct and character (see also ethics).

multiverse(s) (multiverse theory)   The theory in scientific cosmology that there are many, and possibly infinitely many, universes besides our own.

mutation   In biology, a randomly occurring permanent change of the nucleotide sequence of the genome of an organism.

myth (mythology)   Classically understood as a symbolic story containing important truths or themes, not a fraudulent story or outright falsehood.

natural evil   Evil resulting from natural causes or forces rather than from the actions of human beings.

natural law   Classically, this is the moral law, the law of our human moral nature, but in modern usage, this can mean scientific law.

natural science   An academic discipline (such as physics, chemistry, and biology) that studies the objects, phenomena, or laws of the physical world.

natural selection   A key mechanism of evolution involving the differential survival and reproduction of individuals that differ in phenotype.

natural theology   The intellectual enterprise of giving positive arguments for theistic and Christian belief as well as defending against negative arguments.

naturalism   The philosophical worldview resting on the metaphysical position that physical nature is the fundamental reality and that no deity exists or relates to the world, often involving strong empiricist epistemology and related views (see also metaphysical naturalism).

necessity   Ontologically, a state of affairs that must obtain or, logically, a proposition that must be true.

neo-Darwinism   See new synthesis.

neurophilosophy   The philosophy of neuroscience, which is the interdisciplinary exploration of the relevance of neuroscientific studies to issues and arguments in the philosophy of mind.

neuroscience   Considered a branch of biology, the scientific study of the nervous system, including the brain.

new synthesis (modern evolutionary synthesis, neo-Darwinism)   The combination of Darwinian evolution through natural selection and Mendelian genetics, which describes the mechanism of how characteristics are transmitted from parents to children.

nihilism   The view that nothing exists or has value.

noetic   Pertaining to believing and knowing.

normative ethics (substantive ethics)   The branch of ethics dealing with actual (first-order) obligations, typically in terms of acts or rules.

Ockham's razor (also the principle of parsimony, simplicity)   The principle, named after the late medieval philosopher William of Ockham, that the hypothesis postulating the fewest number of entities to explain a phenomenon is preferable.

omnipotence (omnipotent)   The attribute of God of having all of the power it is possible for God to have.

omniscience (omniscient)   The attribute of God of having all of the knowledge that it is possible to have.

ontology (ontological)   The branch of philosophy, often associated with metaphysics, that deals with what has being or what kinds of things have being.

organic   Living or produced by living things.

organism   An individual living thing with interdependent parts making up one whole.

original sin   The Christian theological belief that all humanity is in a state of sin stemming from the sin of the first human or humans.

orthodoxy (without capitalization, or classical Christianity)   The framework of common or ecumenical beliefs endorsed by the Seven Great Councils of the early Christian centuries.

Paleolithic (Age, Era, Period)   The early prehistoric phase of the Stone Age, beginning about 2.5 million years ago and ending about 10,000 years ago.

paleontology (paleontologist)   The field of science that studies life and ecologies existent in the distant past as based on fossils from the pertinent geological periods.

paradigm In a community of researchers, the shared assumptions, values, ideas, and problems that govern a normal period of scientific activity.

phenotype (phenotypic) The observable traits of an individual.

physicotheology A type of natural theology, prominent in seventeenth- and eighteenth-century England, which assumes that the existence of God can be concluded from inferences based on the study of nature.

pragmatism (pragmatic) The distinctively American philosophy that ideas or theories have value and can be called true because acting on them proves useful for human purposes.

predestination The theological view that the ultimate destiny of each person is determined by God.

primary cause The unique creative power that began everything and the guiding power underlying the ongoing events of the world.

probability The measure of the likeliness or chance that an event will occur, quantified as a number between 0 (impossibility) and 1 (certainty) (see also antecedent probability).

Protestantism A major branch of Christianity beginning in the sixteenth century from the reform or protest movement led by such religious leaders as Martin Luther and John Calvin.

providence (providential) The view that God provides wise and loving guidance of the world, although opinions vary regarding ideas of general or specific providential activity.

Quakers (Friends, Society of Friends) A religious movement that avoids creeds and clergy and emphasizes that all believers have access to divine truth and guidance.

qualia In philosophy of mind, a term used broadly to refer to introspectively accessible, phenomenal aspects of our mental lives.

quantum mechanics A major branch of physics that describes physical phenomena at the quantum level, atomic and subatomic.

quark An elementary particle and fundamental constituent of matter, which in some combinations form protons and neutrons in atomic nuclei.

random variation See mutation.

rationalism In the Enlightenment, the philosophy that either the content or the form of knowledge is produced by the mind.

realism Ontologically or metaphysically, the philosophical view that there is a real objective world that is not created by our minds and, epistemologically, the view that we have cognitive powers that reliably know this world.

reciprocal altruism Giving aid or benefit to another with the expectation of receiving aid or benefit in return.

reductionism (reductionist) The procedure of describing a complex phenomenon in terms of simpler or constituent parts (methodological) or the thesis that a complex phenomenon is merely the combination of its parts and cannot represent a higher-level reality (metaphysical).

relativism In ethics, the view that there is no universal standard of moral conduct.

religion   A set of beliefs, behaviors, and emotions organized around an idea of the divine or a spiritual meaning of life.

Resurrection (the)   The coming back to life of Jesus Christ three days after having been put to death by crucifixion.

RNA   Ribonucleic acid, a polymeric molecule, which is involved in various biological roles in coding, decoding, regulation, and expression of genes (see also DNA).

scholasticism (scholastic, the Schoolmen)   The medieval school or method of philosophy, combining rigorous logic, metaphysics, theology, and semantics, as taught by academics in the universities from the twelfth to the sixteenth century.

scientific law   A general statement that a given event as cause brings about a certain effect under specified initial conditions.

scientific method   The highly focused intellectual procedures that seek to confirm or disconfirm hypotheses in relation to empirical experience, such as observation and experiment.

second law (of thermodynamics)   In thermodynamics, the general physical principle stating that the entropy of an isolated system that is not in equilibrium will tend to increase over time, approaching a maximum value at equilibrium.

secondary causes   Created beings that by nature require divine or primary causality to initiate and sustain their activity.

self-organization   In origin-of-life studies, the idea that prebiotic molecules under certain conditions possess the property of self-assembly, now thought to be confirmed in such cases as the formation of RNA molecules in hydrothermal vents or in viruses in host cells.

self-replication   In origin-of-life studies, the behavior of a prebiotic system to produce exact copies of itself, as is now thought to be confirmed for RNA molecules under certain conditions.

sensus divinitatis   The theological view that human beings possess a "sense of the divine" or "sense of God," which has been created in them by God.

sentience   The inner subjective ability to feel and experience, usually distinguished from the ability to perceive or think, which are considered higher functions.

sin   The act of disobedience to God and, more fundamentally, the state of being out of relationship with God.

singularity (the)   In cosmological science, the term for the initial gravitational singularity of infinite density in which all of the mass and space-time of the universe was contained and from which quantum fluctuations caused the rapid expansion of the Big Bang.

skepticism (skeptic)   The antirealist view, usually in epistemology but sometimes in moral theory, that we cannot know certain claims to be true, either because of the subject matter being beyond us or because our powers of knowing have deficiencies.

social construction of knowledge   In epistemology, the nonrealist or antirealist view that knowledge is produced or constructed because of our place in a community.

social Darwinism   The philosophy of society, promulgated by Herbert Spencer and others, that the concepts of natural selection and survival of the fittest in biology can be applied to sociology, economics, and political theory in terms of a universal law of progress.

social science (human science)   An academic discipline (such as psychology, sociology, anthropology, and economics) that studies human life, in some cases individually but usually in groups.

sola scriptura   In Christian traditions born of the Protestant Reformation, the principle that the Bible is the supreme authority in matters of doctrine and practice.

solipsism   The belief that only oneself exists and that there are no other selves or minds.

space-time   In physics, the single physical reality constituted by the interweaving of space and time; any mathematical model of space and time as a continuum.

steady-state theory   In scientific cosmology, the obsolete model of the expanding universe in which new matter is continuously created so that constant density is maintained.

struggle for existence   See survival of the fittest.

substantive ethics   See normative ethics.

supernatural, supernaturalism   The view that there is divine being (or beings) in addition to nature that can interact with nature.

supervenience   A concept with wide application in analytic philosophy to the effect that a set of properties A supervenes on another set B just in case no two things can differ with respect to A-properties without also differing with respect to their B-properties.

survival of the fittest   In Darwinian evolutionary theory, a term (borrowed from Herbert Spencer) to express the idea (drawn from Thomas Malthus) that the organisms in nature are in a constant struggle in which, on average, only the fittest would survive; de facto natural selection.

teleological argument   A type of theistic argument that cites the order and regularity of the world as requiring explanation by reference to a supremely intelligent being who orders it for an end or goal.

teleological explanation   A type of explanation that refers to a purpose or intended end state, generally as the intention of an intelligent being.

teleology   The quality of a being as end-directed or goal-directed, either inherently or by direction of another.

theism   The belief in an omnipotent, omniscient, wholly good God.

theistic evolution   The view that theism and evolution can be combined in a larger perspective in a consistent way, thus achieving harmony between theism and a key part of science.

theodicy   An explanation (involving one or more themes) regarding why (or possibly why) God allows evil and suffering.

theology   The intellectual discipline of formulating and systematizing knowledge of God, generally utilizing sources such as scripture and tradition.

theory   See hypothesis.

transcendent   The divine attribute of being ontologically distinct from creation.

Trinity (doctrine)   The major theological concept of God as existing as one being and yet in three divine Persons.

uniformity of nature (principle)   The assumption anchoring scientific investigation that nature is reliably and consistently regular in its past and future operations.

Unitarian (Unitarian Universalism)   Religious denomination affirming that religion is a matter of individual experience such that only the individual can exercise personal conscience to decide what to believe.

universal acid   Daniel Dennett's term for Darwinian theory because it not only revolutionized biology but also corrodes or eats through all traditional beliefs and practices pertaining to God, morality, human persons, and the like.

vacuum fluctuation   In quantum physics, the temporary change in the amount of energy in a point in space, which may have been important in the origin of the structure of the universe.

variation   See mutation.

worldview   A comprehensive and general philosophical explanation of reality, knowledge, morality, and human beings that has implications for all major areas of life and the world.

REFERENCES

Adams, Marilyn. 1999. *Horrendous Evils and the Goodness of God.* Ithaca, NY: Cornell University Press.

Alexander, Dennis. 2008. *Creation or Evolution: Do We Have to Choose?* Oxford: Monarch Books.

Anselm, St. 1903. *Anselm: Proslogium, Monologium, an Appendix on Behalf of the Fool by Gaunilo; and Cur Deus Homo.* Translated by S. N. Deane. Chicago: Open Court.

Aquinas, St. Thomas. 1975. *Summa Contra Gentiles* [*SCG*]. Translated by A. C. Pegis. Notre Dame, IN: University of Notre Dame Press.

Aquinas, St. Thomas. 1981. *Summa Theologica* [*ST*]. Translated by Fathers of the English Domnican Province. Westminster, MD: Christian Classics.

Aquinas, St. Thomas. 2012. *Disputed Questions on the Power of God* [*DQP*]. Translated by R. J. Regan as *The Power of God.* New York: Oxford University Press.

Augustine, St. 1955. "Enchiridion" in *The Confessions and Enchiridion.* Translated and edited by Albert Outler. Louisville, KY: Westminster John Knox.

Augustine, St. 1982. *On the Literal Meaning of Genesis,* 2 vols. Translated and annotated by J. H. Taylor. New York: Newman Press.

Augustine, St. 1998. *Confessions.* Translated by H. Chadwick. Oxford: Oxford University Press.

Augustine, St. 2009. *The City of God.* Translated by Marcus Dods. Peabody, MA: Hendrickson.

Ayala, Francisco. 1970. "Teleological Explanations in Evolutionary Biology." *Philosophy of Science* 37: 1–15.

Ayala, Francisco. 2007. *Darwin's Gift to Science and Religion.* Washington, DC: Joseph Henry Press.

Bada, J. L., and A. Lazcana. 2009. "The Origin of Life." In *Evolution: The First Four Billion Years.* Edited by M. Ruse and J. Travis, 49–79. Cambridge, MA: Harvard University Press.

Barbour, I. 1988. "Ways of Relating Science and Theology." In *Physics, Philosophy, and Theology: A Common Quest for Understanding,* 21–48. Vatican City: Vatican Observatory.

Barnes, J., ed. 1984. *The Complete Works of Aristotle.* Princeton, NJ: Princeton University Press.

Barrett, P. H., P. J. Gautrey, S. Herbert, D. Kohn, and S. Smith, eds. 1987. *Charles Darwin's Notebooks, 1836–1844.* Ithaca, NY: Cornell University Press.

Barrow, J. D., and F. J. Tipler. 1986. *The Anthropic Cosmological Principle.* Oxford: Clarendon Press.

Behe, M. 1996. *Darwin's Black Box: The Biochemical Challenge to Evolution.* New York: Free Press.

Bergson, H. 1907. *L'évolution Créatrice.* Paris: Alcan.

Berry, R. J., ed. 1991. *Real Science, Real Faith.* Eastbourne, UK: Monarch.

Blackmore, Susan. 2000. *The Meme Machine.* Oxford: Oxford University Press.

Brooke, John Hedley. 2014. *Science and Religion: Some Historical Perspectives.* Cambridge: Cambridge University Press.

Burtt, Edwin. 1948. *The Metaphysical Foundations of Modern Physical Science.* London: Routledge & Kegan Paul.

Calvin, J. 1960. *Institutes of the Christian Religion.* Philadelphia: Westminster Press.

Carr, B. J., and M. J. Rees. 1979. "The Anthropic Principle and the Structure of the Physical World." *Nature* 278 (April): 605–12.

Carter, Brandon. 1974. "Large Number Coincidences and the Anthropic Principle in Cosmology." *IAU Symposium 63: Confrontation of Cosmological Theories with Observational Data.* Dordrecht: Reidel. 291–298; republished in *General Relativity and Gravitation,* with an introduction by George Ellis, 43, no. 11 (2011): 3225–3233.

Catechism of the Catholic Church. 1994. Liguori, MO: Liguori.

Chalmers, David. 1995. "Facing Up to the Problem of Consciousness." *Journal of Consciousness Studies* 2, no. 3: 200–219.

Chambers, R. 1844. *Vestiges of the Natural History of Creation.* London: Churchill.

Chomsky, Noam. 2001. *Language and the Problems of Knowledge.* Cambridge, MA: MIT Press.

Churchland, Patricia. 1986. *Neurophilosophy: Toward a Unified Science of the Mind/ Brain.* Cambridge, MA: MIT Press.

Churchland, Patricia. 1987. "Epistemology in the Age of Neuroscience." *Journal of Philosophy* 84, no. 10: 544–53.

Churchland, Paul. 1984. *Matter and Consciousness.* Cambridge, MA: MIT Press.

Clark, Thomas. 2007. *Encountering Naturalism: A Worldview and Its Uses.* Somerville, MA: Center for Naturalism.

Collins, Francis. 2006. *The Language of God: A Scientist Presents Evidence for Belief.* New York: Free Press.

Collins, Robin. 1999. "A Scientific Argument for the Existence of God: The Fine-Tuning Design Argument." In *Reason for the Hope Within.* Edited by Michael Murray, 47–75. Grand Rapids, MI: Eerdmans.

Conway Morris, S. 2003. *Life's Solution: Inevitable Humans in a Lonely Universe.* Cambridge, UK: Cambridge University Press.

Cosmides, L. 1989. "The Logic of Social Exchange: Has Natural Selection Shaped How Humans Reason? Studies with the Wason Selection Task." *Cognition* 31: 187–276.

Coulson, Charles Alfred. 1958. *Science and Christian Belief.* Oxford: Oxford University Press.

Crick, Francis. 1982. *Life Itself: Its Origin and Nature.* New York: Simon & Schuster.

Crick, Francis. 1994. *The Astonishing Hypothesis: The Scientific Search for the Soul.* New York: Scribner.

Crick, Francis. 1996. *Of Molecules and Man.* Seattle: University of Washington Press.

Crick, Francis, and Leslie Orgel. 1973. "Directed Panspermia." *Icarus* 19, no. 3: 341–48.

Darwin, C. 1859. *On the Origin of Species by Means of Natural Selection, or the Preservation of Favoured Races in the Struggle for Life.* London: Murray.

Darwin, C. 1861. *Origin of Species,* 3rd ed. London: Murray.

Darwin, C. 1871. *The Descent of Man, and Selection in Relation to Sex* (2 volumes). 1st ed. London: Murray.

Darwin, C. 1882. *The Descent of Man, and Selection in Relation to Sex.* 2nd ed. London: Murray.

Darwin, C. 1958. *The Autobiography of Charles Darwin (1809–1882).* Edited by N. Barlow. London: Collins.

Darwin, C. 1985–. *The Correspondence of Charles Darwin.* Cambridge, UK: Cambridge University Press.

Darwin, E. 1803. *The Temple of Nature.* London: Johnson.

Darwin, Francis. 1887. *The Life and Letters of Charles Darwin,* vol. 2. London: Murray.

Davies, Paul. 1982. *The Accidental Universe.* Cambridge, UK: Cambridge University Press.

Davies, Paul. 1995. "The Birth of the Cosmos." In *God, Cosmos, Nature and Creativity.* Edited by Jill Gready. Edinburgh: Scottish Academic Press.

Davies, Paul. 2003. "Complexity and the Arrow of Time." In *From Complexity to Life,* 72–92. New York: Oxford University Press.

Davies, Paul. 2007. *Cosmic Jackpot: Why Our Universe Is Just Right for Life.* New York: Houghton–Mifflin.

Davis, Stephen T. 1984. "Is It Possible to Know That Jesus Was Raised from the Dead?" *Faith and Philosophy* 1: 147–59.

Dawkins, R. 1976. *The Selfish Gene.* Oxford: Oxford University Press.

Dawkins, R. 1983. *Universal Darwinism: Evolution from Molecules to Men.* Edited by D. S. Bendall, 403–25. Cambridge, UK: Cambridge University Press.

Dawkins, R. 1986. *The Blind Watchmaker.* New York: Norton.

Dawkins, R. 1995. *A River out of Eden.* New York: Basic Books.

Dawkins, R. 1997. "Religion Is a Virus." *Mother Jones.* http://www.motherjones.com/politics/1997/11/religion-virus, accessed November 2, 2015.

Dawkins, R. 2006. *The God Delusion.* New York: Houghton, Mifflin, Harcourt.

Dawkins, R., and J. R. Krebs. 1979. "Arms Races between and within Species." *Proceedings of the Royal Society of London, Series B* 205: 489–511.

Dawkins, R. 2014. "Science Discredits Religion." In *Philosophy of Religion: Selected Readings.* Edited by Michael Peterson, William Hasker, Bruce Reichenbach, and David Basinger, 5th ed., 546–48. New York: Oxford University Press. Reprinted from Richard Dawkins, "When Religion Steps on Science's Turf." *Quarterly Review of Biology* 72 (1997): 397–99.

de Duve, Christian. 1995. *Vital Dust: Life as a Cosmic Imperative*. New York: Basic Books.

de Waal, Frans. 2006. *Primates and Philosophers: How Morality Evolved*. Princeton, NJ: Princeton University Press.

Deacon, Terrence. 2003. "The Hierarchic Logic of Emergence: Untangling the Interdependence of Evolution and Self-Organization." In *Evolution and Learning: The Baldwin Effect Reconsidered*. Edited by B. Weber and D. Depew. Cambridge, MA: MIT Press.

Dembski, William. 1999. *Intelligent Design: The Bridge between Science and Theology*. Downers Grove, IL: InterVarsity Press.

Dennett, D. C. 1984. *Elbow Room: The Varieties of Free Will Worth Wanting*. Cambridge, MA: MIT Press.

Dennett, D. C. 1995. *Darwin's Dangerous Idea: Evolution and the Meanings of Life*. New York: Simon & Schuster.

Dennett, D. C. 2006. *Breaking the Spell: Religion as a Natural Phenomenon*. New York: Viking Press.

Dennett, Daniel, and Alvin Plantinga. 2011. *Science and Religion: Are They Compatible?* New York: Oxford University Press.

Diego, Francisco. 1997. Interviewed in *Stephen Hawking's Universe: The Big Bang*. DVD. New York: Educational Broadcasting.

Dijksterhuis, E. J. 1961. *The Mechanization of the World Picture*. Oxford: Oxford University Press.

Dobzhansky, Theodosius. 1973. "Nothing in Biology Makes Sense Except in the Light of Evolution." *American Biology Teacher* 35: 125–29.

Dobzhansky, Theodosius. 1974. "Chance and Creativity in Evolution." In *Studies in the Philosophy of Biology*. Edited by F. J. Ayala and T. Dobzhansky, 307–38. London: Macmillan.

Documents of Vatican II, The. 1966. Edited by W. M. Abbot, S.J., and translated by J. Gallagher. New York: Guild Press.

Dostoevsky, F. [1880] 2007. *The Brothers Karamazov*. Translated by C. B. Garnett. Raleigh, N. C.: Hayes Barton Press.

Draper, Paul. 2008. "Evolution and the Problem of Evil." In *Philosophy of Religion: An Anthology*. Edited by L. Pojman and M. Rea, 5th ed., 207–19. Belmont, CA: Wadsworth.

Driesch, H. 1908. *The Science and the Philosophy of the Organism*. London: Black.

Durkheim, E. 1912. *Elementary Forms of Religious Life*. Oxford: Oxford University Press.

Dyson, Freeman. 1979. *Disturbing the Universe*. New York: Harper & Row.

Eckland, Eric, Jack Szostak, and David Bartel. 1995. "Structurally Complex and Highly Active RNA Ligases Derived from Random RNA Sequences." *Science* 269: 364–70.

Eddington, Sir Arthur. 1931. "The End of the World: From the Standpoint of Mathematical Physics." *Nature* 127, no. 3203: 447–53. doi:10.1038/127447a0.

Ehrman, Bart. 2000. *The Historical Jesus*, part 2. Chantilly, VA: Teaching Company.

Einstein, Albert. 1950. *Out of My Later Years*. New York: Philosophical Library. Reprinted from Albert Einstein, "Physics and Reality." *Journal of the Franklin Institute* 221 (1936): 349–82.

Eliot, T. S. 1935. *Murder in the Cathedral*. London: Faber and Faber.

Ellis, G. 2011. "Does the Multiverse Really Exist?" *Scientific American* 305, no. 2: 38–43.

Farley, J. 1977. *The Spontaneous Generation Controversy from Descartes to Oparin*. Baltimore: Johns Hopkins University Press.

Farrell, John. 2005. *The Day without Yesterday: Lemaitre, Einstein, and the Birth of Modern Cosmology*. New York: Basic Books.

Findlay, J. N. 1948. "Can God's Existence be Disproved?" *Mind* 37, no. 226: 176–83.

Flew, Antony. 2007. *There Is a God: How the World's Most Notorious Atheist Changed His Mind*. New York: HarperOne.

Gilkey, L. B. 1959. *Maker of Heaven and Earth*. Garden City, NY: Doubleday.

Gingerich, Owen. 2006. *God's Universe*. Cambridge, MA: Belknap Press of Harvard University Press.

Goetz, Stewart, and Charles Taliaferro. 2008. *Naturalism*. Grand Rapids, MI: Eerdmans.

Goodwin, B. 2001. *How the Leopard Changed Its Spots*, 2nd ed. Princeton, NJ: Princeton University Press.

Gosse, P. H. 1857. *Omphalos; An Attempt to Untie the Geological Knot*. London: Van Voorst.

Gould, S. J. 1985. *The Flamingo's Smile: Reflections in Natural History*. New York: Norton.

Gould, S. J. 1989. *Wonderful Life: The Burgess Shale and the Nature of History*. New York: Norton.

Gould, S. J. 1994. "The Evolution of Life on Earth." *Scientific American* 271, no. 4: 84–91.

Gould, S. J. 1996. *Full House: The Spread of Excellence from Plato to Darwin*. New York: Paragon.

Gould, S. J. 1997. "Nonoverlapping Magisteria." *Natural History* 106: 16–22.

Gould, S. J., and R. C. Lewontin. 1979. "The Spandrels of San Marco and the Panglossian Paradigm: A Critique of the Adaptationist Programme." *Proceedings of the Royal Society of London, Series B: Biological Sciences* 205: 581–98.

Haldane, J. B. S. 1927. *Possible Worlds and Other Essays*. London: Chatto & Windus.

Hall, A. R. 1954. *The Scientific Revolution 1500–1800: The Formation of the Modern Scientific Attitude*. London: Longman, Green.

Harré, Rom, with J. Arson and E. Way. 1994. *Realism Rescued: How Scientific Progress Is Possible*. London: Duckworth.

Hasker, William. 1999. *The Emergent Self*. Ithaca, NY: Cornell University Press.

Haught, John. 2000. *God after Darwin: A Theology of Evolution*. Boulder, CO: Westview Press.

Hawking, Stephen, and Leonard Mlodinow. 2010. *The Grand Design*. New York: Bantam Books.

Heidegger, M. 1959. *An Introduction to Metaphysics.* New Haven, CT: Yale University Press.

Hick, J. 1961. "Necessary Being." *Scottish Journal of Theology* 14, no. 4: 353–369.

Hick, J. 1980. *God Has Many Names.* Philadelphia: Westminster Press.

Hick, John. 2010. *Evil and the God of Love.* New York: Palgrave Macmillan.

Hitchens, Christopher. 2010. "Unanswerable Prayers." *Vanity Fair* October: 158–63. http://www.vanityfair.com/culture/2010/10/hitchens-201010, accessed November 2, 2015.

Hook, Sidney. 1961. "Naturalism and First Principles." In *The Quest for Being.* Buffalo, NY: Prometheus Books.

Hoyle, Fred. 1975a. *Astronomy and Cosmology: A Modern Course.* San Francisco: Freeman.

Hoyle, Fred. 1975b. *Astronomy Today.* London: Heinemann.

Hume, D. [1748] 2000. *An Enquiry Concerning Human Understanding.* Edited by Tom L. Beauchamp. New York: Oxford University Press, 2000.

Hume, D. [1779] 1947. *Dialogues Concerning Natural Religion.* Edited by N. K. Smith. Indianapolis: Bobbs–Merrill.

Hume, D. [1757] 1963. *A Natural History of Religion. Hume on Religion.* Edited by R. Wollheim. London: Fontana.

Hume, D. [1739–1740] 1978. *A Treatise of Human Nature.* Oxford: Oxford University Press.

Huxley, J. S. 1912. *The Individual in the Animal Kingdom.* Cambridge, UK: Cambridge University Press.

Huxley, J. S. 1927. *Religion without Revelation.* London: Benn.

Huxley, J. S. 1943. *TVA: Adventure in Planning.* London: Scientific Book Club.

Huxley, T. H. 1870. *Lay Sermons, Addresses, and Reviews.* London: Macmillan.

Huxley, T. H. 1874. "On the Hypothesis That Animals Are Automata, and Its History." In *Collected Essays. Volume I, Methods and Results*, 195–250. London: Macmillan.

Huxley, T. H. 1893. Lecture on "The Darwin Memorial," delivered on June 9, 1885, in Thomas H. Huxley, *Darwiniana: Essays.* London: Macmillan.

Huxley, T. H. 2009. *Evolution and Ethics with a New Introduction.* Edited by M. Ruse. Princeton, NJ: Princeton University Press.

Huyssteen, J. Wentzel van. 2006. *Alone in the World?: Human Uniqueness in Science and Theology.* Grand Rapids, MI: Eerdmans.

Irenaeus, St. 1869. "Against Heresies." In *Ante-Nicene Christian Library. Translations of the Writings of the Fathers*, vol. IX. Edited by A. Roberts and J. Donaldson. Edinburgh: T&T Clark.

James, Wm. 1880. *The Principles of Psychology.* New York: Holt.

John Paul II. 1997. "Message to the Pontifical Academy of Sciences" (October 22, 1996). Reprinted in *The Quarterly Review of Biology* 72, no. 4: 381–83.

Joyce, Richard. 2006. *The Evolution of Morality.* Cambridge, MA: MIT Press.

Kant, I. 1959. *Foundations of the Metaphysics of Morals.* Indianapolis: Bobbs–Merrill.

Kauffman, S. A. 1993. *The Origins of Order: Self-Organization and Selection in Evolution.* Oxford: Oxford University Press.

Kauffman, S. A. 2003. "The Emergence of Autonomous Agents." In *From Complexity to Life*. Edited by Niels Gregersen. New York: Oxford University Press. Chapter abbreviated and modified from Stuart Kaufmann, *Investigations*. New York: Oxford University Press.

Kim, Jaegwon. 2005. *Physicalism or Something near Enough*. Princeton, NJ: Princeton University Press.

Kingsley, Charles. 1874. "The Natural Theology of the Future." In *Westminster Sermons*, v–xxxiii. London: Macmillan.

Kitcher, P. 2007. *Living with Darwin: Evolution, Design, and the Future of Faith*. New York: Oxford University Press.

Kuhn, T. 1962. *The Structure of Scientific Revolutions*. Chicago: University of Chicago Press.

Kuhn, T. 1977. *The Essential Tension: Selected Studies in Scientific Tradition and Change*. Chicago: University of Chicago Press.

Kuhn, T. 1993. "Metaphor in Science." In *Metaphor and Thought*. Edited by Andrew Ortony, 2nd ed., 533–42. Cambridge, UK: Cambridge University Press.

Lakoff, G., and Johnson M. 1980. *Metaphors We Live By*. Chicago: University of Chicago Press.

Leibniz, G. W. 1973a; 1714. "On the Ultimate Origination of Things." Translated by G. H. R. Parkinson and M Morris. In *Leibniz: Philosophical Writings*. Edited by G. H. R. Parkinson. London: J. M. Dent & Sons.

Leibniz, G. W. 1973b; 1718. "Principles of Nature and of Grace Founded on Reason." Translated by G. H. R. Parkinson and M Morris. In *Leibniz: Philosophical Writings*. Edited by G. H. R. Parkinson. London: J. M. Dent & Sons.

Leibniz, G. W. 2001. *Theodicy: Essays on the Goodness of God, the Freedom of Man and the Origin of Evil*. Translated by E. M. Huggard. Wipf & Stock.

Lemaître, Georges. 1931. "The Beginning of the World from the Point of View of Quantum Theory." *Nature* 127: 706.

Lenoir, Timothy. 1982. *Strategy of Life*. Dordrecht: Reidel.

Lewis, C. S. 1947. *The Abolition of Man*. New York: Macmillan.

Lewis, C. S. 1955. *Surprised by Joy: The Shape of My Early Life*. New York: Harcourt, Brace.

Lewis, C. S. 1962. *The Problem of Pain*. New York: Macmillan.

Lewis, C. S. 1980. "Is Theology Poetry?" In *The Weight of Glory*. Edited by W. Hooper. New York: HarperCollins.

Lewis, C. S. 2001. *Miracles*. New York: Harper Collins.

Lewontin, R. C. 1974. *The Genetic Basis of Evolutionary Change*. New York: Columbia University Press.

Linville, Mark. 2009. "The Moral Poverty of Evolutionary Naturalism." In *Contending with Christianity's Critics*. Edited by Paul Copan and William Lane Craig. Nashville: Broadman and Holman, 58–73.

Lorenz, K. 1941. "Kant's Lehre vom a priorischen im Lichte geganwartiger Biologie." *Blatter fur Deutsche Philosophie* 15: 94–125. Translated and reprinted as "Kant's Doctrine of the 'a priori' in the Light of Contemporary Biology." In *Learning, Development, and Culture; Essays in Evolutionary Epistemology*, 121–43. Chichester: Wiley, 1982.

Lovelock, J. E. 1979. *Gaia: A New Look at Life on Earth.* Oxford: Oxford University Press.

Lucretius. 2001. *On the Nature of Things.* Translated by M. Smith. Indianapolis: Hackett.

MacArthur, R. H., and E. O. Wilson. 1967. *The Theory of Island Biogeography.* Princeton, NJ: Princeton University Press.

Mackie, J. 1977. *Ethics.* Harmondsworth, UK: Penguin.

Maimonides, M. 1936. *The Guide for the Perplexed.* Translated by S. Friedlander. London: Routledge.

Mascall, E. L. 1956. *Christian Theology and Natural Science.* New York: Ronald Press.

McGinn, Collin. 2000. *The Mysterious Flame.* New York: Basic Books.

McGrath, Alister. 2011a. *Darwinism and the Divine: Evolutionary Thought and Natural Theology.* Oxford: Wiley–Blackwell.

McGrath, Alister. 2011b. *Surprised by Meaning: Science, Faith, and How We Make Sense of Things.* Louisville, KY: Westminster John Knox.

McMullin, Ernan. 1991. "Plantinga's Defense of Special Creation." *Christian Scholar's Review* xxxi, no. 1: 55–79.

McShea, D., and R. Brandon. 2010. *Biology's First Law: The Tendency for Diversity and Complexity to Increase in Evolutionary Systems.* Chicago: University of Chicago Press.

Medawar, Peter. 1985. *The Limits of Science.* Oxford: Oxford University Press.

Meyer, Stephen C. 2009. *Signature in the Cell: DNA and the Evidence for Intelligent Design.* New York: HarperCollins.

Mill, J. S. 1863. *Utilitarianism.* London: Parker, Son, and Bourn.

Miller, K. 1999. *Finding Darwin's God.* New York: Harper & Row.

Monod, Jacques. 1971. *Chance and Necessity: An Essay on the Natural Philosophy of Modern Biology.* Translated by A. Wainhouse. New York: Knopf.

Moore, Aubrey. 1890. "The Christian Doctrine of God." In *Lux Mundi.* Edited by C. Gore, 41–81. London: John Murray.

Muir, J. 1966. *John of the Mountains: The Unpublished Journals of John Muir.* Edited by L. M. Wolfe. Madison: University of Wisconsin Press.

Mumma, Howard. 2000. *Albert Camus and the Minister.* Brewster, MA: Paraclete Press.

Nagel, Ernest. 1954. "Naturalism Reconsidered." *Proceedings and Addresses of the American Philosophical Association* 28: 5–17.

Nagel, Thomas. 1974. "What Is It Like to Be a Bat?" *The Philosophical Review* 4: 435–450.

Nagel, Thomas. 2012. *Mind and Cosmos: Why the Materialist Neo-Darwinian Conception of Nature Is Almost Certainly False.* New York: Oxford University Press.

Newbigin, Leslie. 1995. *The Open Secret: An Introduction to the Theology of Mission.* Grand Rapids, MI: Eerdmans.

Newman, J. H. 1870. *A Grammar of Assent.* New York: Catholic Publishing Society.

Newman, J. H. 1973. *The Letters and Diaries of John Henry Newman, XXV.* Edited by C. S. Dessain and T. Gornall. Oxford: Clarendon Press.

Numbers, Ronald. 1992. *Prophetess of Health: Ellen G. White and the Origins of Seventh-day Adventist Health Reform*, rev. ed. Knoxville: University of Tennessee Press.

Numbers, Ronald. 2006. *The Creationists: From Scientific Creationism to Intelligent Design,* exp. ed. Cambridge, MA: Harvard University Press.

O'Connor, Timothy. 1994. "Emergent Properties." *American Philosophical Quarterly* 31, no. 2: 91–104.

Oden, Thomas. 2002. *The Rebirth of Orthodoxy: Signs of New Life in Christianity*. San Francisco: HarperOne.

Oden, Thomas. 2009. *Classical Christianity*. New York: HarperCollins.

Orgel, Leslie. 1998. "The Origin of Life—A Review of Facts and Speculations." *Trends in Biochemical Sciences* 23, no. 12: 491–95.

Orgel, Leslie. 2006. "In the Beginning." *Nature* 439: 915.

Paley, William. [1802] 1809. *Natural Theology: Or, Evidences of the Existence and Attributes of the Deity*, 12th ed. London: Faulder.

Pannenberg, Wolfhart. 1971. *Basic Questions in Theology*, vol. II. Translated by G. H. Kehm. Philadelphia: Westminster Press.

Papineau, David. 1993. *Philosophical Naturalism*. Oxford: Blackwell.

Peacocke, Arthur. 2003. "Complexity, Emergence, and Divine Creativity." In *From Complexity to Life: On the Emergence of Life and Meaning*. Edited by Niels Henrik Gregersen, 187–205. New York: Oxford University Press.

Penfield, Wilder. 1975. *The Mystery of the Mind: A Critical Study of Consciousness and the Human Brain*. Princeton, NJ: Princeton University Press.

Penrose, Roger. 1989. *The Emperor's New Mind*. Oxford: Oxford University Press.

Persinger, Michael A., Kevin Saroka, Stanley A. Koren, and Linda S. St.-Pierre. 2010. "The Electromagnetic Induction of Mystical and Altered States within the Laboratory." *Journal of Consciousness Exploration & Research* 1, no. 7: 808–30.

Peterson, Michael. 1982. *Evil and the Christian God*. Grand Rapids, MI: Baker.

Peterson, Michael. 1998. *God and Evil: An Introduction to the Issues*. Boulder, CO: Westview Press.

Peterson, Michael. 2010. "C. S. Lewis on Evolution and Intelligent Design." *Perspectives on Science and Christian Faith: Journal of the American Scientific Affiliation* 62, no. 4: 253–66.

Peterson, Michael. 2011. "Deep Resonances between Science and Theology." In *The Continuing Relevance of Wesleyan Theology: Essays in Honor of Laurence W. Wood*. Edited by Nathan Crawford, 139–58. Eugene, OR: Wifp & Stock.

Peterson, Michael. 2013. "The Problem of Evil." In *The Oxford Handbook of Atheism*. Edited by Stehen Bollivant and Michael Ruse. Oxford: Oxford University Press, 71–88.

Peterson, Michael. 2017. "A Theological Evaluation of Evolutionary Ethics." In *The Cambridge Handbook of Evolutionary Ethics*. Edited by Robert Richards and Michael Ruse. Cambridge, UK: Cambridge University Press.

Peterson, Michael, and Michael Ruse. 2013. "Do Science and Faith Conflict: A Debate," accessed November 1, 2014, http://seedbed.com/feed/faith-science-conflict-video-debate/.

Peterson, Michael, William Hasker, Bruce Reichenbach, and David Basinger. 2012. *Reason and Religious Belief: An Introduction to the Philosophy of Religion*, 5th ed. New York: Oxford University Press.

Peterson, Michael, William Hasker, Bruce Reichenbach, and David Basinger, eds. 2014. *Philosophy of Religion: Selected Readings*, 5th ed. New York: Oxford University Press.

Plantinga, A. 1980. *Does God Have a Nature?* Milwaukee, WI: Marquette University Press.

Plantinga, A. 1991. "When Faith and Reason Clash: Evolution and the Bible." *Christian Scholar's Review* 21, no. 1: 8–32. Reprinted in D. Hull and M. Ruse, eds., 1998, *The Philosophy of Biology*, Oxford: Oxford University Press, 674–97.

Plantinga, A. 1993. *Warrant and Proper Function*. New York: Oxford University Press.

Plantinga, A. 2000. "Pluralism: A Defense of Religious Exclusivism." In *The Philosophical Challenge of Religious Diversity*. Edited by K. Meeker and P. Quinn, 172–92. New York: Oxford University Press.

Plantinga, Alvin. 2004. *Christian Faith and the Problem of Evil*. Edited by Peter van Inwagen, 1–25. Grand Rapids, MI: Eerdmanns.

Plantinga, Alvin. 2011. *Where the Conflict Really Lies: Science, Religion, and Naturalism*. Oxford: Oxford University Press.

Plato. 1892. *Theatetus*. In *The Dialogues of Plato* 3rd edition. vol. 4. Translated by Benjamin Jowett. Oxford: Oxford University Press.

Plato. 1974. *The Republic*. Translated by G. M. A. Grube. Indianapolis, IN: Hackett Press.

Polkinghorne, John. 2007. *One World: The Interaction of Science and Theology*. West Conshohocken, PA: Templeton Press.

Polkinghorne, John, and Michael Welker, eds. 2000. *The End of the World and the Ends of God: Science and Theology on Eschatology*. Harrisburg, PA: Trinity Press International.

Popper, K. R. 1974. "Reduction and the Incompleteness of Science." In *Studies in the Philosophy of Biology*. Editors F. J. Ayala, and T. Dobzhansky, 259–84. Berkeley: University of California Press.

Putnam, H. 1975, *Mathematics, Matter and Method*, Cambridge, MA: Cambridge University Press.

Putnam, H. 1981. *Reason, Truth, and History*. Cambridge, UK: Cambridge University Press.

Rahner, Karl. 1982. *Foundations of Christian Faith: An Introduction to the Idea of Christianity*. New York: The Crossroad Publishing Company.

Reid, Thomas. 2010 [1788]. *Essays on the Active Powers of Man*. Edinburgh: Edinburgh University Press.

Richards, R. J., and M. Ruse. 2015. *Debating Darwin: Mechanist or Romantic?* Chicago: University of Chicago Press.

Richerson, P., and R. Boyd. 2005. *Not by Genes Alone: How Culture Transformed Human Evolution*. Chicago: University of Chicago Press.

Rowe, William. 2006. "Friendly Atheism, Skeptical Theism, and the Problem of Evil." *International Journal for Philosophy of Religion* 59: 79–92.

Rowe, William. 2014. "Evil and Theodicy." In *Philosophy of Religion: Selected Readings*. Edited by Michael Peterson, William Hasker, Bruce Reichenbach, and David Basinger, 5th ed., 365–73. New York: Oxford University Press. Reprinted from William Rowe, *Philosophical Topics* 16, no. 2 (1988): 119–32.

Ruse, M. 1973. *The Philosophy of Biology*. London: Hutchinson.

Ruse, M. 1979a. *The Darwinian Revolution: Science Red in Tooth and Claw*. Chicago: University of Chicago Press.

Ruse, M. 1979b. *Sociobiology: Sense or Nonsense?* Dordrecht, The Netherlands: Reidel.

Ruse, M. 1982. *Darwinism Defended: A Guide to the Evolution Controversies*. Reading, MA: Benjamin/Cummings.

Ruse, M. 1986. *Taking Darwin Seriously: A Naturalistic Approach to Philosophy*. Oxford: Blackwell.

Ruse, M., ed. 1988a. *But Is It Science? The Philosophical Question in the Creation/Evolution Controversy*. Buffalo, NY: Prometheus.

Ruse, M. 1988b. *Homosexuality: A Philosophical Inquiry*. Oxford: Blackwell.

Ruse, M. 1988c. "Evolutionary Ethics: A Phoenix Arisen." In *Issues in Evolutionary Ethics*. Edited by Paul Thompson, 225–47. Albany, NY: SUNY Press.

Ruse, M. 1996. *Monad to Man: The Concept of Progress in Evolutionary Biology*. Cambridge, MA: Harvard University Press.

Ruse, M. 1998. *Taking Darwin Seriously: A Naturalistic Approach to Philosophy*, 2nd ed. Buffalo, NY: Prometheus Books.

Ruse, M. 2001. *Can a Darwinian Be a Christian? The Relationship between Science and Religion*. Cambridge, UK: Cambridge University Press.

Ruse, M. 2003. *Darwin and Design: Does Nature have a Purpose?* Cambridge, MA: Harvard University Press.

Ruse, M. 2005. *The Evolution–Creation Struggle*. Cambridge, MA: Harvard University Press.

Ruse, M. 2006. *Darwinism and Its Discontents*. Cambridge, UK: Cambridge University Press.

Ruse, M., ed. 2009. *Philosophy after Darwin: Classic and Contemporary Readings*. Princeton, NJ: Princeton University Press.

Ruse, M. 2010. *Science and Spirituality: Making Room for Faith in the Age of Science*. Cambridge, UK: Cambridge University Press.

Ruse, M. 2012. *The Philosophy of Human Evolution*. Cambridge, UK: Cambridge University Press.

Ruse, M. 2013. *The Gaia Hypothesis: Science on a Pagan Planet*. Chicago: University of Chicago Press.

Ruse, M. 2015. *Atheism: What Everyone Needs to Know*. Oxford: Oxford University Press.

Ruse, M. and E. O. Wilson. 1986. "Moral Philosophy as Applied Science." *Philosophy* 61: 173–92.

Russell, R. J. 2008. *Cosmology: From Alpha to Omega, the Creative Mutual Interaction of Theology and Science*. Minneapolis: Fortress Press.

Sagan, Carl. 1980. *Cosmos*. New York: Random House.

Sagan, Carl. 1985. *Contact*. New York: Simon & Schuster.

Schneider, J. 2010. "Recent Genetic Science and Christian Theology on Human Origins: An 'Aesthetic Supralapsarianism.'" *Perspectives on Science and Christian Faith* 62: 196–212.

Searle, John. 1992. *The Rediscovery of the Mind*. Cambridge, MA: MIT Press.

Smith, George. 1980. "The Case against God." In *An Anthology of Atheism and Rationalism*. Edited by Gordon Stein. Buffalo, NY: Prometheus Press.

Spencer, H. 1857. "Progress: Its Law and Cause." *Westminster Review* LXVII: 244–67.

Stegner, Victor. 2014. *God and the Multi-verse: Humanity's Expanding View of the Cosmos*. Buffalo, NY: Prometheus Press.

Stoeger, William. 1999. "The Immanent Directionality of the Evolutionary Process, and Its Relationship to Teleology." In *Evolutionary and Molecular Biology: Scientific Perspectives on Divine Action*. Edited by Robert J. Russell, William Stoeger, and Francisco Ayala, 163–90. Rome: Vatican Observatory.

Swinburne, R. 1977. *The Coherence of Theism*. Oxford: Clarendon Press.

Swinburne, Richard. 2004. *The Existence of God*, 2nd ed. Oxford: Oxford University Press.

Tattersall, Ian. 2004. "Innovation in Human Evolution." In *The Epic of Evolution: Science and Religion in Dialogue*. Edited by James Miller. Upper Saddle River, NJ: Pearson Prentice Hall.

Tilley, Terrence. 2000. *The Evils of Theodicy*. Eugene, OR: Wipf & Stock.

Thompsen, Dietrick. 1985. "The Quantum Universe: A Zero-Point Fluctuation?" *Science News*, August 3: 71–75.

Trigg, Roger. 2014. "A Defense of Religious Realism." In *Philosophy of Religion: Selected Readings*. Edited by Michael Peterson, William Hasker, Bruce Reichenbach, and David Basinger, 5th ed., 21–26. New York: Oxford University Press.

Trivers, R. L. 1971. "The Evolution of Reciprocal Altruism." *Quarterly Review of Biology* 46: 35–57.

Venema, Dennis. 2010. "Seeking a Signature." *Perspectives on Science and Christian Faith: Journal of the American Scientific Affiliation* 62, no. 4: 276–83.

Ward, K. 1996. *God, Chance and Necessity*. Oxford: Oneworld.

Wavell, S., and W. Iredale. 2004. "Sorry, Says Atheist-in-Chief, I Do Believe in God after All." *The Sunday Times,* December 12, sec. 1: 7.

Weinberg, S. 1977. *The First Three Minutes: A Modern View of the Origin of the Universe*. New York: Basic Books.

Weinberg, S. 1993. *Dreams of a Final Theory: The Scientist's Search for the Ultimate Laws of Nature*. New York: Vintage Books.

Weinberg, S. 1994. "Life in the Universe." *Scientific American* Oct., no. 1: 44–49.

Weinberg, S. 1999. "A Designer Universe?" *New York Review of Books* 46, no. 16: 46–48.

Weizsäcker, C. F. von. 1964. *The Relevance of Science*. New York: Harper.

Wesley, John. 1988. *Wesley's Fifty-Two Standard Sermons*. Edited by N. Burnwash. Salem, OH: Schmul Publishing.

West, S. A., and A. Gardner. 2013. "Adaptation and Inclusive Fitness." *Current Biology* 23: R577–84.

Whewell, W. 1840. *The Philosophy of the Inductive Sciences.* London: Parker.

Whewell, W. [1853] 2001. *Of the Plurality of Worlds. A Facsimile of the First Edition of 1853: Plus Previously Unpublished Material Excised by the Author Just before the Book Went to Press; and Whewell's Dialogue Rebutting His Critics, Reprinted from the Second Edition.* Chicago: University of Chicago Press.

Wielenberg, Erik. 2009. "A Defense of Moral Realism." *Faith and Philosophy* 26, no. 1: 23–41.

Wigner, Eugene. 1960. "The Unreasonable Effectiveness of Mathematics in the Natural Sciences." *Communications on Pure and Applied Mathematics* 13: 1–14.

Wilkinson, David. 2010. *Christian Eschatology and the Physical Universe.* London: Bloomsbury T&T Clark.

Williams, G. C. 1966. *Adaptation and Natural Selection.* Princeton, NJ: Princeton University Press.

Wilson, E. O. 1975. *Sociobiology: The New Synthesis*, Cambridge, MA: Harvard University Press.

Wilson, E. O. 1978. *On Human Nature.* Cambridge, MA: Harvard University Press.

Wilson, E. O. 2002. *The Future of Life.* New York: Vintage Books.

Wittgenstein, L. 1965. "A Lecture on Ethics." *The Philosophical Review* 74: 3–12.

Wittgenstein, L. 1998. *Tractatus Logico-Philosophicus.* Translated by C. K. Ogden. Mineolo, NY: Dover Publications.

Wright, N. T. 1993. "The New Unimproved Jesus." *Christianity Today.* September 13.

Wright, N. T. 2011. *Scripture and the Authority of God: How to Read the Bible Today.* New York: HarperOne.

Wright, N. T. 2014. *Surprised by Scripture: Engaging Contemporary Issues.* San Francisco: HarperOne.

Wykstra, Stephen J. 1984. "The Humean Obstacle to Evidential Arguments from Suffering: On Avoiding the Evils of 'Appearance.'" *International Journal for Philosophy of Religion* 16: 73–93.

Yancey, Philip. 2014. *Vanishing Grace.* Grand Rapids, MI: Zondervan.

Zimmer, Carl. 2009. "On the Origin of Life on Earth." *Science* 323: 198–99.

INDEX